O9-AIG-645

Daily
Guideposts
2016

Guideposts
New York

Daily Guideposts 2016

Published by Guideposts Books & Inspirational Media
110 William Street
New York, New York 10038
Guideposts.org

Copyright © 2015 by Guideposts. All rights reserved.

This book, or parts thereof, may not be reproduced, stored in a retrieval system, or transmitted in any form or by any means, electronic, mechanical, photocopying, recording or otherwise, without the written permission of the publisher.

Acknowledgments
Every attempt has been made to credit the sources of copyrighted material used in this book. If any such acknowledgment has been inadvertently omitted or miscredited, receipt of such information would be appreciated.

Scripture quotations marked (AMP) are taken from the *Amplified Bible*. Copyright © 1954, 1958, 1962, 1964, 1965, 1987 by the Lockman Foundation.

Scripture quotations marked (ASV) are taken from *American Standard Version of the Bible*.

Scripture quotations marked (CEB) are taken from the *Common English Bible*. Copyright © 2011 by Common English Bible.

Scripture quotations marked (CEV) are taken from *Holy Bible: Contemporary English Version*. Copyright © 1995 American Bible Society.

Scripture quotations marked (ESV) are taken from the *Holy Bible, English Standard Version*, copyright © 2001 by Crossway Bibles, a division of Good News Publishers. Used by permission. All rights reserved.

Scripture quotations marked (GNB) are taken from the *Good News Bible* © 1994 published by the Bible Societies/HarperCollins Publishers Ltd. UK, Good News Bible © American Bible Society 1966, 1971, 1976, 1992. Used with permission.

Scripture quotations marked (GNT) are taken from the *Good News Translation*. Copyright © 1992 by American Bible Society.

Scripture quotations marked (GW) are taken from *God's Word Translation*. Copyright © 1995 by God's Word to the Nations. Used by permission of Baker Publishing Group.

Scripture quotations marked (JPS) are taken from the 1917 or 1985 edition of *Tanakh: A New Translation of the Holy Scriptures according to the Traditional Hebrew Text*. Copyright © 1985 by the Jewish Publication Society. All rights reserved.

Scripture quotations marked (KJV) are taken from the *King James Version of the Bible*.

Scripture quotations marked (MSG) are taken from *The Message*. Copyright © 1993, 1994, 1995, 1996, 2000, 2001, 2002 by Eugene H. Peterson.

Scripture quotations marked (NAS) are taken from the *New American Standard Bible*, copyright © 1960, 1962, 1963, 1968, 1971, 1972, 1973, 1975, 1977, 1995 by the Lockman Foundation. Used by permission.

Scripture quotations marked (NIV) are taken from *The Holy Bible, New International Version*. Copyright © 1973, 1978, 1984, 2011 by Biblica, Inc. Used by permission of Zondervan. All rights reserved worldwide. www.zondervan.com

Scripture quotations marked (NJB) are taken from *New Jerusalem Bible*. Copyright © 1985 by Darton, Longman & Todd and Les Editions du Cerf.

Scripture quotations marked (NKJV) are taken from *The Holy Bible, New King James Version*. Copyright © 1982 by Thomas Nelson, Inc.

Scripture quotations marked (NLT) are from the *Holy Bible, New Living Translation*. Copyright © 1996, 2004, 2007 by Tyndale House Foundation. Used by permission of Tyndale House Publishers Inc., Carol Stream, Illinois 60188. All rights reserved.

Scripture quotations marked (NRSV) are taken from the *New Revised Standard Version Bible*. Copyright © 1989 by the Division of Christian Education of the National Council of the Churches of Christ in the United States of America. Used by permission. All rights reserved.

Scripture quotations marked (RSV) are taken from the *Revised Standard Version of the Bible*. Copyright © 1946, 1952, 1971 by the Division of Christian Education of National Council of Churches of Christ in the United States of America. Used by permission.

Scripture quotations marked (TEV) are taken from *Today's English Version of the Bible*. Copyright © by American Bible Society 1966, 1971, 1976, 1979 (Deuterocanonicals/Apocrypha), 1992; Anglicizations British and Foreign Bible Society 1994.

Scripture quotations marked (TIB) are taken from *The Inclusive Bible: The First Egalitarian Translation*. Copyright © 2007 by Priests for Equality. All rights reserved.

Scripture quotations marked (TLB) are taken from *The Living Bible*. Copyright © 1971 by Tyndale House Publishers, Wheaton, Illinois 60187. All rights reserved.

Andrew Attaway photo by Doug Snyder; Evelyn Bence photo by David Singer; Brian Doyle photo by Hob Osterlund; Rick Hamlin photo by Julie Brown; Jim Hinch photo by Martin Klimek; Debbie Macomber photo by Dane Gregory Meyer; Erin MacPherson photo by bloomaustin .com; Roberta Messner photo by Craig Cunningham; Ginger Rue photo by Sherwood Cox; Gail Thorell Schilling photo by Doug Schwarz; Elizabeth Sherrill photo by Shawn G. Henry; Stephanie Thompson photo by Shevaun Williams; Marion Bond West photo by Michael A. Schwarz.

Cover and interior design by Müllerhaus
Cover and monthly page opener photos by Shutterstock
Indexed by Patricia Woodruff
Typeset by Aptara

Printed and bound in the United States of America
10 9 8 7 6 5 4 3 2 1

Hello, friend.

When we decided the theme for *Daily Guideposts 2016* would be "Abide in Me," I had no idea how meaningful those words of Jesus would become in my life. I'm a wife and mom, raising two young boys in New York City. Needless to say, life is hectic. One night this past winter, as I sat in the ER with my one-year-old, I felt very tired. Then I remembered a *Daily Guideposts* devotional by Erin MacPherson. She, too, was sitting in the hospital with her son. She found peace in remembering that when she leaned on God, she could face anything. Her reminder to rest in the Lord soothed my spirit.

"Abide in me, and I in you. As the branch cannot bear fruit by itself, unless it abides in the vine, neither can you, unless you abide in me....As the Father has loved me, so have I loved you. Abide in my love" (John 15:4, 9, ESV). As I've read through these 366 devotions, I'm reminded of God's sustaining presence.

This year marks the fortieth edition of *Daily Guideposts.* Its pages are bursting with honest reflections on living faithfully. Catch up with longtime friends Penney Schwab, Daniel Schantz, and Carol Knapp. Welcome back Debbie Macomber and embrace newcomer Logan Eliasen.

We said good-bye to Shari Smyth, Joshua Sundquist, Linda Neukrug, Brigitte Weeks, and Ashley Wiersma, who are pursuing other things.

Travel with Karen Barber in the series "A Prayerful Lent." And during Advent, revel with Bill Giovannetti in "The Gift of Small Moments." More heartfelt moments such as these await you in *Daily Guideposts 2016*. You'll experience that connection with God, Whose desire is for you to abide in Him all the days of your life.

Faithfully yours,

Keren Baltzer, *Daily Guideposts* Editor

CONNECT WITH US ONLINE

We love hearing from our readers! Whether you use Facebook or send handwritten letters, we want to connect with you. Find us at DailyGuideposts.org and Facebook.com/dailyguideposts, e-mail DailyGPEditors@guideposts.org, or write to *Daily Guideposts* Editor, Guideposts Books, 110 William Street, New York, NY 10038.

DAILY GUIDEPOSTS IN YOUR IN-BOX

Enjoy *Daily Guideposts* wherever you are! Receive each day's devotion on your computer, tablet, or smartphone offered only to members of the *Daily Guideposts* family. Visit DailyGuideposts.org/DGP2016 and enter this code: abide.

JANUARY

"Abide in me, and I in you. As the branch cannot bear fruit by itself, unless it abides in the vine, neither can you, unless you abide in me."

—John 15:4 (ESV)

Friday, January 1

But when he, the Spirit of truth, comes, he will guide you into all the truth. He will not speak on his own; he will speak only what he hears, and he will tell you what is yet to come. —John 16:13 (NIV)

The first day of the new year began with a spectacular sunrise, bright oranges and pinks peeking out over the leafless trees in our front yard, enticing us out of our fire-warmed house, with cocoa in hand, to enjoy the view. It ended with a trip to the hospital. My daredevil of an eight-year-old son, Joey, crashed his bike, resulting in a dislocated jaw and several cuts that needed stitches.

My heart was worn out, done with the new and craving the comfort of the old. I sat in that doctor's office and silently fumed. The year had started so beautifully, only to disintegrate in an instant, into a mess of pain and fear.

Unbidden, a verse I had memorized long ago rushed into my mind: "Remain in me, as I also remain in you... [and together we] will bear much fruit" (John 15:4–5, NIV). I took a deep breath and looked at my son, battered and bruised but okay.

"I'm ready, Lord. Bring on the new year," I whispered, knowing that 2016 would certainly bring spectacular sunrises full of color and promise, but it also would bring terrible crashes, moments of tremendous pain and desperate sorrow, times when I would have no choice but to wonder how to take another step forward.

Through it all, I have no choice but to choose—intentionally, wholeheartedly, and lovingly—to abide in God. Because together we are going to bear much fruit.

Lord, reveal Yourself to me this year through the good and the bad. Amen. —Erin MacPherson

Digging Deeper: Psalm 23

Saturday, January 2

For God, who gives seed to the farmer to plant, and later on good crops to harvest and eat, will give you more and more seed to plant and will make it grow so that you can give away more and more fruit from your harvest. —2 Corinthians 9:10 (TLB)

When I started writing for the fortieth anniversary edition of *Daily Guideposts*, I thought about how many changes there have been in our lives. The Internet, mobile phones, DNA testing, suitcases on wheels, and GPS have all come about while *Daily Guideposts* has been walking us through life's changes and challenges.

This is also the twenty-fifth edition of *Daily Guideposts* that I have written for. I started in 1987 and missed a few years in between, but this makes twenty-five books total. Amazing changes occurred in my own life since then. I became a single parent, worked three part-time jobs to help get my four kids through college, wrote over forty thousand radio commercials, ran a crash pad for airline pilots in my Wisconsin home for ten years, moved to Florida, welcomed nine grandchildren, met Jack, visited twenty-eight countries, married Jack, and lived happily ever after. Well, at least, that's how I hope it plays out.

Today, instead of making New Year's resolutions that I may not be able to keep, I'm going to compile a list of goals to accomplish in the next twenty-five years: more volunteer activities, travel adventures, and caring for my older relatives and friends when they need me.

Reading and writing for *Daily Guideposts* has definitely boosted my faith as I go about the business of making the most out of life. I've been inspired by so many *Daily Guideposts* readers, writers, and editors over the years that it feels like we're one big family navigating through life's ups and downs together. And here we go again. Happy New Year!

Father, thank You for this big family and for the millions of blessings that have come about because of forty years of *Daily Guideposts*. —Patricia Lorenz

Digging Deeper: 1 Peter 2:2–4, Jude 20–23

Then Jesus spoke to them again, saying, "I am the light of the world. He who follows Me shall not walk in darkness, but have the light of life." —John 8:12 (NKJV)

For over twenty years now, at the beginning of the new year, I search for my "word for the year." I generally start by asking God which one word He would like me to focus on.

I've traveled amazing journeys with a single word and learned deep spiritual lessons. One year the word was *magnify*. It seemed that every time I opened my Bible, *magnify* would pop up. That was the year I learned I had to magnify the Lord and count my blessings rather than dwell on resentments and past hurts.

Another year my word was *believe*. After a lifetime of struggles with my weight, God was telling me I had to believe it was possible for me to let go of excess pounds.

As the new year approached, I considered the word *light*. Jesus asked us to be a light unto the world. It seemed like such an obvious choice, so I asked for verification from the Lord. As it happened my husband, Wayne, and I were traveling and had settled down in our hotel room, weary from a long trip and more than ready for rest. Unfortunately, we couldn't find the switch to turn off the bathroom light. I looked, Wayne looked, and we finally gave up, too exhausted to care. When my head pressed against the pillow, I smiled. *Okay, God, message received.*

Lord, may Your light shine brightly in my heart and my life, and may others see it and know its source is You.
—Debbie Macomber

Digging Deeper: Matthew 4:16

Monday, January 4

FINDING REST: Keeping the Sabbath

And on the seventh day God finished the work that he had done, and he rested on the seventh day from all the work that he had done. —Genesis 2:2 (NRSV)

"Even our Lord rested on the seventh day, didn't He?" our friend Rich asked.

I could see my husband, Charlie, trying to avoid being thrown by the question even as he laughed uncomfortably. We'd been talking to Rich and his wife about how difficult it is for Charlie to back away from all of his work and volunteer activities. He has a hard time saying no to anyone, and once he says yes, he becomes 100 percent committed. This attitude, while appreciated by all those he works with, was making it hard for him to relax or do any of the things he enjoyed, not to mention the things I wanted him to do.

"Let's face it," said Rich, "when we can't stop ourselves from working, it may be more about what we need rather than what God wants from us."

This comment caught me up short too. How much of my wanting Charlie to do less was about what I wanted rather than what he needed? Did I really want him to spend more time playing his guitar and reading or washing windows and painting the porch?

When God rested on the seventh day, He rested from labors that were not egotistical or selfish in any way. Such a selfless day of rest may not always be easy for us, but from the day God created us, He expected us to at least try to keep a Sabbath, in Him and with Him.

Creator God, help us to fashion our Sabbath with pure hearts fixed on resting in You. Amen. —Marci Alborghetti

Digging Deeper: Genesis 2:3, Matthew 5:48

Tuesday, January 5

O sing to the Lord a new song; sing to the Lord, all the earth! —Psalm 96:1 (RSV)

Elinor Miller was a stalwart of the church choir back home in California. What a magnificent voice she had; a true mezzo—resonant, rich, rising to the rafters.

I was a much less confident singer in my youth but could never say no when our choir director asked me to sing a solo on a Sunday. When it came time to perform, I was invariably a bundle of nerves. Mrs. Miller was my constant encourager. "You really carried that line," she'd say. "What a natural tenor voice you have. You sounded great." Other people in the congregation would give me compliments, but hearing it from Mrs. Miller counted the most. She knew her music, knew voices. If she said I was okay, I must have been okay.

Over the years, on visits back home, I would see Mrs. Miller, still leading the alto section, still sounding magnificent. Then not long ago I got a call from Mom. Mrs. Miller was reading and enjoying my book *10 Prayers You Can't Live Without*—she wanted me to know. The other piece of news was more sobering: she had just been diagnosed with pancreatic cancer.

I wished I could visit Mrs. Miller, talk about old times, be the one giving her some encouraging words. Instead, prayer would have to do the work. But only weeks later the message from her son, Michael, appeared on Facebook. "Yesterday, my mom joined the heavenly choir."

I e-mailed him, told him how I loved his mom, how grateful I was to her. In a matter of minutes he responded: "Rick, I was just thinking this morning that I needed to be in touch with you. I wanted to let you know how much joy she got from your book. She kept saying that she'd let me read it as soon as she finished it. She said it was as though you were speaking to her."

If my book had only one reader, I would have wished it to be her. *Heavenly choir indeed*, I thought. *Mrs. Miller, save a place for me.*

May my words and thoughts be pleasing to You and Yours, Lord. — Rick Hamlin

Digging Deeper: Psalm 104:33, Ephesians 5:19

Wednesday, January 6

"If we are thrown into the blazing furnace, the God we serve is able to deliver us from it....But even if he does not...we will not serve your gods or worship the image of gold you have set up." —Daniel 3:17–18 (NIV)

After suffering a miscarriage, we'd been blessed with another chance—a happy announcement that I was again pregnant. One in four pregnancies ends in miscarriage, so my isolating and life-changing experience had been revealed to me as fairly common, if rarely discussed. Somehow, knowing I wasn't alone comforted me. I allowed myself to rejoice.

I practically skipped into my first appointment, eager to see the grainy gummy bear of a baby on the ultrasound screen. "I'm so sorry," the doctor said. "There's no heartbeat."

What kind of God does this? I wailed. *What kind of God deserts us at our very lowest?* I poured myself into Scripture, searching for anything I could find. With my first miscarriage, I looked for stories of hope. With my second, I looked for answers and signs of survival.

I came to Daniel. There, King Nebuchadnezzar commanded his people to fall down and worship the golden image he'd crafted. Those who wouldn't do as he ordered would be thrown into a blazing furnace. The king received word that three Jews had disregarded his mandate. Before throwing Shadrach, Meshach, and Abednego into the fire, he asked, "What God will be able to rescue you from my hand?"

The trio replied that the God they served was able to deliver them from the fire and added something I never noticed before: "But even if He does not, we want you to know that we will not serve your gods or worship the image of gold." *Even if He does not.*

In the weeks that followed, I found those words dwelling in my heart. God had not spared me from this anguish, but I knew He would see me through it to the other side.

God, remind me that peace comes not from having my needs met, but by finding my hope in You. —Ashley Kappel

Digging Deeper: Isaiah 45:22, Daniel 3

She hath done what she could.... —Mark 14:8 (KJV)

When my friend Harold died, his daughter noted that he "had the ministry of showing up." At children's programs and recitals. Missions programs. Church classes taught by nervous novices as well as seasoned experts. Celebratory open houses as well as sparsely attended funerals.

A few weeks ago I thought of Harold and his reputation while waiting for the opening notes of a grammar-school winter concert. I'd come to support a youngster in my neighborhood whose family couldn't attend her performance. That unseasonably cold night I was following Harold's example. But I'm not always so faithful or generous. I cringe to remember scenes from years past: my finking out on Daria's wedding, my no-show at David's Christmas party, my unexplained absence from Carla's book club meeting. Each time, my inability to be there disappointed someone, as if I had discounted a friend's value.

I can't be everywhere or involved in every activity, I tell myself and justifiably so. I don't have to be at *every* scheduled church event. I don't have to accept *every* invitation. I don't have to be *everyone's* BFF. Saying *yes* to everything, I know, leads to burnout and fragmentation.

Yet, I'd be honored to be remembered as someone who simply, habitually showed up, offering a smile, a hand, maybe a high five. Becoming that person is my New Year's resolution.

God, in this new year that's spread before me, help me to honor my family and my friends by being steadfastly present. —Evelyn Bence

Digging Deeper: Romans 12:10, 13:10

Friday, January 8

"His master replied, 'Well done, good and faithful servant! You have been faithful with a few things; I will put you in charge of many things. Come and share your master's happiness!'" —Matthew 25:23 (NIV)

"Mommy, just look at me!" My son grabbed my face.

There's nothing like small hands and an exasperated little-boy voice to pierce a mother's heart.

Here I was, in desperate prayer day after day, begging God to bring home my daughter, when all the while I was neglecting what was right in front of me. I had let myself get so wrapped up in the Congo adoption community—sending messages back and forth with fellow adoptive parents, talking on the phone, speculating as to when things would start moving again and we'd be able to bring our children home—that I wasn't being a good mother to the child already under my roof.

God had blessed and entrusted me with Brogan. Was I being faithful to this boy whom I already had? It was a much-needed wake-up call.

With my son's warm palms cupping my face and his big blue eyes staring into mine with hurt and frustration, it struck me that I was taking one of God's biggest blessings in my life for granted.

And finally I gave Brogan what he had been asking for all morning: my full attention.

Lord, let me never forsake the responsibilities and blessings in front of me for the sake of what You've not yet given. —Katie Ganshert

Digging Deeper: 1 Thessalonians 5:18, James 1:17

Saturday, January 9

Oh, the depth of the riches and wisdom and knowledge of God! How unsearchable are his judgments and how inscrutable his ways! —Romans 11:33 (ESV)

Call it synchronicity or God's mysterious ways, but my *Daily Guideposts* devotion for January 4, 2002, led to my being a judge for the Miss Wyoming Scholarship Program Pageant. I had described feeling old and frumpy while I awaited the arrival of Miss Wyoming at a local elementary school as part of my news beat. A kindergartner broke my self-sabotaging reverie when she hugged my knees and asked, "Are you Miss Wyoming?"

About a month later, Randi, the current director of the program, wrote to tell me that my devotion fell on the very day she had to decide whether to resign from her position. She interpreted my story as a sign that she should stay. Not only that, but she invited me to help judge the upcoming pageant. All expenses would be paid, except airfare. I declined only because I was living in New Hampshire at the time and had no budget for travel.

The following winter, Randi invited me again. This time I could accept. Mid–May, my kind hostess drove more than one hundred miles to the airport to fetch me and treated the other four judges and me to sightseeing, dinners, and, of course, the glittering pageant.

Throughout my stay, I observed Randi radiate bonhomie to judges and contestants alike. She encouraged the young women, and they blossomed in her presence. I couldn't imagine anyone better suited for the position than she. Thank God for *Daily Guideposts.*

Lord, You use me in ways I cannot anticipate. May I always be ready. —Gail Thorell Schilling

Digging Deeper: Romans 12:6–8, 1 Timothy 4:14

"Choose the good." —Isaiah 7:15 (KJV)

As Corinne and I raise our family, I find myself going back and trying to understand the things that made my childhood idyllic. Although we never had a lot of money and there were many demands associated with being a preacher's kid, the first word that comes to me is *safe*.

The family traditions that my mom and dad struggled to uphold had a lot to do with those positive feelings, with Sundays nearing the top of the list. For my sister, Keri, and me, missing church wasn't an option. We were always there, where my father had been a minister since I was nine months old.

Mom, Keri, and I would sit in the same pew, toward the back, listening to the words he took so seriously. He had worked all week in a genuine effort to help guide his beloved flock. I can still hear the music and see the sun pouring through the stained-glass windows, covering the walls with beautiful light.

Finally after the last hymn was sung and the benediction pronounced, it was time for our after-church ritual—Chinatown! Andy, our friend from Hong Kong, would welcome our family to the restaurant with a quick wave and a waiting table.

We would relish a long lunch, catching up, enjoying one another.

I'm grateful that I had parents who made sure that after we worshipped together, we also laughed together over a steaming plate of lo mein. Corinne and I are determined to give our little family the same.

Heavenly Father, thank You for traditions and the sense of safety that honoring You as a family brings. —Brock Kidd

Digging Deeper: Job 34:4, Ecclesiastes 2:24

Monday, January 11

WHAT THE SAINTS HAVE TAUGHT ME
Jerome, Companion in Bible Study

Then he opened their minds so they could understand the Scriptures. —Luke 24:45 (NIV)

I first encountered saints in medieval paintings. One figure intrigued me: Saint Jerome was always accompanied by a lion. I started reading about him and then about others, discovering that my ignorance of saints had deprived me of some wonderful companions. Whenever work took me to Europe, I'd try to visit the hometowns of my newfound friends. Unique individuals, no two alike; if saints have one thing in common, it's the secret of abiding in Christ, whatever challenge life throws at them.

Jerome (331–420) was a scholar who retired to the wilderness to study God's Word uninterrupted. A lion, according to legend, went to him with a painful thorn in his paw. Jerome pulled it out, and the lion became his constant companion.

The real story, I discovered, was even better. Jerome was dissatisfied with the awkward Greek translation of the Old Testament—the only version Christians had—and set out to learn the original Hebrew. The Pope heard about it and asked for Jerome's help. Few people could read Greek. Could Jerome translate the Bible into the people's language, Latin?

Jerome spent the rest of his life devoted to this enormous task. He had a companion in his work, but it wasn't a lion. In an age when women were considered incapable of mental activity, Jerome chose a female collaborator. Paula was a wealthy widow, already fluent in Greek, who, to assist Jerome, learned Hebrew, gave her fortune to the poor, and worked daily at his side.

For medieval artists, this intimate companionship between an unmarried man and woman was scandalous! So as Jerome produced the Bible used for over 1,500 years, they painted a lion at his side instead.

Lord, let the example of Jerome and Paula increase my love of Scripture! —Elizabeth Sherrill

Digging Deeper: Psalm 89:15

Tuesday, January 12

"Surely the Lord is in this place...."
—Genesis 28:16 (NIV)

I received an unsettling phone call from my doctor. "Mrs. Garmon, you're severely anemic. You need to see your gastroenterologist to make sure you're not bleeding internally." Although she spoke in a gentle tone, I could hear the concern in her voice.

My gastroenterologist fit me in quickly, ordered more blood work, and prescribed iron. "We need to do a colonoscopy to rule out cancer." Her pale blue eyes locked with mine. "I'd like to wait until your iron level increases, but that's a bit risky." She smiled. "Try not to worry."

I refused all fear until the morning of my procedure. Now lying on a gurney, awaiting anesthesia, I wondered, *Is it possible not to be afraid?* Worst-case-scenario thinking had plagued me for most of my life, and being put to sleep had always been particularly scary for me. In the past, I had shaken so violently, my teeth would chatter.

No telling what the doctor might find, I thought now. A couple of tremors ran through me. *Oh no, not again. Fear is so exhausting.*

"They're ready for you," a nurse said and wheeled me back.

Waiting for my anesthesia, a thought so astounding came to me that I laughed.

"What's so funny?" the nurse said. "I love good jokes."

"Something just dawned on me: I can't perform my own colonoscopy or control the results, so I might as well relax."

She patted my hand. "We'll take good care of you. God will too."

The most peaceful feeling enfolded me; all of the shaking ceased. I knew "surely the Lord is in this place."

Father, no shaking, no fear! Thank You. —Julie Garmon

Digging Deeper: Psalms 115:11, 118:6

Wednesday, January 13

BEING RENEWED: Blessed Assurance

Even the darkness will not be dark to you; the night will shine like the day, for darkness is as light to you. —Psalm 139:12 (NIV)

"Taking the trash out," my husband, Gene, called to me. He rolled the large container to the curb every Wednesday night. I was absorbed in a book. Maybe twelve minutes passed. Suddenly, I looked up and missed him. As I hurried out the garage door, I heard him bellowing, "Over here, hurry." Even at night, I managed to see him lying on the ground. As I knelt by him, he said grimly, "I've broken my hip. Call an ambulance."

I flew back inside to grab my cell phone and coat. Back at his side, I eased my lap underneath his head and threw the coat over him. Then I dialed the dreaded 911. When the ambulance arrived, one of the EMTs said, "It's gonna hurt, sir. But we'll try to be gentle."

Gene groaned loudly as they lifted him. The red lights of the ambulance flashed rapidly; I was still wearing my fuzzy bedroom slippers. The entire scene seemed unreal, and, in a moment, our quiet lives had changed. Fear was slipping up behind me. I couldn't form words to pray. Just then, I glanced upward as the back doors of the emergency vehicle shut with Gene inside. *Oh my!* How bright the night was. Stars twinkling as only stars can, a glimmering moon, and black velvet sky—the exact same brilliant sky I'd gazed up at as a child lying on a quilt in my front yard.

Lingering for just a moment longer, I inhaled deeply as though breathing in some kind of blessed assurance given off by the startling beauty of the heavens. God was there just like always. He saw us all right and would go through whatever lay ahead with us.

Thank You, Father, for all the ambulances You ride in. —Marion Bond West

Digging Deeper: Genesis 1:1–8, Malachi 3:6

Then God said, "Let us make humankind in our
image, according to our likeness...."
—Genesis 1:26 (NRSV)

Here's what I love about Legos: they're endlessly
creative. That's what Benjamin was discovering.
At age four, he was finally old enough to build
confidently with them. We sat at the dining room
table, which we've taken to calling Lego City because
it's crowded with a Lego garbage truck, tow truck,
dump truck, and various other handmade buildings
and vehicles too strange for names. The sound of his
little hand raking through the bin in search of the
right piece was the sound of my own childhood. I
stopped building to watch him.

"Look, Daddy," he said, holding up something
that looked like a cross between a unicycle and a
flatbed truck.

"Awesome," I said. "What does it carry?"

"These boxes," said Benjamin, picking up some
square pieces. "It's taking them to the dump."

I tried to remember what it was like to build
like that, discovering how Legos can be combined
and recombined endlessly. *Like our own minds*, I
thought, *our own personalities assembled from so many
experiences that could have produced anything, but they
produced us.*

And now Benjamin was becoming his own person too. I remembered something J. R. R. Tolkien once wrote, that one aspect of God's image in us is our ability to create. Here we were, playing Legos, but we were also sharing in God's ongoing work. We were making good things: a fun afternoon; our easygoing relationship; and in one small but deeply satisfying way, we were learning a little more about our Creator.

**Our minds are gifts from You, God.
Help us to use them well.** —Jim Hinch

Digging Deeper: 2 Corinthians 5:17, Revelation 21:5

Friday, January 15

... And after the earthquake, a fire, but the Lord was not in the fire; and after the fire a still small voice. —1 Kings 19:12 (NKJV)

Think with me about that meeting you had at work or last week's Bible study. Who talked first? Who talked most? Who talked least? To whom did you listen?

In larger groups, I tend to be the quiet guy. That rankles some people. "You hardly said a word in the meeting. Why don't you like my proposal?" a friend demanded of me.

"It might be great," I said. "I need just a bit of time to think about it."

"Really? Why?"

We had a great conversation about those who speak quickly and with great energy ("talkers talk it out") and those who are more reflective and cautious ("quiet ones think it out"). By week's end, I'd become and remained my colleague's most loyal supporter. Paired together, our different styles complemented each other and we made a great team.

These days I teach leadership at a seminary, and I almost always tell this story. I've learned—too often the hard way—that in group settings, we tend to overvalue people who are like us and underappreciate people who aren't. So next time you're in a meeting or Bible study, ask yourself how you're hearing that person who's so very different from you and how you might learn from how God created them.

You have created us to be different for reasons, God. Help us to see those differences and then learn from them instead of dismissing them.
—Jeff Japinga

Digging Deeper: 1 Kings 19:1–21, Psalm 23, Ephesians 4:1–13

Saturday, January 16

The Lord is good to all, and His mercies are over all His works. —Psalm 145:9 (NAS)

I was watching a video online that my girlfriend had recommended. Various people shared their interpretations of the "good life." Then the viewing audience was asked, "What is the good life for you?" Almost immediately I had an answer: "He has shown you, O man, what is good; and what does the Lord require of you but to do justly, to love mercy, and to walk humbly with your God?" (Micah 6:8, NKJV).

As I thought about these "good life" phrases, I was drawn to "love mercy." This seemed more than an occasional act of kindness. If God wanted only three things of me, and loving mercy was one of them, then it was something to go out of my way for.

Not long after I watched the video, my mother encountered a serious health issue. Living alone at ninety-one, she was too frail to handle it herself. My husband and I—having just relocated nearer her—decided I should move in. So began weeks of sleeping on the sofa, making myself available to her.

It was challenging. Mom grieved her loss of independence, her slowness, her difficulty with things that used to be easy. Her shoulders and knees pained her. She could be bossy. There were moments I bristled...struggled to be patient...felt confined.

Over and over the words from Micah revived me: *love mercy.* Here was my chance to live the good life! To make this time of caring for my mother a pleasure between us.

Loving mercy felt sent to me from God—something that grew and grew. Life moved beyond good. It became great.

Compassionate Christ, Your entire life was a journey in mercy. There is no higher service. —Carol Knapp

Digging Deeper: Isaiah 49:15–16, Mark 8:1–10, 2 Corinthians 1:3–4

Sunday, January 17

Therefore, since we have been justified by faith, we have peace with God through our Lord Jesus Christ. —Romans 5:1 (ESV)

The other morning at church, the pastor began a series of sermons on faith with the first definition that made sense to me after decades of atheism. "Now faith is being sure of what we hope for and certain of what we do not see" (Hebrews 11:1, NIV). Actually, the wording of the version he read was somewhat different from my husband's earlier edition of the NIV: "Now faith is confidence in what we hope for and assurance about what we do not see." Perhaps that's why the pastor understood this definition to be about *confidence* and *assurance*, whereas, for the struggler I once was, faith was synonymous with *hope*.

I had hoped throughout the decades of my atheism. And, though by now I've believed in God longer than I hadn't, my faith is still more reliant on hope than certainty. Faith just doesn't come naturally for me. I have to reach for it daily, and the reaching is all about hope that what I've been taught, what I relearn daily, what Scripture routinely claims, is true: God loves us so much He sent His Son to save us from ourselves.

So it surprised me to come to a full turnaround in my understanding of the passage. I saw, with certitude, that my grasping hope wasn't faith exactly, though it has sufficed these many years. Rather, my faith came about through God's response to my hope—His willingness to be grasped and held and depended upon. I marveled at our invisible God's power to claim us for His own.

Thank You for Your love, Father, and the convincing authority of Your words. —Patty Kirk

Digging Deeper: Romans 15:4

How good and pleasant it is when God's people live together in unity! —Psalm 133:1 (NIV)

I skimmed the newspaper article and beamed at the photo of my son's seven-year-old freckled face and bright red puffer jacket. On that day, ten years ago, Kalin had marched proudly among a sea of people to commemorate Dr. Martin Luther King Jr.'s national holiday.

Dr. King's work had made it possible for us—a motley crew of African Americans, Caucasians, Hispanics, and Asians from every corner of our small suburban town in Tennessee—to walk together in unity. We could almost hear his voice resonating through the rolling hills around us: "Let freedom ring from Lookout Mountain of Tennessee....From every mountainside, let freedom ring!"

Scanning the photo, I once again witnessed what had moved the photographer to capture the image of my son. While we adults stood side by side, my son walked hand in hand with a ten-year-old boy named Brandon. Brandon and Kalin had become fast friends and were thrilled to find each other at the march that day.

I wasn't surprised at all when these two boys chose to walk together. Kalin couldn't have cared less that Brandon was white, and Brandon couldn't have cared less that Kalin was black. They were friends, and that friendship existed outside the realms of race or culture.

Lord, may Dr. King's dream of unity live on in us.
—Carla Hendricks

Digging Deeper: John 17:22–23, 1 Corinthians 1:10, Colossians 3:13–14

Tuesday, January 19

Ye are all the children of God by faith in Christ Jesus. For as many of you as have been baptized into Christ have put on Christ. —Galatians 3:26–27 (KJV)

For the past four years, I've been getting treatment for my depression at a clinic. The clinic has many advantages: it's close to home, it has a great staff and facilities, and we can afford it. But it has a downside too. Since it's a training clinic, doctors rotate in and out every two years.

I've developed a very good relationship with my therapist for the last two years. I've been able to go with him into the most painful and problematic parts of my life. I trust him. It's hard to establish that kind of trust, and I was worried about having to start the whole process again.

Trusting people enough to share my heart with them isn't easy for me. I'm afraid that if I let them see through the public me, the private me will repel them.

It's not a rational response; it's an automatic emotional reaction that's very hard for me to work through.

Unfortunately, my difficulties with trust aren't confined to other people; they get in the way of my relationship with God. Over and over again, Scripture urges us to trust the Lord. There's no false front I can put up to fool God; whether I like it or not, He can see right through me. And that's pretty scary.

For me, the above verses from Galatians help me to see past the fear. When I came to Christ, I put on Christ. And when the Father looks at me, it's not my sins and inadequacies He sees; it's His Son, Who has taken them up and clothed them with Himself. That's where I should be looking too.

Lord Jesus Christ, teach me how to trust in You.
—Andrew Attaway

Digging Deeper: Psalm 33:21, Proverbs 3:5,
1 Timothy 1:14

Wednesday, January 20

"I will bring healing to you and cure you...."
—Jeremiah 30:17 (JPS)

There is a bench in the master bathroom next to the tub. It provides a clear view of my husband's side of the bed, and since Keith had to sleep sitting up in order to breathe, an occupant of the bench could see him clearly. On the morning before my husband died, our cat L.E. had curled onto the bench, her green eyes fixed on him. For more than thirty hours, she never moved from that spot.

The year before, when Keith had had to spend several days in the hospital, L.E. was frantic, wandering from room to room looking for him, meowing forlornly. She had always demanded he fuss over her. I expected that after he died she would be as stricken as I was. But once the men from the funeral home took Keith's body from the house, L.E. left the bench and came into the kitchen to eat. I knew that she understood he wasn't coming back.

Two months after Keith died, L.E. came to me to be petted for the first time and then vanished under the bed for several days, except for meals and the litter box. The next time she came to me, she stayed longer and vanished for a shorter time. When Keith had been gone for six months, L.E. climbed onto my lap, tucked her head under my chin, and purred. I began to think she had stored up the love Keith had given her and now was sharing it with me.

I know You created love that could not be lost, Lord, and I am grateful You found a way to remind me of that when I needed reminding so very much.
—Rhoda Blecker

Digging Deeper: Exodus 15:2; Psalms 36:6–7, 118:1

"The Lord is my helper; I will not fear. What can man do to me?" —Hebrews 13:6 (NKJV)

I awake with a pounding heart and a sense of dread. I have a doctor's appointment this afternoon. "Lord, help me face this day," I pray.

Maybe some doughnuts from the bakery will cheer me, but when I twist the ignition key, the car won't start. *Oh, great. Just what I need. Something else to worry about!*

I do my own repairs, so I am soon up to my elbows in tools and test instruments. I feel like Sherlock Holmes probing for that one elusive clue that will unravel this mystery. I enjoy removing parts, discovering the engine's deepest secrets. It feels masculine tugging hard on wrenches, stretching my arm muscles. I twist and bend, looking for concealed bolt heads. Soon I am breathing hard, but it's stimulating, refreshing.

Then comes that eureka moment: *It's the coolant temperature sensor! A cheap, easy fix!* An hour later I turn the key and the engine fires to life. I feel a huge sense of conquest, man over machine. I am John Henry, the steel-driving man!

I am grinning from ear to ear when my wife opens the kitchen door. "It's time for lunch. And don't forget, you have a doctor's appointment."

I did forget! So absorbed was I in my work that there was no room for anxiety.

The appointment went all right, and on the way home I gave myself a lecture. "Next time you are facing a threat, find something to occupy your mind. If not car repair, then gardening or helping Sharon clean house."

It's easier to carry two suitcases than one because the load is better balanced and sometimes one problem balances out another.

Lord, I am embarrassed to be so afraid of doctors, but thank You for helping me to manage my fears.
—Daniel Schantz

Digging Deeper: Deuteronomy 20:1, 2 Kings 6:16

Friday, January 22

"Be still...." —Psalm 46:10 (KJV)

"Charles, will you please get my phone?" I ask my four-year-old grandson. "It's on the blue couch."

He leaves and then quickly returns to the kitchen. "Mimi, you don't have a blue couch," he says.

I smile, as I dust the flour off my hands and lead him to the living room. I pull up the gray slipcover that hides the blue couch. "Here it is." I laugh.

The blue couch. When it got too threadbare and stained, I couldn't bear to replace it, so I covered it.

My father gave me the couch when my daughter, Keri, was born. On his frequent visits, it became our place to "be." We'd sit with steaming coffee and enjoy the early mornings. We didn't need to talk. Being together was enough. After he left his earth suit behind and went on to worlds we don't yet know, the blue couch remained my "being" place. At first, I would go there to remember Daddy. But over time it became a sort of portal to something larger. In the silence of the blue couch, I always felt closer to God.

The blue couch, to me, is a pointer to a simpler way. It suggests the truth behind God's invitation: "Be still, and know that I am God." In the silence, suddenly I discover my first and best clue to finding God. He is here, now, in the stillness, waiting.

Let me be still, Father. Let me meet You here, now. —Pam Kidd

Digging Deeper: Psalms 23:2, 37:7; Mark 4:39

Saturday, January 23

Do not be conformed to this world, but be transformed by the renewal of your mind…. —Romans 12:2 (ESV)

I got to my aerobics class a little late, which meant there were no exercise mats left. *You know everyone goes to the gym in January,* I self-scolded. *You can't be late in January.* So I did the best I could without a mat.

After class, I noticed a stack of flyers entitled "Keys to Forming a New Habit." I picked up a copy and glanced over all of the familiar suggestions about setting attainable goals, measuring small steps of progress, avoiding negative self-talk, and rewarding yourself for success.

Then I was off to the grocery store and got all the way to the checkout area, when I realized I'd left my cloth grocery bags in the car. Our store now charges for plastic ones, so I left my cart in the deli section and darted back through the snow-covered parking lot to retrieve my bags.

A week later, I was feeling proud of myself for getting to aerobics earlier for several days in a row. Walking out, I spotted the same stack of flyers about forming new habits and smugly decided I knew the most effective key: the best way to form a habit of doing something right is by doing it wrong.

I went on to the grocery store, got all the way to the checkout line, and discovered I'd left my cloth bags in the car . . . again.

Lord, Your grace gives me countless opportunities to do something right after doing it wrong. I'm thankful, especially when it involves more than an exercise mat or grocery bags. —Carol Kuykendall

Digging Deeper: Job 5:17, Proverbs 10:17

Woe unto you, scribes and Pharisees, hypocrites! for ye pay tithe of mint and anise and cummin, and have omitted the weightier matters of the law, judgment, mercy, and faith.... Ye blind guides, which strain at a gnat, and swallow a camel.
—Matthew 23:23–24 (KJV)

At any church service, Catholic or otherwise, I whisper these eight words: "Lord, I am not worthy to receive You." I know I am a sinner. The realization that I join the human race in this distinction provides no comfort.

I am also an environmentalist—and a mighty hypocritical one at that. I spend summers on a motor scooter, saving on gas and saving the environment...and spend winters driving a fifteen-miles-per-gallon truck because I simply cannot let it go. I take short showers, except on days when I can't quite wake up, which are most days. I chastise my daughters for leaving lights on, but the lights *I* leave on...well, that's different.

One could argue it's human nature. I suppose. Still, I'm surprised hypocrisy didn't make the list of seven deadly sins. Hypocrisy has this added gem: arrogance. *(Here's what you ought to do. Trust me. I know better. Meanwhile, I have no intention of doing anything like that.)*

Maybe that's what rankled Jesus. He seemed to hold special wrath for those who were full of high sentence but no real commitment. Unlike avarice or sloth, hypocrisy can sound so good: it has the smell and taste of solid advice, an experienced voice. In reality, it's a dressed-up hoax and fancy fib—no matter how well-intended.

A final note: I lied. (Another sin.) I don't just say those eight words every Sunday; I answer them with ten more: "But only say the word and I shall be healed."

I have bet my salvation on those words. Here's hoping for the salvation of our collective island home.

Lord, forgive me for arrogantly preaching one thing while conveniently practicing another.
—Mark Collins

Digging Deeper: Psalm 24:1, Matthew 6:2

Monday, January 25

"Therefore I tell you, do not worry about your life...." —Matthew 6:25 (NIV)

I woke up this morning, Monday, and all my worries were marching on me like an army. There were financial issues, work deadlines, a medical test I kept putting off, an old friend struggling with depression whom I just couldn't seem to reach out to. It was one thing after another, guilt and anxiety. Did I mention it was Monday?

I'm one of those people for whom Monday mornings are a frequent struggle. I've given up trying to figure out why. I mean, shouldn't Sundays prepare me for Mondays? Was my faith so hollow that I gave in to all of my troubles before the week had even started? *Lord*, I wanted to pray, *I'm sorry I'm such a faithless wretch.*

All at once I remembered a craggy old voice emanating from the back room of a church basement, the voice of one of the old-timers at a twelve-step program I'd attended for years: "One thing at a time!"

That was this old guy's prevailing wisdom for just about any difficulty: *One thing at a time.* It is a popular slogan of the program, and hearing it rumble from deep within this otherwise taciturn fellow always made me smile.

Now, on this Monday morning, I needed to hear it. And I did, as clearly as if he were sitting in my living room. *One thing at a time.*

I sat on the edge of my bed and, one by one, handed each of my worries to God: finances, work, health, relationships. Every time I reached out my hand and spread my fingers wide, releasing my worries quite deliberately to a loving power greater than any trouble that could ever befall me. With each release, my mind eased, my perspective shifted, and I felt myself smile just a little, which is big for a Monday.

Okay, Lord, the week can start. I'm ready, now that I've put my worries before You and I've put You before my worries. —Edward Grinnan

Digging Deeper: Luke 12:25–26

Tuesday, January 26

The law written in their hearts, their conscience also bearing witness.... —Romans 2:15 (KJV)

There's a farewell reception for a fellow employee today. She is finally leaving after years of epic and smarmy incompetence and lies and devious politicking. Everyone else in my office gets ready to go, many of them grumbling but they are going anyway, and I am adamant that I am not going, no way. I think she was a terrible employee who misspent not only her own time and creativity but the time and possible sweet work of many other people, and that bothers me for lots of reasons—mostly that our work is to elevate kids. So in my view she hurt crucial and holy work, and it would be a whopping lie for me to stand at a reception and clap politely or even, God help us, shake her hand and wish her well.

Everyone leaves for the reception, and I sit here stewing and harrumphing and thinking about the egregious lies she told me and the slippery underhanded things she did, and I redouble my insistence that I am not going, no way. Then I get up and go. Deep inside me is something—a voice, a governor, a knowledge?—that warns me when I am being a particular fool, which I regret to say is often. This is one of those times. The Creator breathed life into this woman. The Creator made but one of her, *ever*, and who am I to sneer and pronounce judgment? Was I in attendance when the Creator laid the fundaments of all that is? I was certainly not. So who am I to be arrogant?

My job is not to judge, but to witness, to hope, to believe that light can dawn in the most fearsome darkness. Even here, in this relatively tiny matter, I must try to stand up and do that which is reverent and sings the miracle of the Gift. So I go...snarling just a little.

Lord, help me get this huge beam out of my own eye so that I can see a tad more clearly to remove the mote in my foolish sister's eye. —Brian Doyle

Digging Deeper: 1 John 2:27

Wednesday, January 27

For now we see through a glass, darkly; but then face to face.... —1 Corinthians 13:12 (KJV)

I'd expected my eye exam to be routine. Instead, the optometrist spent ten minutes looking at my right eye through a slit lamp. "I found a cluster of abnormal cells inside your eyeball," he told me. "I'm not certain what has caused them, but it could be quite serious. You'll need to see a retinologist as soon as possible."

The optometrist provided information and tried to reassure me that most eye problems can be treated successfully. Even so, I thought about those abnormal cells several times a day. I imagined them multiplying, taking over my right eye, then the left one. The possibility of losing my sight was terrifying. Almost everything I do for fun—reading, live and televised sports, crossword puzzles, playing the organ—requires eyesight. I alternated between asking God to spare me from blindness and begging Him to help me accept whatever would come.

Three weeks later I saw the retinologist. His exam was brief but thorough. "You definitely have a cluster of abnormal cells," he said, "but the spot is small and on the periphery of the eyeball. You don't have any sight-threatening conditions, and I don't recommend treatment other than checkups every six months or so."

I was stunned. "But what caused the cells?" I asked. "Why are they there? What if they grow?"

He shook his head. "I have no explanation. Some things just are. Accept that and be as happy to receive good news as I am to give it."

Good advice—for my eyes and for every aspect of my life. I won't always have explanations or answers, but God knows all and cares for me. For that I am exceedingly thankful.

Thank You, Father, for walking with me even as I question the mysteries of life. —Penney Schwab

Digging Deeper: Job 38:1–10, Isaiah 35:3–10, Colossians 1:26–27

Thursday, January 28

"For the Lord searches every heart and understands every desire and every thought...."
—1 Chronicles 28:9 (NIV)

When my son Henry first asked, "Can we get a dog?" I hoped it was a fleeting want that would disappear. It's not that I don't like dogs. It's just that I've never had a dog, never wanted a dog and, to be completely honest, dogs scare me a little—not to mention we have four cats.

Months passed, and instead of Henry's desire waning, getting a dog moved its way to the top of his wish list. So one night, I halfheartedly searched online for adoptable dogs. I browsed a local pet rescue Web site, scrolling over photos of big dogs with comments like "for a house without young kids" and "not cat-friendly" to a small, shaggy, cream-colored furball named Schroeder. His sad eyes called out to me.

"Tony!" I yelled. "Come here!" I pointed to the picture. "What do you think?" Before my husband could answer, I said, "I like him. I really like him."

Tony was less impressed, but we talked about it, prayed about it, and filled out the application. Three days later we got the call. Schroeder was ours.

And now, Schroeder, shortened to Soda, is here, all thirteen pounds of him. Henry is in heaven. He's already said it's the best day of his life six times.

Walking our brand-new dog down the street, I can't get over how amazing it is that God put us together: this little furry fella who came all the way from death row in a Georgia shelter and me, fortysomething years old, walking a dog for the very first time in my life. Who knew? I'm a dog person, after all.

Thank You, Lord, for helping me discover a place in my heart I didn't know was there, for giving me a little boy who yearned for a dog, and for guiding me to simply say, "Yes." —Sabra Ciancanelli

Digging Deeper: Matthew 10:29, Luke 12:6

Do not lay up for yourselves treasures on earth, where moth and rust destroy.... —Matthew 6:19 (NKJV)

All I owned was a duffel bag and a saddle when I first showed up at the cattle ranch as a college intern. Unofficially adopted into the family, I eventually built a house of my own. And then stuff happened. Relatives gave me heirlooms—here a couch; there an end table; old books. My house got so cluttered, there wasn't room for me anymore.

Enough! I thought. I started downsizing, but it turned into a harder job than I anticipated. I didn't want to get rid of anything valuable. I found a box labeled "Great Aunt Nan's dishes"; I didn't recognize the handwriting. Inside were three very old plates and a butter dish. Of course, I had to keep those.

A friend came to help me haul away the excess but was disappointed at how little I was actually parting with. "Who was Nan?" she asked, glancing at the box I'd just shifted to the Keep pile.

"She was, uh..." I hesitated but then admitted, "I don't even know which side of the family she's from."

Was I cherishing memories or hoarding things because they might be worth something? To me, they were just some old plates stored in a dust-covered box. Truthfully, they might be valuable to someone, but they weren't to me. I was being selfish. It was time I let them go to someone who might actually appreciate their utility and worth.

Help me to discern, Lord, between keeping things for greed or for good, and that my true treasures are awaiting me in heaven, not on earth. —Erika Bentsen

Digging Deeper: 2 Corinthians 9:7, Philippians 3:19–20, 1 Timothy 6:18

Saturday, January 30

Have mercy on me, O God, because of your unfailing love. Because of your great compassion, blot out the stain of my sins. —Psalm 51:1 (NLT)

My wife, Margi, and I pride ourselves on keeping a clean house. But after a few years with kids and dogs, even the tidiest home might need professional carpet cleaning.

When we started getting ready for that day, we had a minirevelation. *We're not as clean as we think we are*—at least not in the rooms frequented by certain precious children, who will remain unnamed.

Years of juice stains, dog hair, foot traffic, and snacks were adding up. The net effect was gross, especially in places that rarely saw the light of day. There was no giant spill, no massive dirty area. Just a lot of little spills adding up over time.

I looked into my own heart. There were no big sins. No high crimes or misdemeanors. Nothing that would shame my family. But had the small stains multiplied over time? Was there a growing collection of little sins? Had I become so desensitized that I couldn't even see them?

I moved furniture around and continued cleaning. I was reminded of how my Sunday school teachers said to "keep short accounts," that I shouldn't go too long without checking in with God and making sure there was nothing between us.

Thank God for a dirty rug.

Dear Father, help me keep short accounts. Preserve me from growing numb to things that sully my walk with You. —Bill Giovannetti

Digging Deeper: Jude 24, 25

Sunday, January 31

Your face, Lord, I will seek. —Psalm 27:8 (NIV)

I pulled on my muck boots and stepped out the back door, whispering prayers. *"I need..."* My golden retriever, Sunrise, bounded over to me. She punched my right hand with her nose, which meant she wanted me to throw the ball. Tucking my hand in my pocket, I scolded, "Not now. I'm late for church and I still have to feed the horses." But my sour tone didn't deter her. She traipsed behind me into the pasture and then the barn, bumping my right hand every time it dangled by my side.

I murmured prayers as I loaded the hay on the sled. When I turned around, I nearly tripped over the eighty-five-pound shadow that kept staring at my right hand. "Sunrise, I said no!" I bristled and stomped out of the barn. The sled bumped behind me.

As I tossed the last flake of hay in the feeders, I wrapped up my long list of prayer needs and thought, *I wonder what the message in church is going to be?* I looked forward to receiving words that I could use during the week.

While the sled hissed behind me, Sunrise bounded up and down and banged my hand. "Can't you just be happy being with me?" I growled. "Why are you always after my hand?"

As soon as the words left my mouth, I heard, *She's a reflection of you.*

It was true. All morning my prayers to God were need-oriented and I focused on what I could glean from church. It was time to seek His face and figure out how I could give back to Him.

In the morning, Lord, remind me that the most important thing is to seek You. —Rebecca Ondov

Digging Deeper: 1 Chronicles 16:11

GOD'S ABIDING LOVE

1 _____

2 _____

3 _____

4 _____

5 _____

6 _____

7 _____

8 _____

9 _____

10 _____

11 _____

12 _____

13 _____

14 _____

15 _____

16 _____

17 _____

18 _____

19 _____

20 _____

21 _____

22 _____

23 _____

24 _____

25 _____

26 _____

27 _____

28 _____

29 _____

30 _____

31 _____

FEBRUARY

*"As the Father has loved me,
so have I loved you. Abide in my love."*

—John 15:9 (ESV)

Monday, February 1

Being confident of this, that he who began a good work in you will carry it on to completion until the day of Christ Jesus. —Philippians 1:6 (NIV)

Shortly after resigning as pastor at Hudson Valley Fellowship, I decided to visit different congregations. My wife, Elba, and I attended the Baptist church in our town, and the pastor read from Galatians 5:22-23: "But the fruit of the Spirit is love, joy, peace, patience, kindness, goodness, faithfulness, gentleness, and self-control. Against such things there is no law."

I had read this passage hundreds of times, but it got my attention. *Did I embody the fruit of the Spirit? Which qualities did I lack?*

Two weeks later, we visited a Missionary Alliance congregation, twenty miles south of our town. The youth minister was preaching his farewell sermon, and his Scripture selection was the same text from Galatians. Was this a coincidence or was God trying to get my attention?

After some time spent in looking at this passage and spiritual reflection, I discovered that "gentleness" was a characteristic I needed God to help me develop further. Growing up in a tough neighborhood in New York City, I quickly learned that gentleness was seen as a weakness, not a strength. The tough, in-your-face, no-nonsense, and sometimes harsh person that I can be needed to soften up!

I must confess that my life is a work in progress but, with God's help, change is within reach.

Lord, change is never easy, but with Your guidance it is possible. —Pablo Diaz

Digging Deeper: 2 Timothy 3:16, James 1:22–24

Tuesday, February 2

Whoever serves, as one who serves by the strength that God supplies—in order that in everything God may be glorified through Jesus Christ. . . . —1 Peter 4:11 (ESV)

Since my first visit to Saint Paul's, I had felt loved and appreciated. As a new church member, I needed ways to use my gifts, but all my familiar roles were filled: soloist, cake decorator, newsletter writer, Sunday school teacher. What could I contribute?

My pastor offered me a part-time position as a secretary. I was to assist the administrator with typing and other mundane tasks while she recuperated from surgery.

Staff received me with warmth. However, any notions of creative writing and socializing soon gave way to the reality of outwitting the high-tech copier to crank out reams of documents in solitude. I made spreadsheets and answered several phone lines, once disconnecting the bishop's office! I filed invoices, often in the wrong places. Skyrocketing stress prevented me from catching typos and caused me to make even more. ("Food Panty" was definitely the worst!)

Yet Monday through Friday, I witnessed the inner workings of "weekday church." Scores of people lugged bags from the food pantry and thrift shop. Many received money for medicine. Countless volunteers (CEOs, nurses, PhDs) tagged secondhand clothes and doled out canned goods and compassion.

I left my position once the administrator returned. Now I contribute to choir, hospitality, and writing, but my awkward secretarial contribution taught me firsthand that a gracious spirit is a gift more blessed than perfection.

Lord, thanks for reminding me that I don't have to be perfect to serve You. —Gail Thorell Schilling

Digging Deeper: Matthew 5:5, Romans 12:5–6

Wednesday, February 3

"Even to your old age I am he, and to gray hairs I will carry you. I have made, and I will bear; I will carry and will save." —Isaiah 46:4 (ESV)

Help me see Your beauty in this, I pray silently. We're in the car on the way home from visiting my ninety-three-year-old mother-in-law.

The first time I met Sybil, almost twenty years ago, I was struck by her eyes—ocean blue, so clear and bright, that I found myself looking deeply into them as if I just might see a distant gull soaring in the sunset.

Over the last few years, Sybil has battled a number of health problems, the most devastating being dementia, which causes her to need round-the-clock nursing care. As Sybil's memories began to fade, she said the same prayer over and over again: her five children's names, in their birth order. Often she would pause and ask how they were, each one, unaware she was speaking to her youngest and forgetting that her oldest had died years ago.

To explain these things was unbearable, so her prayer would continue. The same question would arise: "Are they all right?" The same answer: "Yes, they're all good." And her eyes would twinkle as she would respond, "Yes, yes. Good." But now, even the names and memories of her children have slipped somewhere—heaven, I hope—and her sharp crystal eyes have softened to beautiful sea glass.

On the drive from the nursing home, I put my hand on my husband's and just hold it there, searching for something to say and not finding anything. We sit with the hum of the motor. Even the boys in the backseat are quiet. They, too, know there are no words. I look out the window at the sun in the distance and go to my familiar prayer:

> **Dear God, help me see Your beauty in this. Help me to trust Your plan and feel blessed to be a witness.** —Sabra Ciancanelli

Digging Deeper: Psalm 28:7, Isaiah 28:29

Thursday, February 4

"And the Word was made flesh...full of grace and truth." —John 1:14 (KJV)

I was walking to my car when I saw a man coming toward me. *Oh no, not again*, I thought. It was obvious that he was homeless, hadn't had a bath in a while, and didn't plan to buy food with whatever money he might ask of me.

A day earlier, I'd had a similar encounter as I walked down this same street with a friend. "These guys spend all their time begging," he had said. "I don't support that sort of behavior. If you give him money, he'll just get drunk."

Now this man was approaching me. "Do you have any money to spare, sir? I'm awfully hungry."

I stopped dead-still. A story my dad had shared with me played across my mind. It was by a nineteenth-century theologian who told of his childhood. When walking with his father, they came upon a blind man begging for money. His father pressed a bill into his son's hand and told him to put it in the man's cup. He did as he was told and returned to his father. "You didn't tip your hat to the man," the father said. The son answered, "But, Dad, he's blind." To which the father replied, "Yes, but what if he's faking?"

"This, Brock, is a story of grace," my dad said.

I smiled at the man who stood before me. I slipped some money into his hand. "God bless you," he said.

I'm sure I saw God's love filling his eyes, and that set me to wondering about grace. Was it mine to give—or his?

Dear Lord, thank You for the lessons that You bless us with from the most unlikely people and places.
—Brock Kidd

Digging Deeper: Numbers 6:25, 2 Corinthians 12:9, 1 Peter 5:5

Friday, February 5

Whatever is pure, whatever is lovely, whatever is admirable—if anything is excellent or praiseworthy—think about such things. —Philippians 4:8 (NIV)

"There's nothing on this slide," I muttered to myself as I fiddled with minor adjustments on the microscope. I was supposed to be looking at some sort of pond organism for my college biology class, but I couldn't find a thing. I had tried raising the viewing platform, changing the magnification, and cleaning the lens. Still nothing. I let out an exasperated groan. I just wanted to go home. I was tired of the day, this class, and looking into an empty microscope. I leaned toward my lab partner. "Did you find anything on yours?" I asked.

"Sure I did. I see dozens of little things kicking around." He looked over at my equipment. "Did you adjust your microscope?"

"Yeah. I still can't see anything."

He moved over for an inspection. "Whoa, man, you're way out of focus," he said. He spun the dial several times. "Try that."

I put my eye up to the lens. Twenty-some tiny organisms were creeping across my viewing field. The once-empty slide was rife with living things. I stared in amazement.

Maybe I needed a change of focus too. I hadn't been in the best mood today. I had grumbled about everything, from my professor to the lab equipment. But what if I decided to think about the positives instead of the negatives? The A on my quiz. The opportunity to learn about God's creation. My helpful lab partner.

I paused and thanked God for the blessings I had ignored in my negativity. And just like my slide, what had been empty became full of life.

Father, thank You for biology and microscopes and tiny creeping things. And help me to see what is excellent and praiseworthy in them all. —Logan Eliasen

Digging Deeper: Proverbs 17:22, Colossians 3:2

Saturday, February 6

The eternal God is your refuge, and his everlasting arms are under you. —Deuteronomy 33:27 (NLT)

The doctor who was about to replace my hip bone with a manufactured one came into the pre-op room. "Are you nervous?" he asked.

"Yes."

"Me too," he joked, signing his initials on my right thigh.

I smiled and tried to relax. I'd fought this hip replacement for three years, until the pain became too limiting. Now here I was; there was no turning back. I had confidence in my doctor. Most of all, I had confidence in my Lord. I repeated Psalm 28:7 (NLT): "The Lord is my strength and shield. I trust him with all my heart."

After two hours, I was out of surgery. Everything went well; now I needed to recover. The next two weeks passed in a fog of painkillers and sleep. I stayed focused on just getting through.

Normally I talk with God throughout the day. Now I was acutely aware of my need for Him but unable to gather my thoughts. How would I get through if I couldn't even pray? Then one day, lying in my study, it hit me: my family and friends were doing the praying that I could not. Their prayers, not mine, would make the difference. Peace instantly filled me.

Lord, thank You that when I'm too weak to even pray, I have the prayers of others and Your everlasting arms.
—Kim Henry

Digging Deeper: Psalm 42:1–2, 5; Isaiah 46:4

Sunday, February 7

Search me, O God, and know my heart: try me, and know my thoughts: And see if there be any wicked way in me, and lead me in the way everlasting.
—Psalm 139:23–24 (KJV)

I squirm in the uncomfortable wooden pew. I am healing after rupturing a disk in my back two years ago while fighting a wildfire on our family's cattle ranch. There are still many days when sitting for any length of time is torturous. Trying to concentrate on the pastor's message only makes the pain in my back radiate more intensely.

"C'mon, God, stop this pain," I pray through gritted teeth. "I'm here to listen to Your message, remember?"

Immediately I feel contrite. Am I trying to goad God into making me feel better? Am I treating Him like a genie in a lamp, here to perform at my beck and call?

"Forgive my weakness, Lord!"

I came to church to worship God as best I could. He doesn't ask any more or less of me. Even if I can't focus on the sermon, I can focus my thoughts on Him. Worship also means worshipping through pain. That I can do gladly.

Please help me overcome my struggle with pain, Lord. Help my imperfect flesh dwell on Your perfect love with all my heart. Lead me in Your way.
—Erika Bentsen

Digging Deeper: 1 Chronicles 28:9

Monday, February 8

BEING RENEWED: Seeking Help

"With all our tribulation and in spite of it, I am filled with comfort...." —2 Corinthians 7:4 (AMP)

Family and friends surrounded me while Gene was in surgery. The surgeon would repair a spiral break that involved his left hip and femur. He'd said Gene couldn't put any weight on that leg for three months. I was deeply concerned about his recovery. But I felt guilty about a ridiculous concern for myself. I didn't want anyone to know I couldn't sleep in my house alone. When darkness closes in, I become wide awake.

Gene's surgery went well, and everyone left. I sat by his bed in the semidarkened room. He slept quietly. I grabbed my cell phone at the first hint of a ring.

"Mom," my son Jeremy said, "I want you and Gene to know I'm going to be there for you. Y'all have been there for me all these years. Even when I didn't deserve your help. I'm going to stay with you for three months. I'll be working, but I'll spend the nights and do whatever needs doing. I'll keep the kitchen sink spotless—just the way Gene does. You just name what you need, and it will be done. You don't have to worry about anything. Okay?"

"Okay," I whispered and put the phone back in my purse. Jeremy had been the clown of our family and kept everyone laughing. He still does. Jeremy, who had such a passion for hard work. Dear Jeremy, who'd fought addictions and bipolar disorder fiercely, courageously. Jeremy, who'd come so near giving up on himself but didn't. We'd be living together again after all these years. A huge measure of sweet comfort unfolded in my heart like a soft blanket.

Father, thank You for meeting each need so graciously.
—Marion Bond West

Digging Deeper: Isaiah 51:12; 1 Thessalonians 4:18

Tuesday, February 9

"Lord, to whom shall we go? You have the words of eternal life." —John 6:68 (NIV)

We're getting ready to move. I don't want to leave our home, Andrew *really* doesn't want to, and the kids *really, really* don't want to go. But we've had too many years of not quite making ends meet and need to sell our apartment while the market's good.

I wake up in the morning with a to-do list a mile long, praying, "Lord, give me the strength!" Half the time what I mean is "Lord, make this easier!" God has reminded me—more than once—that when He gives me strength to do hard things, it's still my job to put that strength to work. So I've figured out how to plaster large sections of wall and retile the bathroom. I've taught the kids to prime and paint. I've purged closets and given away toys and books.

Every few days one of the children asks, "But, Mom, where will we go?"

I reply, "We won't know until we have a contract for sale." We can't look for a rental apartment until we have a closing date.

I'm careful to make the move seem doable to the children, though I lie awake in bed at night trying to figure out the logistics. I remind them (and myself) that the cross we're asked to bear right now is uncertainty. Wherever we end up, it won't be far away. Wherever it is, we'll be with one another—and God will be with us.

Jesus, in every transition I go through, help me move closer to You. —Julia Attaway

Digging Deeper: James 1:17

Wednesday, February 10

"I, I am he who blots out your transgressions for my own sake, and I will not remember your sins." —Isaiah 43:25 (ESV)

I'm on a stepladder, retrieving Easter decorations. There's a carved cross for the buffet, ornamental eggs for the hurricane vase, a wicker rabbit for our table. But the small handmade basket with flowered paper and "Mom" written in child's print will stay in the box. It brings regret.

The basket had been a surprise gift from my son. He made it when he was ten and had saved his allowance to buy chocolate to place inside. On Easter morning, after all the boys had found their baskets, he'd declared, "There's one more basket! We have to look! I know!"

I'd misunderstood. Often my ten-year-old had wanted a bit more than he'd been given, and so I snapped, "You have your basket! Be happy with what you have! It's frustrating when you're not satisfied." My son's smile faded, and when he led me to the hidden gift for me, I ached.

Now, deep in adolescent struggle with that same son, I regret that morning still. I long for his wide-open smile and the extravagant gesture of little-boy love. I long to pull him into my arms, peer into his heart, take his hand, and peek playfully behind curtains and chairs.

But today is Ash Wednesday—a day to confess my iniquities, my shortcomings. And with that comes my need for Jesus's perfect, redeeming work on the Cross. Standing there on the ladder, box in hand, I wonder, *Can I allow Jesus's blood to cover my long-held regret?* I set the box on the floor, tug the flaps, lift the basket, and run my fingers over my son's scrawl, over my own name. I can place this basket on the piano; over and over again it can remind me of enduring grace.

Lord, thank You for removing my sin and shame. Amen. —Shawnelle Eliasen

Digging Deeper: Acts 3:19, Titus 3:5, 1 John 1:9

Thursday, February 11

WHAT THE SAINTS HAVE TAUGHT ME
Caedmon, Companion of Self-Doubters

The Lord is my strength and song.... —Exodus 15:2 (KJV)

I could see the ruins of the monastery far across the North Yorkshire moors. Whitby Abbey was the first Christian settlement in this whole part of England, founded in 657 by Saint Hilda. The saint who fascinated me, however, was not this Anglo-Saxon noblewoman, but a humble cowherd who labored on the abbey's farm.

Like most people then, Caedmon could neither read nor write. That was the domain of the monks and nuns. Farm workers' lives were hard. The only entertainment was the singing contest each evening, when they gathered around the fire, passing a small harp from hand to hand. Poor Caedmon! He grew tongue-tied at the sight of the harp. Panicking at the thought of singing, he'd creep away and hide among the cows in the barn.

One bitterly cold night when he'd bedded down beside the animals, a bright figure appeared in the dark stable. *Sing to me!* the apparition said.

"I can't sing," the cowherd stammered. "I'm hiding here, so they won't ask me."

Sing, Caedmon. Sing about creation!

And from the cowherd's mouth poured a glorious poem in praise of God the Creator.

What a crazy dream! Caedmon thought when he woke next morning. Yet he remembered every word of his song. Incredulous, he rushed out and recited it to other farmhands. The astonished farm manager took him to Abbess Hilda, who could scarcely believe the beauty of this hymn in the "uncouth" English language. Monks translated Scripture passages for the cowherd; Caedmon turned each verse into eloquent song. For the rest of his life, the first-known English-language poet lived at the abbey, creating hymns that carried the good news across the land.

Give me words, Father, to sing Your praise.
—Elizabeth Sherrill

Digging Deeper: 2 Samuel 22:50

Friday, February 12

"I will sing a new song to you, O God; upon a ten-stringed harp I will play to you." —Psalm 144:9 (NRSV)

At the age of eighty-eight, the actress Cicely Tyson returned to Broadway for a plum role in Horton Foote's play *The Trip to Bountiful*. She played Carrie Watts, a homesick, elderly woman eager to return to her erstwhile hometown. In doing so, Tyson not only stole hearts but also won rapturous ovations and the first Tony Award of her storied career.

I watched Tyson play Watts as a little hapless and helpless but a lot feisty and energetic, and it occurred to me that the character and her journey are in many ways analogous to the seeker's life. Her son and daughter-in-law do not—cannot—understand her mind or heart. So Watts relies on her faith in the powerful but unseen, as well as on the assistance of strangers, to get where she needs to go.

The play's most memorable moment comes as Watts sits in a bus station, waiting for the ride that could bring her a little closer to home. Suddenly, she launches into the old hymn "Blessed Assurance." "This is my story, this is my song," she sings, "praising my Savior all the day long."

The audience soon joined Tyson in song. It was wondrous, hundreds of voices joined in this theater-turned-church. *Was this the Spirit's leading? Was it the emotional manipulation of the audience by a brilliant actress?* Perhaps it was both; it doesn't matter.

In that moment, I saw all of our stories coming together with Carrie Watts's. None of us, however eager to get on with the journeys we believe God has prepared, travel alone. Our testimonies, lived and spoken, help one another.

God of celebration, remind us how our stories and songs come together in You. —Jeff Chu

Digging Deeper: Psalm 100:1–5, Colossians 3:16

In all circumstances take up the shield of faith, with which you can extinguish all the flaming darts of the evil one; and take the helmet of salvation, and the sword of the Spirit, which is the word of God.
—Ephesians 6:16–17 (ESV)

What was supposed to be a fun, romantic evening spiraled quickly into a nightmare. My husband and I were enjoying a date when the text came: Congolese immigration would no longer allow adopted children to leave the country. This would be effective for up to twelve months. And here we thought we'd be bringing our daughter home in three!

Needless to say, my husband and I didn't finish our date. I was sick to my stomach. We hurried home to get online, so we could figure out what was going on. The US Embassy in the Democratic Republic of Congo confirmed the news. It didn't take long for my mind and heart to spin into a black hole of worry and doubt.

Two of my friends, also adopting children from the Congo, were spinning alongside me, until one of them offered up a Bible verse. That's all it took. Suddenly, these two friends were firing off Scripture references: Exodus 14:13–14, Nahum 1:7, Matthew 10:29, Hebrews 10:22–23.

My friends were wielding the one and only, all-sufficient weapon God has given us to fight the enemy. Even though their knees were shaking and their hearts were breaking, they drew their swords, and I felt like I could breathe again.

God, Your Word is power and truth. When the world spins out of control and worry and doubt close in, help me to bravely hold up Scripture. —Katie Ganshert

Digging Deeper: Zechariah 4:6, Hebrews 4:12

Sunday, February 14

How precious is your steadfast love, O God!
—Psalm 36:7 (ESV)

I wasn't looking forward to Valentine's Day. After fourteen years of marriage, I was going through a divorce and didn't want any reminders of how happy other people were with their sweethearts.

My friend Jody called and asked if she could run by.

"Come on over," I said. "I'm certainly not doing anything."

Soon Jody arrived at my door, holding a vase filled with a dozen red roses and a box of chocolates. "These aren't from me," she said.

I looked at her, confused. "Then . . . who?"

"They're from God," Jody explained. "I asked God to make sure that today, of all days, you would know how much He loves you. I know if God were here in the flesh, He'd bring you flowers and chocolates and tell you how much He adores you. I'm just making the delivery."

For the next full week, the flowers stayed as beautiful as the day Jody brought them, and every time I saw them on my kitchen table I smiled, knowing how much I was truly loved.

Father, thank You for Your servants who remind me just how close by You always are. —Ginger Rue

Digging Deeper: 1 Thessalonians 4:9, 1 John 4:16

Monday, February 15

The Lord has anointed me to bring good news to the afflicted; He has sent me to bind up the brokenhearted, to proclaim liberty to captives and freedom to prisoners.... —Isaiah 61:1 (NAS)

A while ago I was standing in the gymnasium at a high school in Australia, and I had finished my ranting to the students, and the burly teacher next to me had glared down the hubbub of happiness now that the shaggy American was finally finished with his interminable nasal burble about how every moment is pregnant with miracles and how we are made of the stories we seize from the slew of natter and how defiant grace and courage are prevalent everywhere and in everyone if we look hard enough, and there was a silent instant.

Then a lanky boy in the back row said, "Sir, you are going on and on about stories. What's the single greatest American story ever?"

For once I said exactly the right thing at the right moment, and even now I wonder if some holy spark in me was waiting merrily for this moment. For I said, with startling passion, "The day the sixteenth president of my country said that as of January 1, 1863, no people could be sold in America anymore, no brown children sold in the market, no weeping mothers sold away from their children, no roaring husbands torn from their wives, no more, done, the end. And he got shot in the head for it, and I think he knew he would be murdered for it, and he did it anyway because he knew it was right. And that's the greatest American story of all: that a tall skinny guy from Kentucky did the right thing even when he knew he would get a bullet for it. Does that answer your question?"

There was a long silence and then they roared too, a tide of applause; not for me, not at all for me, but for a guy who did the right thing, no matter what. We can do that, every moment. Happy Presidents' Day.

Lord, thanks for the tall skinny guy from Kentucky. Thank You for his wry sinewy courage, to which we Americans can turn when we hesitate to do the right thing. —Brian Doyle

Digging Deeper: Luke 4:18–19

Enter his gates with thanksgiving, and his courts with praise! —Psalm 100:4 (ESV)

The morning after Dad died, there were a thousand things to do: phone calls to make, e-mails to send, a memorial to plan, a notice to write up for the newspaper. He had been in a wonderful nursing facility for the last few months, Monte Vista Grove, and had been on hospice care for several weeks. As Mom said, "We had the luxury of saying good-bye." Even so, I was surprised when she told me over breakfast that morning what she wanted to do first: "I want to go back to Monte Vista."

"Are you sure, Mom?" I asked. "I can go by myself to pick up his things." The place had been a godsend, Dad's last home, where we could push him in his wheelchair on garden paths. We all loved the caregivers who helped Dad, teased him, cajoled him, sang to him, laughed with him, and made him comfortable. Twice a day for these five months, Mom had gone there to share meals with Dad in the lunchroom, getting to know the other patients. Did she really want to go back now?

"Let's go," she said with determination.

We parked under the oak trees, pushed open the glass door next to the sign that read "I was sick and you visited me." We walked to the nurses' station, past Dad's empty room. Mom greeted the nurses and aides, one by one, giving hugs, words of praise. "I wanted to come by and thank you for all you did," Mom said. I looked on in wonder. Thankfulness came first—thankfulness in her first hours of widowhood, thankfulness in the midst of mourning.

I picked up Dad's things, and then we got back in the car. "I'm glad we did that," Mom said. Thankfulness was the way to move on.

I give You thanks, Lord, for those who have enriched my life. Let me not forget to thank them as well.
—Rick Hamlin

Digging Deeper: 1 Corinthians 1:4

Wednesday, February 17

FINDING REST: A Gift from God

Jacob . . . lay down. . . . And he dreamed that there was a ladder set up on the earth, the top of it reaching to heaven; and the angels of God were ascending and descending on it. And the Lord stood beside him. . . .
—Genesis 28:10–13 (NRSV)

Whenever I read this Scripture, I feel jealous of Jacob. What I wouldn't give to close my eyes to seek rest and have God send a dream to comfort me! My rest is, as often as not, an epic struggle between a too-vivid imagination and a perpetually anxious mind. When the two sides stop their tug-of-war and start working together, it's even worse.

Just as Jacob was on the run from Esau, the brother he had wronged, I am sometimes on the run from worries and problems when I lie down to sleep. I don't always go to bed expecting peace or that God will give me rest, and a dream I had recently makes me wonder if my perspective is the real problem.

I dreamed that I was running laps in a strange place, sometimes on a path, sometimes on a road. The entire dream consisted of my running. When I awakened, I automatically started down the "poor me" path because of another night of restlessness and exhausting dreams.

Then I noticed how I felt: Good! Awake! Energetic! So I started thinking about the dream. How had I really felt during it? Alive, optimistic, strong, amazed that I could keep running. And in my amazement, I'd realized that there was no way I was running so strongly and well on my own; God was giving me the strength.

For the first time after one of my seemingly exhausting dreams, I was fully rested.

Oh, God, help me recognize that I can always access your comfort, waking or dreaming, if I just remember to shift my perspective. Amen. —Marci Alborghetti

Digging Deeper: Genesis 28:16, Psalm 32:6–7

Thursday, February 18

"The promise is for you and your children and for all who are far off—for all whom the Lord our God will call." —Acts 2:39 (NIV)

Today, on the phone, my former student Ali spoke of my daughters as "children of the covenant."

"What does that mean?" I asked her. Homeschooled by missionary parents, Ali often speaks a language I don't understand.

"Oh, you know. You've raised your girls in a Jesus-loving household. Now it's up to God." Ali was telling me to trust in God's promise, something I struggled with.

We'd been talking about a fantasy I have: that the older my daughters get, the closer I will be to contentment. In my shimmering vision, they love God, are in happy relationships, fulfilled in their jobs, living in clean houses, and raising healthy children with parental confidence and foresight I never experienced. But the older my daughters get, the farther away this heavenly vision seems.

Sometimes I think this fantasy is my main impediment to contentment. After all, my home is fairly clean; I love God and my husband and my work; my girls are healthy and thriving and occasionally kindhearted and God-oriented. Still, I'm anything but content when I start worrying about them.

God and every angel who ever visited Earth commands, "Fear not!" I long to obey, but how does one shut down this particular worry?

Today, considering God's many pledges of love to us, I suddenly resaw my fantasy as God's too: What we want for our children is what He wants for us. With one difference: God has the power to make it happen.

Father, Abba, Daddy, we are the children of Your hopes and many promises, the children of Your power and love. Let everything happen according to Your good purposes. —Patty Kirk

Digging Deeper: Proverbs 22:6, Isaiah 54:9–17

Friday, February 19

"Holy, holy, holy is the Lord of hosts; the whole earth is full of his glory." —Isaiah 6:3 (NRSV)

The wind shook my tent. It poked sharp fingers into my sleeping bag. I was camped on snow beside an alpine lake in Yosemite. The snow had fallen the night before and more was expected. A layer of fresh powder blanketed the peaks around me, glowing eerily in the moonlight. The temperature was below freezing and falling.

But I wasn't worried. I sensed God in all of it—the snow, the wind, the cold. So I lay curled for warmth, at peace.

How different from a year ago! I'd hiked this very same trail, solo like now, and I'd been anxious the whole time. It was balmy then, dry as a bone. But I'd been preoccupied, worried about work, pestering God to give me some clear guidance about the future. The louder I raised my voice in prayer, the less I seemed to hear.

This time I tried a different approach. I remembered something a wise friend said: "All of life can be prayer if you let it."

I let my boots hitting the trail be prayer. The dense pines at the trailhead and the rockscapes above the tree line. My tired muscles. My hunger at dinner. The silence of the lake reflecting snow. The moon. The stars. And now the cold and the wind.

It worked. Looking patiently for God in the landscape, I saw Him. Listening for His voice without the noise of my own demands, I heard Him. And seeing Him, hearing Him, I felt His peace in a way I'd never experienced before.

I curled up tighter. I couldn't sleep in this cold wind. But I didn't want to. I was in God's presence. I would savor every moment.

I'll let You do the talking when I pray today, Lord. Speak to me in the beauty of Your creation.
—Jim Hinch

Digging Deeper: Psalm 24:1–2, Zephaniah 1:7

When pride comes, so does shame, but wisdom
brings humility. —Proverbs 11:2 (CEB)

My friend Ann is a pastor of a small church in
Brooklyn, New York. Their actual membership is
about fifty, but on nights when they offer a hot meal
to the homeless or on food-pantry afternoons, their
numbers swell to two hundred or more.

I happened to be there the day the local food-
surplus organization delivered three tons of fresh
green beans to the front lawn of this little church.
Have you ever seen three tons of green beans? I'm
six feet five, and the stack of crates towered over me!
All afternoon, volunteers rotated in and out, cooking
the meal for that night's dinner or bagging the fresh
beans two pounds at a time for the food pantry the
next day.

At one point I found myself bagging beans with
an actor who, in a few hours, would be performing
his role in a Broadway play. "What does it feel like
to come onstage at the end of the play with the
audience standing and clapping?" I asked him.

"Actually, I get more satisfaction from working
here," he said, "because it's not about people saying
thank you to me for something I've done. It's about
me saying thank You to God through what I'm
doing. That's what gives me the deepest satisfaction."

Since that day, I've adjusted the way I think. It's not simply about doing good and being recognized for it; it's about intentionally asking how I might use part of my skill that day to say thank You to God. That subtle change has filled my soul in profound ways.

Thank You, God, for opportunities daily to say thanks through my actions for the great gifts You've given.
—Jeff Japinga

Digging Deeper: Luke 14:7–24, Philippians 2:1–11

Sunday, February 21

"Bear in mind that the Lord has given you the Sabbath...." —Exodus 16:29 (NIV)

I've always heard about the forty days of Lent between Ash Wednesday and Easter. But guess what? The math doesn't compute. It's really forty-six days; the six Sundays don't count. I learned that because we live on this side of the Resurrection, many describe Sundays in Lent as "little Easters," each one a day for worshipping and celebrating Jesus's Resurrection, a day when many choose not to fast but to feast.

Me too! I decided. During Lent, I usually give up my numbing automatic responses for self-gratification to remind myself of what Jesus gave up for me. Most often that's something I mindlessly

78

put in my mouth—something sweet or salty or convenient, like the last bites of cheese-dripping pizza left on a child's plate. I vow to eat more frugally, except on Sundays.

At family gatherings or lunch with our couples group after church or dinner with my husband, I've feasted. It sounds self-serving, but it has set Sunday apart as a day of celebration because Jesus has risen. And that reflects the rhythm of life with Jesus, a pattern of both suffering and celebrating, fasting and feasting. By doing that more intentionally, I become more aware of celebrating little Easters throughout the year.

Lord, I want to live in the rhythm of life with You.
—Carol Kuykendall

Digging Deeper: Romans 8:17, Philippians 3:10

Monday, February 22

"I am. . . ." —Psalm 46:10 (KJV)

When I was fifteen, I had life all figured out. Already, I had modeled a bit and was taken with the attention. I expected that as time went by, I would go on to New York City, where my face would be splashed across magazine covers. I would live on Fifth Avenue, collect Steuben glass, and wear only designer clothes.

Immersed in these self-centered teenage fantasies, I was sitting on the piano bench gazing into the big mirror in our living room when it happened. Unnoticed, my mother had come into the room and caught me wallowing in my vanity. "Pamela, there will always be someone prettier than you and smarter and richer. Concentrate on your heart. That's the only happiness that lasts," she finished, searing each word into my memory.

Embarrassed as I was, I knew I had heard the truth. "Go to that place of the heart where God is," she kept urging me as I developed a more substantial plan for my life. "When you find God within yourself, He'll tell you who you are and who you're meant to be."

I never made it to Fifth Avenue and never owned a single piece of Steuben glass. Mirror-gazing? My mother's words pretty much cured me of that. Fortunately, the things I've done in life have never relied on my looks.

"I Am," God reminds me from deep within my being.

"You are," I answer back.

Father, You are the great I Am. Let my heart be a reflection of You. —Pam Kidd

Digging Deeper: Exodus 3:14, Isaiah 44:6, John 14:6

Be wise in the way you act toward outsiders; make the most of every opportunity. —Colossians 4:5 (NIV)

I always knew that Dad met my mother when they were in college, but I never knew the details. Recently, when visiting Dad and Bev (Mother died in 1979), I asked him the specifics. "I met your mom in the assembly hall at Western Illinois University in 1941. She was a junior, and I was a sophomore. Everyone had to sit in alphabetical order. There she was in the middle of the row: Lucile Knapp. Then an older married couple who were students, Mr. and Mrs. Knappenburger. Then me, Ed Kobbeman. I'd seen her around campus but didn't know her name."

Dad said he was delighted when their last names brought them together. When he leaned over the older couple to talk to Lucile, the couple moved down a seat so Dad could sit next to the woman who had caught his eye.

What if Dad's name had started with a different letter? He may never have met my mother. My siblings and I would not have been born.

What if I hadn't talked my brother and sister into taking a vacation in Florida? We would never have bought a condo together, and I would never have moved there.

What if I'd never started talking to Jack in the pool across the street? We may never have gotten married.

I believe that these *what ifs* are gifts from God, the great orchestra leader. God wanted my dad to meet Mom that day in the assembly hall in 1941. He wanted me to move to Florida and meet Jack in the pool. I think God just wants us to talk to others to get things started.

Next time I feel an urge to talk to someone who looks sad, lonely, out of sorts, or just plain interesting, I'm going to do it. Who knows what might happen if I just open my mouth?

Father, I know it's important to speak up when I'm out and about. Nudge me to use my words to do Your work. —Patricia Lorenz

Digging Deeper: Proverbs 31:26, Philippians 3:12–21

Wednesday, February 24

Look to the Lord and his strength; seek his face always.
—1 Chronicles 16:11 (NIV)

"Will you please pray for me right now?" my friend Sam texted in her moment of distress.

"I'm on it!" I replied before setting aside my phone to continue making dinner. I pulled out a carrot from the refrigerator and began to peel it, thinking about how Sam's husband had lost his job and they were struggling to buy groceries. Next came tomatoes, and I considered how hard it must be for Sam to watch her husband apply for job after job only to be turned down. Then I added an avocado and some lettuce. I finished up the salad and picked up my phone to see another text from Sam. "I'm really struggling. Life feels so heavy."

I swallowed a lump of guilt. I had promised to pray, but instead made salad and allowed my mind to be carried away with my own thoughts. My friend needed to be in front of God, Whom she so desperately needed.

I headed to the couch, where I got down on my knees and lifted Sam and her family up to God. I pleaded with Him to bring her peace and clarity as they figured out the next steps. I prayed that God would bring her hope that went beyond human understanding, so she could walk forward and trust Him to provide even when things seemed dire.

Another text came: "Peace has calmed my soul, my desperation is gone, my hope has been reclaimed."

We need only to ask—not think, not meddle, not solve, not talk—and our great, powerful, all-knowing Provider will do the rest.

Lord, draw my eyes toward You and my knees to the floor when my loved ones need You most. Amen.
—Erin MacPherson

Digging Deeper: Romans 8:26, Philippians 4:6

Thursday, February 25

But you are a chosen generation, a royal priesthood, a holy nation, His own special people, that you may proclaim the praises of Him who called you out of darkness into His marvelous light.
—1 Peter 2:9 (NKJV)

I've always been interested in how I got here. I understand the basics. I was conceived, born, baptized, and eventually found a job and got married. But what about all those dominoes that had to fall just right, down through the centuries, to get me to this spot?

The name Grinnan is Irish, though not common, and there is some dispute whether it is of ancient origin or of later Norman provenance.

Most Grinnans came from farm country in central Ireland, a county called Offaly. I scoured church death records starting in 1845, when a catastrophic blight fell upon the potato crop of Ireland. More than one million Irish would perish of starvation over the next four years and even more would flee or be driven from their lands, sick and destitute. I saw many death certificates for the family name Grinnan in several neighboring parishes. I traced some Grinnans to Liverpool. A friendly scholar explained that's where the so-called famine boats left for the United States. I found the manifests. Yes, precious Grinnans had made it on board. "More than half usually didn't survive the crossing though," he said, shaking his head. "Starvation, disease. Some simply threw themselves overboard in despair."

Yet I made it. My father's father's father survived the crossing. And here I am, the American representation of the gene pool. Nothing could amaze me or sadden me or inspire me more. For none of it was random or meaningless or lucky or unforeseen. Not by a God Who sees all and understands all, Whose ways are not always known to us but never unknown to Him.

Father, You have breathed life into every one of us since the beginning of time so that every life has a purpose. Today, help me to fulfill mine. —Edward Grinnan

Digging Deeper: Psalm 82:8, Isaiah 14:27

Friday, February 26

Now therefore, listen to me, my children; pay attention to the words of my mouth....
—Proverbs 7:24 (NKJV)

My wife's grandmother was a lovely woman who managed to raise two successful daughters despite her eighth-grade education, a retail-job budget, and a husband who was a husband in name only. Shortly after my wife and I were married, I agreed to drive "Little Marie" to Washington, DC. As we entered the Pennsylvania Turnpike in Pittsburgh, I said, "So how've you been, Mrs. Hughes?"

"Well," she said, "I was born January 13, 1912, the coldest day of that year—six pounds, twelve ounces . . ." and she didn't let up for the next 236.7 miles. No detail was spared—none. By the time we reached the George Washington Parkway, we had made it only to 1953. "I'll tell you the rest on the way home," she said.

See? That story took only fifteen seconds to tell, but four and a half hours to hear. We do this shorthand summary all the time: *He's the new guy from the Cleveland office* or *She's the exchange student from Brazil*, as if that somehow says it all. We spend hours writing our résumés, hoping to condense a lifetime onto 8½" × 11" paper with proper margins. It's unfair, really—which details do we leave out in deference to brevity? Instead we retreat to sweeping generalizations and platitudes, hoping clichés can convey what sentiment eludes us.

We're not résumés. We're not synopses. To paraphrase singer Jim White, our lives are "contradictions that are larger than any language can explain." Maybe that's why we pray to Someone Who knows our hearts and not our words, Someone Who knows all of our stories, Someone Who will listen for four and one-half hours while we share exactly just who we are as we find our way home.

Lord, spare us from clichés and platitudes so that we may know each other's hearts. —Mark Collins

Digging Deeper: Job 38:18–23, Psalm 84:3

Saturday, February 27

Let perseverance finish its work so that you may be mature and complete, not lacking anything.
—James 1:4 (NIV)

"C'mon, David, you can do it!" We had taken our seven-year-old grandson, visiting us in north Idaho, to a fitness facility. He'd already made one failed attempt on the thirty-three-foot rock-climbing wall. But he'd seen an older boy try it barefoot and decided to remove his shoes and go at it again.

"Yes, yes!" we cheered as he neared his goal. He would have to free one hand and stretch to ring the bell at the very top. It looked scary from below. He summoned his courage. *Ding!* He had done it!

That night, while I was out, David lost a table game to his grandpa. He asked to play again and won. Telling me about it the next day he said, "I learned from climbing the rock wall that if I didn't give up and tried again, I could make it."

His insight reminds me of a successful "second try" story from the Bible. After Jesus's nighttime arrest leading to His Crucifixion, His disciple Peter denied he ever knew Him, exactly as Jesus had predicted: "Before a rooster crows, you will deny Me three times" (Matthew 26:75). When the rooster announced the dawn, Peter felt like such a failure he "went out and wept bitterly" (Matthew 26:75).

But the account doesn't end there. After the Resurrection, with Jesus's encouragement, Peter tried again (John 21:15–17). He went on to become one of the great voices for Christ to the world. In this story, I see a Savior Who gave His all the first time, so I could have a second try.

Jesus, it's because I've tried again—and sometimes multiple "agains"—that I know You are always reaching for me, giving me hope for a new try.
—Carol Knapp

Digging Deeper: Luke 15:11–24, Romans 8:31–34, 1 Corinthians 15:10, Jude 1:24

Even so the body is not made up of one part but of many. —1 Corinthians 12:14 (NIV)

Only a few are gathered for Sunday service...nineteen, to be exact, counting Blake and Kate's baby. *How long can our church stay open?* I ask myself as I start the prelude. Another, more poignant question follows: *Should we stay open? Is it right to put resources into a building where so few people worship? Could our pastor be better used by God in a larger congregation?*

The Call to Worship and three praise choruses later it's time for announcements, joys, and concerns. Our pastor reads a note thanking us for serving lunch following a funeral. "We especially appreciate your kindness since we don't belong to your church," the writer says. A community Bible school sign-up sheet goes around, and several people volunteer to teach lessons, help with crafts, or prepare food. We are reminded about Thursday's blood drive; our church has sponsored blood drives every two months for over ten years.

Later in the service we pray for a family whose grandfather died and a young man in Marine Corps basic training. We pray for the world, our nation, and our community. We praise God for a woman's successful cancer surgery. We give tithes for church support and offerings for disaster relief and distribution of Scriptures.

By the time the sermon is over and the benediction pronounced, I've received an encouraging gift: the understanding that our church is much greater than nineteen souls in the sanctuary. We are a vital part of Christ's body, striving to be faithful disciples through our worship, prayer, gifts, and service for Him in the world.

Lord Jesus, we rely on your Word: "So don't be afraid, little flock. For it gives your Father great happiness to give you the Kingdom" (Luke 12:32, TLB).
—Penney Schwab

Digging Deeper: Matthew 16:18–19, Revelation 3:8

Monday, February 29

One of his disciples said to him, "Lord, teach us to pray...." —Luke 11:1 (NIV)

Two weeks after Christmas, my neighbor dragged his Fraser fir tree to his side yard. I guessed that he was planning to leave it at the curb for the recycling truck, but the tree stayed in his yard for weeks. I started praying, *Lord, please move my neighbor to move his tree to the curb, so the recyclers can pick it up. Amen.*

That petition became part of my daily prayers. Each night I asked God to touch my neighbor's heart, so he would be moved to properly dispose of his tree. Each morning the tree was still there.

A month later, I was still praying. One morning I went to my driveway to put out my recycling bin and looked over at my neighbor's Christmas tree. I walked over, grabbed it, and headed to the curb. I got the tree there just in time for the recycling truck that was making its way down the street.

Just then my neighbor opened the door and called out, "Thank you! I hurt my back dragging that tree out of the house and didn't know how I was going to get it to the curb."

"Sure thing!" I responded, smiling.

Another neighbor from across the street walked over. "So you finally got him to do the right thing and move that tree?" she asked.

I shook my head. "I asked God to move this man to move his tree," I replied. "Instead, God moved *me* to move the tree."

She smiled, put an arm across my shoulders, and said, "Funny thing, isn't it? The purpose of prayer is not to change what God does but to change who we are."

Thank You, all-powerful and all-knowing God, for the gift of prayer that changes me so I change things. —Melody Bonnette Swang

Digging Deeper: 2 Chronicles 6:35, Psalm 42:8

GOD'S ABIDING LOVE

1 _____

2 _____

3 _____

4 _____

5 _____

6 _____

7 _____

8 _____

9 _____

10 _____

11 _____

12 _____

13 _____

14 _____

15 _____

16 _____

17 _____

18 _____

19 _____

20 _____

21 _____

22 _____

23 _____

24 _____

25 _____

26 _____

27 _____

28 _____

29 _____

March

Whoever dwells in the shelter of the Most High
will rest in the shadow of the Almighty.

—Psalm 91:1 (NIV)

He has told you, O mortal, what is good; and what does the Lord require of you but to do justice, and to love kindness, and to walk humbly with your God?
—Micah 6:8 (NRSV)

About a month after the kidnapping of 276 Nigerian girls from their school, I went to a #BringBackOurGirls interfaith call to prayer. We prayed, sang, and heard Scripture in many languages and from diverse religious backgrounds. We were then charged to talk to those around us and come up with one action that we could take to help end violence against women.

While that is certainly a large call, speaking with my pew neighbor in a prayerful and reflective manner brought forth fruit. I told her that I would do as the New York City "philosophy" suggests: "See something, say something." I tend to keep quiet and to myself, resolving any issues and wrongdoings by taking them to God in prayer. But my adviser pressed me to consider what kind of help my words might offer to those struggling internally.

So now, if someone says something that does damage to women, I speak up. It can be pretty nerve-racking for an introvert, but by doing so, I am claiming space for all women to fully exist. The conversations can be awkward because, let's face it, no one wants to be on the receiving end of accountability. But I've gotten braver and kinder with my language so that I can talk from a place of love—of God.

God of many names, keep me humble as I do Your work. Help keep my eyes looking for the divine in every uncomfortable conversation. —Natalie Perkins

Digging Deeper: Isaiah 1:17

Wednesday, March 2

"Trust in the Lord with all your heart...."
—Proverbs 3:5 (NIV)

I opened our mailbox and immediately suspected that the letter on top, with the unfamiliar, neatly written address, was from a *Daily Guideposts* reader. His name was Roy, and his letter referred to my devotion on New Year's Day 2001 about a Christmas gift my husband, Lynn, had received from a friend in his Bible study group.

It was a framed message beautifully penned in calligraphy that my husband placed on the kitchen counter: *Lynn, trust me. I have everything under control. Jesus.* The words began to shape my pensive attitude about what the new year might hold for me.

Roy, who is also a calligrapher, began penning this message to family and friends, and, before he knew it, he was getting requests to create these gifts for others he didn't even know. "I am humbled and amazed at how this ministry continues to spread the powerful message of God's love for us," he wrote. "I am enclosing a list of the names of those with whom I have shared these meaningful words." Included were several sheets of paper with nearly six hundred names.

I believe one of God's ways of spreading His truth is person to person, writer to reader, reader to friend. What a privilege to be one of the connections in that sacred pattern.

Creator God, You give us our creative ideas and unique connections, which bless us and others. I pray these earthly connections also bless You.
—Carol Kuykendall

Digging Deeper: Psalm 56:4, John 14:1

Thursday, March 3

"For where two or three are gathered in my name, there am I among them." —Matthew 18:20 (ESV)

My first day at Guideposts, I was arranging my desk stuff when a little bell went off at precisely 9:45 AM. A colleague said, "Time for Prayer Fellowship. It's voluntary, but you should come since it's your first day."

I knew little about Guideposts when I took the job. I certainly hadn't expected this, starting the week with a prayer meeting. I headed into the conference room where half the staff sat around a long brown table heaped with letters that contained prayers. People were finding ones to read and occasionally closing their eyes to pray silently. *That's it*, I thought. *I'm in a cult.* I considered sneaking out, grabbing my gear, and then heading for the hills. Too late. The door was closed. I was trapped in Prayer Fellowship.

But as we went around the table and each staffer read one or two requests out loud, I was drawn in. There were the megaprayers for world peace and an end to hunger. But it was the microprayers, the everyday prayers, that moved me most. Someone asked for prayers for his old car, so he could take a job that required him to drive. A wife prayed that her husband would shave his beard—she found it scratchy—but was afraid of hurting his feelings. It came as quite a revelation: people depend on prayer.

The forty-five minutes went by fast, as have the twenty-nine years since. Guideposts has moved its office a couple of times, most recently to downtown Manhattan, but we still have that brown table and we still gather around it every Monday morning, reading prayer requests, though many now come through the OurPrayer Web site and Facebook page. Maybe on Monday you can set that little alert bell on your phone for 9:45 AM and join us in prayer.

Lord, You said that whenever two or more are gathered in Your name, You are there. We want to keep You busy on Monday mornings, for there is no prayer too big or small for You. —Edward Grinnan

Digging Deeper: Psalm 145:18, Philippians 4:6, 1 Thessalonians 5:17

Friday, March 4

Jesus replied, "You don't understand now what I am doing, but someday you will." —John 13:7 (NLT)

When my sister Maria died in her sleep, I thought the grief would lift when I could finally learn what happened. But when the autopsy came back with all the test results normal—no trauma, nothing wrong—I was baffled.

I spent hours on the Internet searching for the truth. I borrowed forensic books from the library. One late night, nose-deep in a medical book, I suddenly realized my mistake: I thought that if I found out *how* she died I would understand *why*. The answer was something I'd never find in a book.

I turned to prayer. I asked God to help me understand. No answer came. I prayed about it more. I changed my prayer to help me find peace without knowing. I still pray about it.

Not long ago a coworker brushed me on the shoulder and said, "Hey, did they ever find out what happened to your sister?"

I shook my head. "She just died."

"Must be hard not knowing," he said.

"It strengthens my faith," I replied. As soon as the words left my mouth, I knew I meant it.

Dear Lord, when doubt and questions trouble me, help me to have faith that there are reasons I'm not to know right now. —Sabra Ciancanelli

Digging Deeper: Job 3:24, Proverbs 3:5–6

Saturday, March 5

For by me your days will be multiplied, and years will be added to your life. —Proverbs 9:11 (NRSV)

It was 7:30 AM. I punched in my sister's telephone number. "Happy fiftieth birthday!" I exclaimed.

"Ugh. That sounds so old," Shelby groaned. Her voice was heavy. Besides celebrating this milestone, she was scheduled to work long hours with her boss today. "When you get this old, there's nothing really special about birthdays anyway."

Why did I procrastinate? I chided myself. I'd been there and knew how she felt. I'd hoped to cheer her up, but her birthday surprise wasn't scheduled for delivery until *after* today. Three states away from each other, we normally don't exchange presents. But when we'd talked last week, Shelby confided dread over her impending birthday. I wanted to make her smile with a surprise and surfed the Web. A tower of treats—four boxes filled with chocolates, stacked on top of one another and tied with a bright-blue ribbon—looked impressive. But she watched her weight. I didn't know if two pounds of chocolate would thrill or annoy my sis, so I put off the idea.

Four days before her birthday, the sugary idea still nagged at me. I ordered, but delivery took five to seven days. I felt silly asking for divine intervention with the candy's arrival, yet I did. I wanted my baby sister to feel special.

Later in the evening, Shelby called. "Thank you so much," she said, oozing with delight. "I'm rationing myself to two pieces a day. At least my first month of being fifty will be sweet!" She giggled.

I fist-pumped the air. The candy's arrival on her birthday was a special gift to me too.

Father, thank You for caring about even the little things that make us feel special.
—Stephanie Thompson

Digging Deeper: Psalm 139:13–16, 1 Peter 4:8

Sunday, March 6

For we walk by faith, not by sight.
—2 Corinthians 5:7 (NRSV)

"Guess what, Dad? I'm actually going to church today," my son told me one Sunday last year. In fact, it was Easter morning, but I didn't want to read too much too quickly into a simple text message.

The "Guess what" part was because he knew I'd be surprised. I have two kids in college. Both were raised in the church, and although their Sunday school experiences were fairly uninspiring throughout the formative years, we always sat together in the pews as a family on Sunday mornings, talking about what was happening and why it was important, as I tried to pass along my passion for a personal relationship with God.

I often say, "Faith didn't 'take' in them. I honestly don't know why." By the time both kids were teenagers, I felt like a failure. Neither of them seemed to have a personal faith of their own. So I prayed and prayed.

You see, when my son texts me from college in Boston about going to church on Easter morning, there's a lot going on.

"I'm glad," I write back after he fails to answer the phone. "Tell me later what you thought of it."

You are the One Who changes our hearts, Lord.
I leave the real work to You! —Jon Sweeney

Digging Deeper: Ephesians 2:4–9

Monday, March 7

When you lie down, you will not be afraid...your sleep will be sweet. —Proverbs 3:24 (NIV)

One year ago, I was blessed with my darling, curious, whirling dervish of a child, Olivia. From her first days, you could see her desire and frustration, even as her tiny hands flailed about, desperate to get out of her swaddle blanket.

As she grew, so did her passion for movement. No snuggle baby here! If Olivia was awake, she was moving, crawling, rolling, climbing, and navigating the stairs over and over again.

Family members and babysitters loved to tell us that she didn't look tired or that she'd never be ready for bed. But her daddy and I knew better. The more Olivia partied and played, the closer we knew she was to surrendering to sleep.

When she hit a frantic pace, waving her arms, standing up and dropping down, or flinging books over her shoulders, I'd take her to the nursery, rock her, and read her a story. It was only then that she'd sigh and relax into my arms.

As I'd sit rocking her, I'd think, *How often does my heavenly Father watch me as I bustle around, tackling my never-ending to-do list and hardly stopping for a minute to eat, much less pray?* It is in that wonderful chaos that He calls me to climb into His arms and simply be.

In my special chair with my favorite blanket, I feel Your presence, Lord. I'm so glad I can rest in You.
—Ashley Kappel

Digging Deeper: Exodus 33:14, Matthew 11:27–30

Tuesday, March 8

For where your treasure is, there your heart will be also.
—Matthew 6:21 (ESV)

"Well, we're not paying an extra five thousand dollars to move those," my wife, Julia, said crossly, looking at the bookcases that took up the longest wall in our living room. They went from the floor to the ceiling, and the books were all double-shelved.

We'd been having this argument for years, but now it had taken on a new urgency. We were thinking of selling our apartment, and the thought of taking all those books with us was more than Julia could handle.

I started to sulk. The books were repositories of the wisdom and knowledge of the centuries. And perhaps more important, they were *my* books. They told the world—and me—who I was.

"How many of those have you read anyway?" Julia asked.

I shrugged. "That's not really the point," I murmured.

"Well, if the point of books isn't reading them, what is their point?"

You have a point there, I thought. "Well…I've read a lot of them," I stammered.

Julia gave me a skeptical look and went back to her work.

For years I'd thought my book collecting, even if it was a vice, was an innocuous one. But I was only fooling myself. Sure, my particular vice wasn't as catastrophic as smoking, drinking, or gambling, but it was eating away at my marriage. It had taken the place my faith and family should have occupied. It had become my identity, crowding out everything else from my heart.

I diddled and dawdled, but eventually I found someone who would box my books, take them away, and even pay me something for them. Now there are only three bookcases against the wall, with space for other things. And there's a little more room in my heart.

Lord, help me to keep my heart open to You and the people You have given me to love. —Andrew Attaway

Digging Deeper: Psalm 51:10, Isaiah 44:9

Wednesday, March 9

> "Whenever you did one of these things to someone overlooked or ignored, that was me—you did it to me."
> —Matthew 25:40 (MSG)

My heart was breaking for my daughter Katie. Without warning, her marriage was ending. The two of us stood side by side in the dining room of her lovely home, packing up her things. We didn't say much. Unspeakable sadness filled my heart. I couldn't imagine how she must be feeling.

Her dark pine table was covered with china, dishes, and crystal—wedding gifts. Their marriage that began so beautifully almost eight years ago was over. We hand-wrapped the once-treasured items in newspapers and placed them in cardboard boxes.

Lord, help Katie smile, I prayed silently. *Let her experience joy again.*

I spent that last night with her in the house, and the next morning we found an apartment. After she paid the deposit, we spotted a woman crying softly, talking to the manager. "I'm so sorry for whatever's happening in her life," Katie said.

"Me too," I responded.

The next day, Katie called. Her voice sounded like she was sixteen again—young, hopeful, full of promise. "Mom, you'll never believe it, but that woman's going through a divorce too! She has no one. She needs beds for her two children and food. After work, I'm meeting her to help her move. I'm ordering them a pizza, bringing toys for her children, and asking my friends to help, and I'm going to see if she can use my dishes."

Bittersweet tears came. Katie was going to make it.

Oh, Father, You arrange love so beautifully. When we reach out to someone overlooked, we ourselves are healed. —Julie Garmon

Digging Deeper: Nehemiah 8:10, Galatians 2:20

Thursday, March 10

BEING RENEWED: A Thin Place
"I have lift up mine hand unto the Lord....
—Genesis 14:22 (KJV)

While Gene was in the hospital, I spent the days with him. God seemed to give me wondrous energy. The surgeon thought his hip would heal, but Gene was discouraged. Truth be told, he'd been depressed long before his accident. I so wanted to help him find joy again.

Preparing to leave one evening, I laid my head on his chest, assuming he'd wrap his arms around me. He didn't.

Oh, God, I don't want to leave him. But I can't stay day and night. I hesitated at the door, unable to move. Finally, I walked to the elevator. My heart stayed in Gene's room.

The elevator was going to be crowded. A clump of people stood before the opening door. One woman balanced a tray of food precariously in her hands. A tiny girl stood close, holding on to the woman's red coat. As the mother moved toward the door, the child lost her grip. Without looking up, perfectly calm, the girl simply stuck her hand high in the air. The mother didn't see her. My instinct took over, and I reached for her small hand. We entered the elevator together, the mother and I finally exchanging smiles.

Oh, the sweetness of that tiny hand in mine, trusting totally. In the lobby, the child and mother disappeared. My hand remained warm from the child's touch.

When I located my car in the dark underground parking lot, even before unlocking it, I raised my hand high in the air. Exiting the darkness into the last golden rays of the sun, I sensed God's holy presence.

Oh, Father, the very same hand that was pierced for me still cares for me. —Marion Bond West

Digging Deeper: 2 Chronicles 30:12, Psalm 10:12

Now, our God, we give you thanks, and praise your glorious name. —1 Chronicles 29:13 (NIV)

After five days of helping my eldest get settled into her apartment—efficiently, calmly, and with motherly confidence—I climbed onto the bus to the airport and waved good-bye. Out of my daughter's sight, I promptly burst into tears. The reality of leaving Elizabeth halfway across the country spread through my guts, my heart, and my body like a pool of liquid grief.

I let myself cry. And cry. Eventually I reminded myself that the magnitude of my hurt was the measure of my love. Then I thought, *No, that's not true. The hole in my heart is only the size of my loss.* My love is much bigger.

Raising Elizabeth has given me beautiful memories, pushed me closer to God, taught me to give sacrificially. Being her mom has been as much about my own growth as it's been about her growing up.

I began to think of all of the ways in which being Elizabeth's mother has been a blessing. There were—are—a lot. Remembering the good things didn't diminish the gaping hole in my heart, but it did make me thankful. And having a thankful heart is a good start for building the next phase of my relationship with my girl.

Lord, letting go of those I love is hard. Thank You for setting the example for how to do it. —Julia Attaway

Digging Deeper: 2 Corinthians 6:18

Saturday, March 12

Great is his faithfulness; his mercies begin afresh each morning. —Lamentations 3:23 (NLT)

Sometimes we don't realize God's grace until it's taken away. For me, this happened in the Congo while visiting a child whom we're in the process of adopting.

This day, in particular, had been a hard one—a she-won't-let-me-put-her-down, I-don't-know-what-she-wants kind of day—in a foreign, impoverished country where nobody spoke my language. I was concerned about her speech. I was concerned about her lack of muscle mass. I was concerned that she was hungry but had problems with eating. We needed to get her home. To start speech therapy. Physical therapy. Food therapy. I was hopelessly overwhelmed. It hit me with so much clarity: *Life will never be the same. This adoption road will never get easier.*

Despair parked itself on my chest. How had I gotten here, to this country, with no guarantee of getting my baby home? I crawled into bed, eyes puffy and bloodshot, wondering how I'd get up in the morning.

But then the morning came. And you know what? I was okay. I could breathe again.

I wonder if God didn't peel away His protective blanket of grace for that one night to let me feel the full weight of despair. Not because He's mean, but because He wanted to show me the evidence of His grace in my life and where I'd be without it. In light of that time, the discomfort I experience on this adoption journey has become a reason to praise God; His grace covers me.

Lord, if I could truly wrap my mind around the magnitude of Your grace, I would never be able to get up off my knees. —Katie Ganshert

Digging Deeper: Psalm 54:4, Isaiah 41:10, Hebrews 4:16

Sunday, March 13

FINDING REST: "God Will Provide"

Moses said, "Eat this today, because today is the Sabbath, a day of rest dedicated to the Lord, and you will not find any food outside the camp. You must gather food for six days, but on the seventh day, the day of rest, there will be none." —Exodus 16:25–26 (GNT)

Several years ago my husband and I were volunteer servers at a soup kitchen in Key West, Florida. The volunteers were presided over by a stern, majestic woman named Sarah, who dealt with everything from homeless families to unruly patrons to making sure there were enough paper plates and plastic forks. One Sunday we showed up with a few other stalwarts. We were going to serve chili and pizza, both to be supplied by local restaurants. We prepared salad and sliced bread as we waited for the food to be delivered... and waited.

By the time we accepted the fact that the food wasn't coming, there were more than one hundred people, including children, lined up outside for the only meal they would have this Sabbath. There was no time to go to the store. Besides, all of us had arrived on bikes or been dropped off.

Sarah was calm. "God will provide" was all she said.

Another volunteer decided to go to the kitchen for extra juice and water; at least we could keep people hydrated in the brutally hot weather. There was a shout from inside. On the large walk-in fridge was a note from the church's youth program leader: "We had to postpone our spaghetti supper at the last minute. Please use what you need!" The fridge was filled with vats of spaghetti and meatballs.

Smiling serenely, Sarah helped us transfer the food to the stovetops, told the crowd we'd be a little late, and fifteen minutes later watched as we fed 114 people.

Almighty God, help me to remember on every Sabbath and on every day that I depend upon You for everything! Amen. —Marci Alborghetti

Digging Deeper: Matthew 6:25, Mark 8:4–5

Monday, March 14

For everyone born of God overcomes the world.... —1 John 5:4 (NIV)

I trudged through the snow from the subway to my job. Winter wonderland had lost its charm months ago. I could see my frustration mirrored in my fellow New Yorkers. We had already endured double the amount of snow we're accustomed to in winter, and here we were wearing snow boots on the first days of spring. *Would it ever end?*

I walked into the office, grumbling about the weather as I took off my coat. While most echoed my sentiments, my boss looked up with a smile and said, "The flowers always triumph over winter."

The image stayed with me throughout the day: tiny, fragile flowers resting patiently under the snow and earth, waiting in confidence to claim their inevitable victory. While I knew warm weather would eventually show up, I had allowed the cold, snowy day to discourage me. How often I shrink in the face of difficulties, feeling too small to conquer the great trials before me. I grumble in doubt instead of calmly waiting for the victory that is already mine.

Thank You, Lord, for the flowers that rest patiently and confidently in Your timing. Help me to trust You like that. —Karen Valentin

Digging Deeper: Habakkuk 2:3

Tuesday, March 15

"Peace I leave with you. My peace I give you. I give to you not as the world gives. Don't be troubled or afraid." —John 14:27 (CEB)

I headed out to the park for my morning run. I had such a passel of worries somersaulting through my brain that I could hardly take in the sun rising behind the clouds, flushing the sky with pink, nor the daffodils opening up in brave yellow flanks on the hillside. Not for nothing did Jesus say, "Consider now the lilies."

I was on my first loop, dreading the hill, my steps slowing, my thoughts stuck on an absurd cycle of looming penury and decrepitude, when I saw a runner in a fluorescent-green jacket coming toward me. Was that Jim? Yes, it was. A history professor and writer, he's always got something interesting to say.

"Can I join you?" he asked.

"Please," I said.

The next two loops flew by as we discussed the book he was writing, the class he was teaching, how our sons were doing, and just how much easier it was to run uphill with a companion.

"Thanks a lot," I said as we parted ways. "You were just what I needed."

"You were too," he said. "I never go that fast by myself."

"I've forgotten already what I was worrying about."

All the way home my eyes were open to the beauty of the day. Call it endorphins, call it sunshine, I'd say friendship was my boon companion. I recalled something preacher and writer Max Lucado once said: "When you're really down, when you're losing faith from excessive worry, get with your loving friends. They'll lead you back to God."

Two loops with my pal Jim did just that.

I give thanks, Lord, for the bounce that friends always put in my step. —Rick Hamlin

Digging Deeper: Proverbs 12:25, Ecclesiastes 4:9

Wednesday, March 16

After fasting forty days and forty nights, he was hungry. —Matthew 4:2 (NIV)

Today I got a text from my daughter Charlotte. "Want to give up meat for Lent with me?"

Unsolicited conversations of a spiritual nature are so rare, so delightful, with either of my daughters. *Answered prayer!* I thought.

Immediately afterward, though, I began to doubt that her text had anything to do with God or Lent. Although she's thin and healthy and eats heartily, Charlotte loves weird fasts and diets. Just last month she and some friends had gone on a crazy two-day juice cleanse involving pricey liquids: a bitter green one, a fatty one made of cashews, and lemonade laced with cayenne and maple syrup. Was her desire to give up meat for Lent just such a game?

I prayed for the right response, some way to focus the conversation and the ensuing fast on spiritual matters without causing her to shut me down as preachy.

After praying, I was still unsure how to reply, so I consulted my colleague Jake, a Presbyterian minister's son who, I often joke, is my own personal Holy Spirit. Though younger than I, Jake always offers helpful advice. "Ask her what she wants to put in its place," he said.

I knew what he meant. I also knew what Charlotte's answer would be: vegetables, tofu, nuts, pasta.... Nevertheless, as typically happens when I consult Jake, I felt empowered.

"Okay," I texted back. "That's a meaningful sacrifice. Let's also think of a way to be spiritually intentional about it." I suggested possible strategies and then hit Send. I didn't really expect a reply.

Imagine my delight when I got one: "Okay." Not a full-out statement of commitment, but still.

Dear God, show me how to make You real to others, to help them know You. —Patty Kirk

Digging Deeper: Matthew 6:16–18

Thursday, March 17

WHAT THE SAINTS HAVE TAUGHT ME
Patrick, Companion When You're Wronged
But I say unto you, Love your enemies....
—Matthew 5:44 (KJV)

I used to dread St. Patrick's Day. The Irish-American kids at school wore green, sang Gaelic songs, and made it clear that it was a bad thing not to be Irish.

So I was gratified when I discovered that Patrick wasn't Irish either. Son of a government official in Roman Britain, he was a cultured Latin-speaking Briton. When Patrick was a child, Ireland was the stuff of nightmares—a pagan land of marauding pirates who periodically swept down on his civilized Christian homeland.

In 405, when Patrick was sixteen, the nightmare came true. A gang of Irish raiders attacked his coastal village, dragged him to their boat, crossed to Ireland, and sold him as a slave. Tending his master's sheep on a rocky mountainside, all but naked through the long winters, always hungry, what sustained him was a single thought: *Escape!*

It was six years until his master's absence gave him the chance. Running by night, hiding by day, he finally made his way to the coast and across the sea to Britain where, in gratitude for his deliverance, he decided to devote his life to God.

It was at the seminary in France where he was studying for the priesthood that the strange dreams began. He heard Irish voices begging him to come back and bring them the Gospel. And, of course, Patrick did go back. For thirty years he traveled ceaselessly throughout the island, teaching, baptizing, planting churches, and bringing learning and peace to the land where he had received only cruelty.

Father, You gave Patrick grace not only to forgive but to turn wrong into blessing. Teach me, too, to forgive and bless. —Elizabeth Sherrill

Digging Deeper: Luke 6:28

Friday, March 18

Jesus said unto her, I am the resurrection and the life: he that believeth in me, though he were dead, yet shall he live. —John 11:25 (KJV)

Good Friday was just one week away. I was contemplative as I thought of Jesus's sacrifice for me. I imagined Him hanging from the Cross, blood running from His beaten body. I envisioned the crown of thorns on His head and the nails in His hands and feet. I also thought of the victory of that Cross, that the Savior rose on the third day, conquering death.

For this I was happy...until I spotted those Easter lilies at a store. They were beautiful and white, each with three full blooms. They reminded me of Jesus's Resurrection, but they also reminded me of two miscarriages years ago. That Easter, I hadn't felt joy and hope; I was still reeling from the loss. Sure, I had a loving husband and a sweet five-year-old son and a Savior Who'd died and rose from the dead for me, but I wasn't eager to sing "Because He Lives."

One thing I was eager to do was purchase a lily in memory of the precious children I'd lost to be displayed in church. I never had the privilege of holding those babies or kissing the tips of their noses or rocking them to sleep, but I could choose to remember them.

Good Friday reminds me that living brings pain and difficulties and death. It also reminds me that it promises joy and hope and new life.

Lord, help me to remember the pain of Good Friday and to never forget the victory of Easter.
—Carla Hendricks

Digging Deeper: Romans 6:8–11,
1 Thessalonians 4:13, 1 Peter 1:3

Saturday, March 19

A PRAYERFUL LENT: The Gift of Being Last

"Then Simon Peter came along behind him and went straight into the tomb...." —John 20:6 (NIV)

It was almost closing time at the Garden Tomb in East Jerusalem, and our group of five was the last through the iron gate. With no time to spare, a gentleman ushered us quickly up a shaded pathway to stone benches. I sat looking longingly over my shoulder at the garden we had hurried through—beautiful flowers, lush trees, small spots tucked away just begging for me to come and meditate on Christ's Crucifixion, burial, and Resurrection. But we'd arrived too late, and there was no time for us to linger.

Our guide hit the highlights of how the strange limestone formation might have been Golgotha, the place of the skull, because of the two slanting holes in the cliff's facelike eye sockets. This garden area had been a vineyard at one time, discovered when they uncovered an ancient stone winepress. Quickly, we were escorted down to the small square hole in a steep, straight cliff that had been a quarry.

The previous tour group finished snapping photos inside the tomb. Suddenly, it was entirely empty. The five of us stepped into the chamber together. We fit perfectly, gazing in awe at a stone-carved trough where Christ's body may have rested. "Let's sing 'Christ the Lord Is Risen Today,'" one of our group members said. We fell into song in lovely harmony as the walls of the tomb echoed our joy.

Dear Jesus, sometimes being last can become the first thing that You bless. Thank You. —Karen Barber

Digging Deeper: Matthew 19:30, 28:5–6

Sunday, March 20

A PRAYERFUL LENT
Seeking Reconciliation

"If you are offering your gift at the altar and there remember that your brother has something against you.... go and be reconciled to your brother...."
—Matthew 5:23–24 (NIV)

I was worshipping at Christ Church inside the Jaffa Gate in Old Jerusalem. When it was time for Communion, I knelt at the altar with my hands cupped to receive the bread. The minister broke off a small, crisp piece of matzo. When he gave it to me, he pressed it firmly down into my palm, breaking it as a symbol of Christ's sacrifice.

I walked toward some church members who were stationed in an alcove by the altar, available to pray for anyone who needed it. *I could use some prayer for my ministry*, I thought, approaching a woman and a man. The woman quietly prayed for my work, but I was surprised to hear the man say, "Lord, I have a perception that perhaps she should pray about giving any relationship in her life that is strained to God."

What? I thought in confusion as I made my way back to my seat. *I honestly can't think of any.*

The prayer had been so unexpected that I decided to meditate on it. *Well, I guess there's that woman at church whose actions I don't like. I really don't care to be around her.*

I remembered the broken Communion wafer and prayed:

Lord, You forgive me my sins. May I be more charitable and loving toward others and be reconciled to them in my heart. Amen. —Karen Barber

Digging Deeper: Matthew 6:12, Ephesians 4:31–32

Monday of Holy Week, March 21

A PRAYERFUL LENT: The Inner Walk

"I . . . enabled you to walk with heads held high."
—Leviticus 26:13 (NIV)

Lying still in an MRI machine, getting a brain scan, was the last place I expected to be two weeks before my prayer mission trip to Israel. I'd suddenly developed extremely high blood pressure and started taking medication. Then I had fallen getting out of bed, hitting my head, and landed in an emergency room with severe vertigo.

"Keep your head completely still," the nurse said. As the machine closed in around me, I realized praying was the only way to make it through the next forty-five minutes and I thought, *Picture yourself on your morning prayer walk where you commune with God.*

During a series of loud, obnoxious noises from the machine, I stood at my "trust spot" where I needed to cross a busy road. When the noises gave way to a quick beat, I crossed the street. As each series of noises came, I remembered details of previous times of communion with God on the quiet subdivision road. The huge oak tree where thousands of acorns littering the sidewalk reminded me of God's lavish provision. Rain gushing down the curb cleansed the pollen and debris from the road. A big landscape rock had me meditate on Christ praying on the rock in Gethsemane. As the machine made a noise like the sound of someone pulling a bow across a huge out-of-tune instrument, I felt utterly dependent on God, yet at peace with letting go of all of my own grand plans. *You'll be at that very place in Gethsemane soon.*

Finally, the machine stilled and the padded table moved out of it.

Dear Father, enable me to have a vivid inner walk with You in all of life's circumstances. Amen.
—Karen Barber

Digging Deeper: Deuteronomy 5:33, Psalm 86:11

Tuesday of Holy Week, March 22

A PRAYERFUL LENT: Seeking Healing

"And he was healed from that moment."
—Matthew 17:18 (NIV)

With not even two weeks to go before my trip, I continued to have serious problems with dizziness. *Will I be steady enough to go?* I'd been reading the Gospels in preparation, and now I paid close attention to the accounts of miraculous healings. Time after time it seemed that those who came to Jesus were healed, like the paralyzed man getting up off his mat—and walking!

I closed my Bible and prayed, "God, please heal me."

Suddenly, a thought came: *You must seek healing. The people who were healed by Christ had been seeking healing for a long time.*

With my trip deadline looming, I urgently needed help to get well. I contacted my doctor again. He referred me to a physiotherapist who taught me eye-focus exercises that would help. I scoured the

Internet for advice. I bought an elastic bracelet that hit a pressure point on the wrist to help with seasickness. I have always hesitated to ask others to pray for me, but I began admitting my need to more and more people. As a result, I had twice as many folks praying for me than if I hadn't reached out.

I wasn't completely over the dizziness when I boarded the plane, but I was well enough to manage. I had sought healing, and slowly but surely I was receiving it.

Dear Father, give me the ability to seek and follow the healing paths You are opening for me today, tomorrow, and the day after that. Amen. —Karen Barber

Digging Deeper: 2 Kings 5:11–14, Mark 9:29

Wednesday of Holy Week, March 23

A PRAYERFUL LENT: Spontaneous Joy

Others cut branches from the trees and spread them on the road. —Matthew 21:8 (NIV)

Our minivan was squeezing down an extremely narrow lane in Nazareth when our hostess said, "You may not be able to get out of the parking lot tomorrow morning because of the Palm Sunday processional."

"Palm Sunday?" I asked in surprise. "We celebrated Palm Sunday weeks ago back home."

"It's Eastern Orthodox Palm Sunday," she explained, "and all of the Christian churches in Nazareth have decided to celebrate on the same day this year." What a wonderful surprise to know we would be in the hometown of Jesus on Palm Sunday!

We arrived for services where two gigantic palms, at least fifteen feet high, arched over the cross up front. After the opening hymn ("How Great Thou Art" sung in Arabic), children from the congregation skipped forward to the altar. Instead of receiving palm branches as we would back home, these children were given small olive sprigs. *It makes sense, judging by the enormous size of the local palm fronds*, I thought. They processed down the center aisle, waving them as we stood, clapped, and sang a word that was the same in Arabic and English: *Hosanna! Hosanna!*

I learned that some believe since Jesus rode the donkey down the Mount of Olives into Jerusalem, many of the branches spread before Him may have been olive boughs. You use what's closest at hand for a spontaneous celebration.

Dear Lord, help me to use the ordinary parts of life available today to spontaneously join in praising You. Amen. —Karen Barber

Digging Deeper: Luke 19:35–38, John 12:12–19

A PRAYERFUL LENT: Choosing to Praise

I will praise God's name in song and glorify him with thanksgiving. —Psalm 69:30 (NIV)

As we walked onto the dock to board a boat on the Sea of Galilee, I reached for my camera. It was gone! I panicked, remembering I had hung it on a door hook in a bathroom stall. I sprinted back and searched the ladies' room twice; no luck. I walked back to the boat, dejected because I would be unable to capture the once-in-a-lifetime memories awaiting us on our trip.

I found a seat, and when we were in the middle of the lake, the captain, who was a Messianic Jew, took out his electric guitar to lead us in praise songs. *Oh, I wish I had a camera to photograph the large group of Russian Christians dancing and raising their hands in praise!*

As my thoughts quieted, I had a choice to make. I could continue to lament my lost camera or I could join the praise party of a lifetime. I got up out of my chair and began to sway and sing with the joyous crowd as we learned the Hebrew words to "How Great Is Our God." I felt my spirits lift and a smile break out on my face.

Finally, the music stopped and the captain steered the boat back to the dock. That's when I remembered I had my phone with me—and it took pictures!

Dear God, as I praise You today, may my spirits be lifted above my sorrows, losses, and problems. Amen.
—Karen Barber

Digging Deeper: 2 Samuel 22:50, Psalm 30:11–12

Good Friday Day of Prayer, March 25

A PRAYERFUL LENT: Have Love in All You Do

Pray for the peace of Jerusalem....
—Psalm 122:6 (NIV)

We had taken a day's drive to pray along the northern border of Israel. Now we were in Jerusalem, in awe of the complex intertwining of diverse people, history, and religions. Although I had signed up for this prayer mission trip, I was feeling inadequate about praying for such insurmountable problems.

A friend had arranged for us to meet a priest named Father John, director of the Notre Dame Center that runs an enormous landmark hotel for pilgrims and a Center for Healing. Father John was obviously very important, yet when we met him, he acted as if he had all the time in the world to entertain three strangers.

"When I was chosen by my order to be in charge of the center, occupancy was extremely low and it was in financial crisis," he told us. "I'd never stayed in a hotel, much less knew how to manage one.

'God, there must be some mistake,' I prayed. But God assured me He would help me in the task."

Then one of our group asked Father John, "Is there something specific we can pray for you?"

He smiled. "That I would have love in all I do."

In that moment God had given me two perfect answers to my feelings of inadequacy about my ability to pray for gigantic problems. I could be assured that God would help me in the task. And if I prayed "just for love," all of the seemingly unsolvable problems would be covered.

Father, I pray for Your love as the ultimate healing answer. Amen. —Karen Barber

Digging Deeper: Romans 8:26–27, 1 Corinthians 13:4–7

Please join us for Guideposts Good Friday Day of Prayer. Find out more at guideposts.org/ourprayer.

Holy Saturday, March 26

A PRAYERFUL LENT: Uncovering Faith

"Go," he told him, "wash in the Pool of Siloam...." So the man went and washed, and came home seeing." —John 9:7 (NIV)

The evening we arrived in Jerusalem from Galilee, I was suddenly overcome with severe vertigo. I sat forlorn on the sofa. *I've been fine for a whole week now. I hope this doesn't keep me from going on our walking tour of Old Jerusalem tomorrow!*

Immediately, an answering thought came. *Go. If you become dizzy, you can always sit down or hold on to one of your friends.* It was just enough of a response to calm my fears.

Months earlier I had hired a private guide for our tour. When he asked us if there was anything in particular we wanted to see, for some reason I had told him, "The Pool of Siloam."

The next day our guide took us across the City of David and then down through Hezekiah's tunnels, which were narrow passages dug in the rock to divert a spring into the city in case of siege. We emerged at the bottom of the Kidron Valley, where we ended up at an area of ancient stone steps near a huge water pipe. "These steps were accidentally discovered in 2004 when the pipe behind you broke and they excavated this area to repair it," our guide told us. "The steps are 225 feet long and led into a huge pool where travelers may have bathed before going up to the temple." Then he read the Scripture to us about the blind man being healed after Jesus instructed him to wash in the Pool of Siloam.

I suddenly saw my vertigo in a different light. It's often a problem like the man's blindness or a broken water pipe—or vertigo—that helps us uncover enough faith to go forth, even when we're not sure we can.

Dear Jesus, You are calling me to move forward in my life, no matter what. May I heed Your invitation. Amen. —Karen Barber

Digging Deeper: Nehemiah 3:15, John 9:1–11

Easter Sunday, March 27

A PRAYERFUL LENT: Finding Christ

"Where is the guest room, where I may eat the Passover with my disciples?" —Luke 22:11 (NIV)

I stepped inside the upper room with its vaulted ceiling held up by a series of pillars. My eyes roamed the interior for some painting, statue, inscription, or symbol of the Last Supper where Jesus broke bread and gave the cup to His disciples. This same place was supposedly the location where the Holy Spirit descended on the early church on Pentecost. They were such momentous happenings in Christianity, yet the room was full of nothing but tour groups and guides competing to be heard.

I sank down on a stone bench by the wall. *How do I find Christ in this empty, noisy, unadorned place?*

A group came in with flat black satchels out of which they unfolded white robes that they donned and said reverent words in Italian. Another group brought in a big box from which they took brightly painted ceramic chalices to place on a stone ledge. A group of Russians entered the room and sat on the floor as the guide read Scriptures to them.

Suddenly, it dawned on me. It was only fitting that the upper room was a place where you needed to bring your own faith instead of expecting that simply showing up would fill you with faith. When Jesus and His disciples gathered in this room, it was a borrowed space that required them to make their own preparations.

I closed my eyes and began to quietly sing, "Let us break bread together on our knees...."

Jesus, help me to prepare and bring my faith into the empty spots in my life that will be filled by Your presence. Amen. —Karen Barber

Digging Deeper: Matthew 26:17–30, Acts 2:1–4

Easter Monday, March 28

A PRAYERFUL LENT: Trying Harder

"Watch and pray.... The spirit is willing, but the flesh is weak." —Matthew 26:41 (NIV)

I was in the most famous prayer site in Christianity, in Jerusalem, at the very rock on which Jesus agonized in prayer right before His arrest and Crucifixion. Yet as I knelt on a pad along the altar rail that surrounded the huge outcropping of limestone rock inside the

Church of All Nations, I was extremely frustrated. I was trying to pray but couldn't concentrate because of the noise all around me.

The church was mobbed with tourists and pilgrims from all over the world who were standing in a long, fitful line for a chance to press forward and briefly touch the sacred rock. I clasped my hands while the person next to me whispered loudly to her friend, "Take a picture of me here!"

I closed my eyes tighter. A priest standing in the altar area intoned in a deep chantlike voice, "Silence, please." The crowd quieted temporarily, but after a microsecond of quiet, a growing avalanche of whispered chatter filled the air again.

This crowd is ruining my ability to pray! I thought grumpily. Then, *Try harder.*

Jesus asked His disciples to pray with Him in the Garden of Gethsemane, though they kept falling asleep. He roused them several times, basically saying, "Try harder." But perhaps Gethsemane-praying is not only about wrestling to do God's will but also about our daily struggles against the inner and outer distractions.

Father, may I learn from Christ in Gethsemane to pray harder when life makes it hard to pray. Amen.
—Karen Barber

Digging Deeper: Luke 18:1, 22:39–46

Tuesday, March 29

"I know every bird of the mountains, and everything that moves in the field is Mine." —Psalm 50:11 (NAS)

Easter is a beloved morning for me. I am outside early in nature, rejoicing in the Resurrection. This year, the first in our north Idaho home on a woodsy mountainside, I sat on the deck, listening to the birds and watching the sun play over the valley spreading before me.

Nearby a chickadee gave its *he-who* call—or so it sounded to me. I noted in my journal it reminded me of Jesus's words to Martha: "I am the resurrection and the life; *he who* believes in Me will live even if he dies, and everyone who lives and believes in Me will never die. Do you believe this?" (John 11:25–26).

Within moments a chickadee—maybe the same one—alighted on the rail. To my utter surprise it hopped on my shoe...along my outstretched leg...and looked trustingly at me from my lap. It jumped to my shoulder...and from there to my head.

Spellbound, I held motionless as it danced around in my hair, its tail feathers momentarily hanging over my glasses' lens. Then it reversed itself and left the way it arrived. Never had I experienced such a thing!

I went inside to tell my husband. Wishful thinking prompted me to say, "Watch from the window. Maybe it will come back." Beyond expectation, it returned! I felt honored that a little wild thing would visit me twice with such trust.

Jesus asked Martha if she believed He was the "resurrection and the life." He wanted her to trust Him for eternal life.

How a small chickadee appeared on an Easter morning to call forth Jesus's beautiful words of hope and to demonstrate exquisite trust is a mystery only God knows.

Son of God, with You "all things are possible" (Luke 18:27). I believe! —Carol Knapp

Digging Deeper: Genesis 1:20–23; John 1:29–34

Wednesday, March 30

Your Father knows what you need before you ask him. —Matthew 6:8 (NIV)

"Time for your pain medicine." I swallowed the pills my husband, David, handed me and hoped for respite from the intense protest of my assaulted leg. My hip joint of bone was gone. In its place were a titanium stem, ceramic ball, and plastic socket. My skin was glued back together. No wonder I hurt.

I needed help with most everything: getting up, lying down, moving, taking medicine, meals. David was living the "or for worse" part of our wedding vows.

I appreciated that he was handling things but yearned for a more romantic expression of his love. I envisioned his hand gently, lovingly brushing my hair from my forehead, though he hadn't ever done that in our thirty-eight years of marriage. He was so busy caring for my physical needs, I didn't feel I could ask him to care for my emotional needs too.

The medicine made me feel sick. One evening, feeling particularly bad, I asked David to check on me occasionally to make sure I was still alive. Sometime later that night I was awakened by his hand on my forehead, gently, lovingly brushing my bangs to the side. I smiled as I drifted off again.

A few days later David left the house to buy groceries. For the first time I had to get my own medicine. Reaching for it, I saw a stack of papers. There was a pile for each medicine, listing every date and time I'd taken it since surgery. As I spread them out, I saw his love written all over them.

God had gifted me with one romantic expression of my husband's love, and with those papers, He made me aware I'd had plenty more.

Lord, thank You for hearing my heart and opening my eyes. —Kim Henry

Digging Deeper: Psalm 20:4, Proverbs 13:12

Hast thou entered into the treasures of the snow?...
—Job 38:22 (KJV)

"Can you believe we're getting more snow?" fumed Liz,
my Pilates instructor. Our class groaned, not because
of the crunches she led us through, but because
we were heartily sick of winter and near-record
precipitation. This late in March, when crocuses
usually began poking through soil, a foot of dirty,
frozen snow still buried the state of New Hampshire.
Ice two to three feet thick, much of it compressed
snow, still covered the lakes. Now a nor'easter and
another foot of the stuff barreled our way.

After class, I reached my car as fresh flakes began
to fall. I sighed and opened my trunk to dig out
my well-used snowbrush. As I did, several single
flakes alighted on my glove where they contrasted
dramatically with the black fleece. Their delicacy
caught me off-guard. I lowered my brush to look—
really look—at each flake: some lacy, some daintily
spiked, all impossibly fragile.

I thought about the old Vermonter Wilson
"Snowflake" Bentley, who in the 1880s braved
the cold with his primitive glass-plate camera
and microlens to discover the fantastic crystalline
structure of individual flakes. He devoted his life to
photographing snowflakes and would have loved a

winter like this. Granted, he didn't have to dig out a car and drive on a highway, but he found beauty where I had found only irritation.

I spent a little extra time brushing my car that afternoon, stopping now and then to admire God's artwork floating onto my gloves.

Lord of all creation, thank You for the loveliness of snowflakes. —Gail Thorell Schilling

Digging Deeper: Psalm 8, Ecclesiastes 3:11

GOD'S ABIDING LOVE

1 _____

2 _____

3 _____

4 _____

5 _____

6 _____

7 _____

8 _____

9 _____

10 _____

11 _____

12 _____

13 _____

14 _____

15 _____

16 _____

17 _____

18 _____

19 _____

20 _____

21 _____

22 _____

23 _____

24 _____

25 _____

26 _____

27 _____

28 _____

29 _____

30 _____

31 _____

APRIL

My people will abide in a peaceful habitation,
in secure dwellings, and in quiet resting places.

—Isaiah 32:18 (ESV)

"For with God nothing will be impossible."
—Luke 1:37 (NKJV)

A speaker at church talked about the courage to pursue our dreams. "What dreams I have, God put in my heart, so that makes it a mandate that I respond to them because they're from God. And remember, you will not know how the dream will be fulfilled, only that through your actions it will be."

I thought back to when I'd found the courage to pursue a dream. For years, I'd wanted to write for Guideposts, but had no idea how to go about it. Then a friend read about the biannual Guideposts Writers Workshop competition and urged me to enter. I was hesitant. Seeing my reluctance, she added, "God doesn't give you the dream without giving you the courage to take the action to pursue it." With that, I wrote my story and submitted it. Accepted or not, win or lose, the point was to act on my dream, to do something about it, toward it.

I'm happy to report that my entry provided the opportunity to fulfill my dream of writing *Daily Guideposts* devotions, which I've done since 1999.

Dreams can be opportunities to step out in faith, not knowing how the dreams will be fulfilled, and that can be scary. But just as the speaker said that night, "If your dreams aren't big enough to scare you, then they probably aren't big enough."

Lord, thank You for giving me big dreams that require a big faith in You.
—Melody Bonnette Swang

Digging Deeper: Deuteronomy 31:6, Isaiah 41:13

Saturday, April 2

"I needed clothes and you clothed me...."
—Matthew 25:36 (NIV)

"Not that one!" my husband said as I pulled a well-worn, down-filled blue parka out of the hallway closet. We were trying to decide which of our many coats to give to the church clothing drive for the homeless in our community. "Each of our kids has worn it to feed the horses in thirty-below weather!" he told me, as if I didn't remember.

"Our closet is not a museum," I answered, not admitting that's what I'd been telling myself as I went through my own closet. The fact is I, too, felt sad at the thought of giving away "Big Blue." You know you're in trouble when a coat has a name.

"I'll take a picture of it and send it to the kids to see if anyone wants it," I decided.

First, our daughter Lindsay answered quickly. "You can't give away Big Blue!"

This is what her sister Kendall said: "No way! Big Blue is better tucked away in the back of your closet than keeping someone else warm. Just kidding! A little sad to part with it, but it has served us well and now can serve others."

So I cleaned up the coat and added it to our giveaway pile.

Lord, You have so richly blessed us. May we bless others with what You've given us. —Carol Kuykendall

Digging Deeper: Deuteronomy 15:7–8, Psalm 82:3–4, Hebrews 13:16

Sunday, April 3

"On the seventh day he rested and was refreshed." —Exodus 31:17 (NIV)

My husband's a certified public accountant and, during tax season, he works pretty much all the time, including Sundays. Tax season, as he sees it, is our ox in the ditch. Kris bears it without complaint. But I complain. "It's not healthy. It's not good for our marriage. And it's not fun."

I nag him to schedule exercise into the end of his workdays, and he follows that plan at the beginning of the season. Soon, though, it reverts to the same late nights, the same stress.

I wish I could rest for him, but I can't. I do take over his share of the housework and fix our electric fence if a cow charges into the yard. And on Sundays, either after or in lieu of church, we have "dates" at the bookstore. He brings his computer, thick file folders, and this gadget that gives him a secure Internet connection, and I bring students' writings to be graded. We drink cappuccinos all day. Such Sundays are pleasant—and I like getting things accomplished—but afterward I need a real Sabbath, a day of rest, a day of getting nothing accomplished.

One Sunday, I'd had enough. "We need a break," I said. "Let's go check out those new bike trails. You've always wanted to."

I'm not sure what persuaded him. That he'd always wanted to? That I wasn't complaining? That he, too, was burned out? We loaded our bikes in the car to leave straight from church. It was cool out and sunny. We cycled twenty miles, stopping for lunch along the trail. Afterward, though my legs were tired, I felt more rested than I had in years.

**Father, help us cease working and,
like You, be refreshed.** —Patty Kirk

Digging Deeper: Exodus 31:12–17, Hebrews 4

For, behold, the winter is past; the rain is over and gone. The flowers appear on the earth; the time of the singing [of birds] has come....
—Song of Solomon 2:11–12 (AMP)

Just when I thought it might never happen, spring has arrived. A record-cold winter with three feet of snow that stayed on the ground for a month is finally over. The bright, strong sun streams in the kitchen window. I'm about to reach for a cup of coffee when a large blur of something catches my eye out by the catalpa tree.

What is that? I think, looking closer to see a tom turkey strutting his stuff, splaying his feathers, and dancing in circles.

We've had one lonely wild turkey rambling about all winter. She struggled to make it to the bird feeder in the deep snow and often resorted to traveling in paths left by deer. But now I see a flock of four has joined her beside budding daffodils in my flower garden.

I watch out the window in awe of the turkeys and how stunningly beautiful, yet absolutely ugly, a creature can be at exactly the same time. "Come quick!" I yell to the boys, who have their noses in their tablets. Grudgingly, they get off the couch and put their faces in the sun and look out the window.

"That's the male," I say, pointing to the turkey hopping in circles. "He's trying to impress the females with his feathers."

"He's trying to get a girlfriend?" Solomon asks. "Cool."

"Maybe he's just happy that it's finally warm," Henry says. "Maybe he's dancing in the sun."

The boys go back to the living room, but I stay at the window to watch the tom turkey put into motion the prayer of gratitude that's been in my head:

Dear Lord, thank You for the sunny days ahead, of warmth and blue sky and green grass and flowers blooming, of the wonders of spring. —Sabra Ciancanelli

Digging Deeper: Genesis 1:14, Ecclesiastes 3:1–8

Tuesday, April 5

Blessed are the merciful, for they will be shown mercy. —Matthew 5:7 (NIV)

Millie and I detect Maurice one hundred feet down the block. Millie's nose rises in the air. I wish I could cover mine. Pretty soon she is dragging me over to her friend's doorway, where he is liquidly slouched.

"Millie!" he cries, arms out, speech garbled, eyes red slits.

Maurice is a wino, not homeless. He is particular about that. Maurice could never manage a home. He says the high point of his day is when he sees "Queen Millie." Then in a wheezy aside he says, "I tell that to all the girls."

By now Millie is trying to bull her way onto his lap. With the toe of my shoe, I inch his paper bag with a fresh pint of Mad Dog 20-20 out of harm's way. We see the homeless, and it's painful to imagine how to help them. We give up because we think they've given up.

Maurice and I are clear on one thing: I don't give him money. We both know what he'll do with it. I know what I did with it back when I was Maurice and begging change on the streets of New York City. Once I bought him a pack of cigarettes. He said he was dying for a smoke, and I thought, *He's dying anyway.* I gave him a sandwich when he looked especially gaunt. He put it by his bag and said, "Maybe I'll get to it later." I gave him an Alcoholics Anonymous meeting book and he tossed it back to me.

It was Millie who struck up the friendship with Maurice. She looks for him during his periodical absences and is overjoyed when he returns, sporting one of those plastic hospital ID bands. Maurice has had lots of those, all different colors—his stripes.

Eventually Millie and I head toward the dog park, she glancing back at her friend. *Friend.* To her that's what he is. She rejoices in his humanity. Have I lost sight of Maurice's humanity? There but for the grace of God go I. Surely I know that. Yet, perhaps, for the grace of God there I should go.

Pour forth Your mercy, Lord, on Maurice, as You did for me. Let me help be the messenger, like Millie, and go there. —Edward Grinnan

Digging Deeper: Hebrews 2:14–18

Wednesday, April 6

So you see, faith by itself isn't enough. Unless it produces good deeds, it is dead and useless. —James 2:17 (NLT)

"Joyce called," my wife, Elba, said. Joyce and I had met when I was an interim pastor at Gilead Church. It had been some time since we last spoke. "Her husband died unexpectedly while she was recovering from hip surgery. I think you should give her a call."

By the time I reached out to Joyce, I could hear that her breathing was labored. "It's very difficult and painful to move around," she said. Then she confided her sadness over not being able to visit her husband in the hospital during those last days. She felt remorse for not having the time to grieve for him since her physical pain was consuming her. "I feel at a loss."

At that moment I knew how I could help. "Joyce, I'd like to send you some stories by Dr. Norman Vincent Peale." She welcomed the idea, and we ended our conversation in prayer.

A few months went by, and I got a beautiful card in the mail. "Thank you so much for your thoughts and prayers and our telephone conversation. I'm finally healed! The stories were a comfort and an inspiration, and my faith has pulled me through. God bless you. Love and prayers, Joyce."

Lord, may I never forget that others are in need of You and of my care in whatever way that might be. —Pablo Diaz

Digging Deeper: Luke 18:39–43, James 2:14–16

Thursday, April 7

"Guard against every kind of greed. Life is not measured by how much you own." —Luke 12:15 (NLT)

Alabama is full of wonderful things: gorgeous beaches, the last foothills of the Appalachians, and more barbecue than is reasonable for anyone to consume. But it also comes with its moments of panic, especially in April, the start of tornado season.

This part of the country calls itself the "Buckle of the Bible Belt." Though it has a lot of faith, it also has a lot of fear, as evidenced by the absence of bread, milk, and water in the grocery store every time the siren sounds for incoming dangerous weather.

Last April, it was just my husband, Brian, our golden retriever, Colby, and me hunkering down in our basement for a few nights. We slept soundly, huddled in our warm blankets.

Now that I'm a mom with a one-year-old, this April feels very different when the siren sounds. There's more urgency, more of an edge to how I feel, knowing that I have to wake little Olivia sleeping in her crib so that we can seek safety from the storm.

As we prepare to head downstairs, I begin to play that childhood game: if I had to suddenly dash for shelter, what three things would I grab? In the past I'd thought about photos, documents, and letters Brian had written to me in college. But this time I look at my sleeping daughter, my gentle dog, and my wonderful husband and feel my fear dissipate. Everything that matters is already gathered close around me.

**Lord, when You blessed me with family,
You gave new meaning to my true life. Help me to
remember that we are safe in Your care always.**
—Ashley Kappel

Digging Deeper: Matthew 8:24–26,
Hebrews 12:18–22

Truly, I say to you, whoever does not receive the kingdom of God like a child shall not enter it. —Mark 10:15 (ESV)

My wife, Emily, persuaded me to read John Green's *The Fault in Our Stars*. I resisted at first. For one thing, I barely read for pleasure anymore because I spend all day poring over legal cases. For another, it's categorized as a Young Adult novel. I don't like to admit it, but I have always had a snobby streak and wasn't enthusiastic about a book written for high schoolers.

I started reading it anyway, largely because I thought it would make Emily happy. I snickered about some highfalutin dialogue, but I was quickly engrossed. The book is a love story about two teenagers with cancer. It could so easily have been melodramatic, but instead it was honest and heartfelt. What Hazel and Augustus felt—from falling in love to the despair of thinking they're going to die—touched my heart with a purity that "adult" books seldom had. It almost seemed that because Green was writing for kids, he didn't need to worry about adults ridiculing him. The result was marvelous.

The Fault in Our Stars helped me to see Jesus's statement about receiving the kingdom of God as a child in a different light. I'd always interpreted this to mean that we must guard against our intellect overwhelming our belief and be as open-minded as children are to God's teachings. I still think that's true, but now I see more depth. Being like children also means letting go of the thoughts that might override our hearts. Children, often less encumbered by cynicism and apathy, are capable of truly honest feelings. And being closer to God is always more about the heart than the head.

Thank You, Lord, for always attacking my cynicism.
—Sam Adriance

Digging Deeper: Philippians 4:7

Saturday, April 9

And if the root be holy, so are the branches.
—Romans 11:16 (KJV)

I was watering a small tree, when my wife wandered outside to watch. "We need to move," she announced abruptly, like a prophet of God. "We are not thriving here. It's costing us too much to maintain this old house. The neighborhood is declining. If we don't move soon, we will be trapped here."

I looked at her blankly, surprised that she suddenly wanted to move after all these years. She gave me that "Irish" look and marched back indoors.

I turned off the hose and pondered the tree I was tending. In five years it had not grown one inch. I took it out and discovered that there was a rock-hard layer of clay under the roots. No wonder it wouldn't grow! I moved the tree to a better spot, and by October it had grown a foot. Then I thought of Sharon's words: "We are not thriving here. We need to move."

At supper I said to her, "You know, maybe you are right. Maybe we need to move."

She perked up.

I went on. "I'm tired of working on this old house. It's a money pit, and you have been very patient about it. Besides, it could be exciting, starting over late in life." And so we moved to a new house, just outside the city limits, where we are indeed thriving.

Yes, there is wisdom in staying put, and we did that for a long time. But now I can see that there is value in putting down new roots in fresh soil: a new neighborhood, a different job, another church home. These can be a tonic to the spirit.

I guess I should listen to my wife more often. The Irish know things.

Lord, help me to know when to sit tight and when to move on. —Daniel Schantz

Digging Deeper: Proverbs 12:12,

Sunday, April 10

Come near to God and he will come near to you. Wash your hands, you sinners, and purify your hearts. . . . —James 4:8 (NIV)

Baking powder—I had forgotten the baking powder. I slammed the waffle iron onto the counter and grabbed a fork to try to pick the crumbled mess from the hot griddle, snarling at my kids that they would have to eat cereal for breakfast instead. Switching on the garbage disposal, I watched the mess float away, wishing I could begin again and start fresh, making amends for the morning that had turned out all wrong.

But I couldn't. We had no time. Church started in just twenty minutes. "Everyone get your Bibles and put on your shoes. We're leaving in two minutes!" I shouted. We scrambled into the car, a frantic cacophony of seatbelts and whines as my husband squealed out of the driveway. Silence settled over the car. I glanced back to three wide-eyed kids, sitting as if they were afraid to even breathe.

"I'm sorry, guys." I took a deep breath. "I wish I hadn't forgotten the baking powder in those waffles."

"No, Mama," my eight-year-old chimed in, "the waffles weren't the problem. The problem is we forgot Jesus."

I closed my eyes, the truth of the morning washing over me. A teaspoon of baking powder in the waffle batter wouldn't have changed anything because in our frenzied rush to get ready for church, we had forgotten the most important thing. Sunday—our every day—is all about Jesus, regardless of what we have for breakfast.

Father God, when I'm harried, worried, or frantic, turn my eyes toward You. Amen. —Erin MacPherson

Digging Deeper: Psalms 29:11, 34:14

Monday, April 11

If ye have faith as a grain of mustard seed…nothing shall be impossible unto you. —Matthew 17:20 (KJV)

When I was nine, Dad took me to my first greenhouse. He chose his tomato plants and selected the seeds: Kentucky wonder beans, cucumbers, corn. I spotted watermelon seeds and asked him to buy those too.

Dad considered. "No, our season isn't long enough. They won't make it."

"Pleeeeease…" I just knew those melons would grow.

Blakie, the owner, puffed his pipe and then winked. "Here," he said, offering the packet. "A little gift from me."

Dad showed me how to plant the black seeds in a hill. I checked daily, thrilled by their progress. Leaves!

Blossoms! By August the vines had several marble-size globes, and toward September one had swelled to the size of a baseball. Dad agreed that the little watermelon might, indeed, make it if the first frost held off.

Then one afternoon I heard dull bells and saw a dozen milk cows shamble out of the pine trees, cross the meadow, and head straight for Dad's corn. Mom grabbed a broom to swish them away, but just as one lumbered aside, another lurched into its place. A few phone calls later, the apologetic owner arrived to herd his escapees the five miles home.

The damage was done. Along with trampled beans and corn, my baby watermelon lay crushed by heavy, dirty hooves. I don't remember crying, but I do remember how my watermelon had changed Dad's mind about melon season and how I learned to trust the little voice that still whispers, *Don't give up.*

Lord of hope, may childlike faith guide me all of my life. —Gail Thorell Schilling

Digging Deeper: Hebrews 1:1

Tuesday, April 12

And the sash of fine twined linen and of blue and purple and scarlet yarns, embroidered with needlework, as the Lord had commanded Moses.
—Exodus 39:29 (ESV)

"Honey, does this go?"

You'd think after half a lifetime of wearing ties that I'd have figured out which color goes with what. It's not like I'm color-blind or don't have reasonably good taste, but I stand there at my closet, my new rust-colored shirt on, staring at a jumble of ties. Finally, I pick one. Then a few more. And more. At my wits' end, I take out Exhibits A, B, C, and D, and bring them to Carol in the kitchen. "Which one goes?" I ask again.

She looks up from the sink and shakes her head. "None of them." Then she takes off her rubber gloves and returns with me to the closet. I sheepishly put away my bad choices. She swiftly pulls out a blue tie with an orange pattern and holds it up to my striped, rust-colored shirt. "Perfect!" she declares. One Christmas, years ago, she sold ties at Brooks Brothers to make some extra money. She's a real pro. But how did she figure out this one was right? "Let me tell you a secret," she says. She points out the orange in the tie. "You see, this orange is exactly in between the rust and the blue. It links the two of them."

I nod, pretending I understand, but I haven't got a clue. "Good," I say. Once again she has saved me from a sartorial nightmare. I kiss her good-bye, "Thanks, sweetie," and head off to work.

Such is the marvel of marriage, the miracle of matrimony. The power of two far exceeds what one can do on one's own, the God-given gifts multiplying. You should have heard what one of my coworkers said: "Great tie, Rick. Goes perfectly." Then another, feigning innocence three steps ahead of me, commented, "Did Carol pick it out?"

I give thanks, Lord, for all the colors of the universe and the perfect partner to help me see them.
—Rick Hamlin

Digging Deeper: Proverbs 18:22, Revelation 19:8

Wednesday, April 13

"Consider the lilies, how they grow: they neither toil nor spin; yet I tell you, even Solomon in all his glory was not clothed like one of these." —Luke 12:27 (NRSV)

No rain, no rain, no rain. Then, suddenly, rain. At long last our severe drought in California had a moment's respite. Storms rolled in, skies darkened, and rain fell—sometimes even poured—though not nearly enough to replenish dry reservoirs.

But wildflowers, the kids and I discovered, are hardier than people. They don't need much to drink. A few days after the rain stopped, we ventured to some nearby trails to hunt for blossoms. They were everywhere: poppies, shooting stars, monkey flower, and my favorite, elegant brodiaea. Who could resist a delicate purple wildflower with a name like that?

The trails were muddy, but we didn't care. We breathed fresh air and went from flower to flower. The kids clutched wildflower identification pamphlets we'd picked up from a kiosk at the trailhead. "I think it's this one!" Benjamin cried, pointing to a picture on the pamphlet as we kneeled to examine a delicate cluster of white blossoms.

As we walked, I thought of the massive damage the drought was doing to farmers, ranchers, and California's elaborate, expensive system for capturing, storing, and transporting water. It's because of that system that so many people can live in a semiarid region prone to drought.

Yet here were these flowers. It had rained just a few days. But that, apparently, was enough. I could almost hear God say to each flower, "You are mine, and I will not abandon you."

I wasn't sure how invested God was in our man-made water system. But I could see His care for His creation right here, on this trail, in the poppies, the monkey flower, and the elegant brodiaea.

Today I will not be discouraged, Lord. I will remember Your unfailing care for me and for all that You have made. —Jim Hinch

Digging Deeper: Jeremiah 2:13, 1 Peter 5:7

Thursday, April 14

For everything created by God is good, and nothing is to be rejected, provided it is received with thanksgiving.
—1 Timothy 4:4 (NRSV)

I've been feeding the birds, mostly chickadees and woodpeckers, all winter. It has been a long season. In fact, one of the snowiest and coldest on record. But last week the remaining bits of snow melted away from the dark corners of my yard. I hadn't seen a woodpecker in weeks, so I finally took down the suet feeders from their hanging places along the garage.

So, of course, what happened this afternoon only a few hours after the suet feeders came down? I was sitting on the back porch, reading a book, and heard a flutter off to my side. I turned and looked. There, on the spot of the garage where I had taken down the last feeder earlier that day, hung a woodpecker. She was perched on the hook where the feeder had been. For a few moments, she turned her head this way and that, looking around, perhaps puzzled. Then she flew off.

I'm not worried. This is why the seasons of life march on. I'll bet that within seconds of her flying away she found a pliable tree to poke and bugs to eat. The mosquitoes are hatched now, too, so may that woodpecker help us out by feasting on them!

Bless You, Lord, Who creates and sustains all things! Bless this gentle creation. —Jon Sweeney

Digging Deeper: 1 Corinthians 2:11–13

Friday, April 15

"Whom the Lord loveth he correcteth; even as a father the son in whom he delighteth." —Proverbs 3:12 (KJV)

I took up fly fishing as a young man. There's something magical about the rod creating beautiful loops that sail the fly on a long arc. If luck is with you, the fly will land gently on a calm drift where a perfect trout awaits. Later, reading *A River Runs Through It* and discovering my commonality with the author, Norman Maclean, who was also the son of a minister, I was hooked for life.

I longed to share this passion for fly fishing with my son, Harrison, and chose my birthday as the ideal time for our first outing together. In preparation, we practiced casting for hours in the backyard.

We drove to a secluded place on the river, put on our waders, and slogged through the stream to the first fishing hole. I could sense Harrison's nervousness as he began to cast out his line. "Over there, H!" I pointed to a trout near the opposite bank. He quickly lifted up his line, attempting to get it close. But the fly landed too hard and the fish darted away.

"Harrison, you need to be a little gentler in your cast." I badly wanted him to get a fish, but I didn't want to be so bossy that he wouldn't want to keep trying.

We spotted another fish, and Harrison cast again. But when the trout rose to sip in the fly, Harrison was too slow and missed hooking the fish. "Harrison, you need to try to be quicker." Again, I caught myself. *He won't love this if you criticize him.*

He didn't give up though. Finally a few tries later, Harrison hooked his first fish. He marveled over the beauty of the rainbow trout and then set it free and looked at me. For a long moment, he didn't say a word and then, "Wow, Dad, can we come back on my birthday?"

Father, help me find Your perfect balance between correcting and loving. —Brock Kidd

Digging Deeper: Proverbs 10:1, 23:24

Saturday, April 16

FINDING REST: Keep It Holy

Remember the sabbath day, and keep it holy.... For in six days the Lord made heaven and earth, the sea and all that is in them, but rested the seventh day; therefore the Lord blessed the sabbath day and consecrated it. —Exodus 20:8, 11 (NRSV)

I can remember the moment when I realized that not everyone celebrated the Sabbath on a Sunday. I was in junior high school with a minor role in the play *Fiddler on the Roof.* There was a Sabbath scene, and the drama teacher explained that for Jews the Sabbath began at sunset on Friday and ended at sunset on Saturday. This seemed extraordinary to me! Wasn't the Sabbath the Sabbath? Irrefutably, immovably on Sunday? Written—literally—in stone?

It took time and study to understand that the Sabbath of the Hebrew people was not on Sunday. An even longer time passed before I understood that Muslims also celebrated the Friday-sunset-to-Saturday-sunset Sabbath.

I've been fortunate enough to become close to an elderly Jewish woman who has helped me understand that, in some ways, Jews keep the Sabbath more reverently than many Christians. "The Sabbath," she explains, "is really a gift. The Almighty gives us a chance to rest, almost forcing us to pause in our ridiculously busy lives—not only to be religious or pious, but to literally stop and acknowledge Him. It's a twenty-four-hour period during which we admit we are not as important as we think, and God's world goes on without us."

Perhaps the actual day of the week isn't as significant as the reasons for it and the way we keep it.

God of all majesty, make my heart right as I strive to keep the Sabbath with gratitude and understanding. Amen. —Marci Alborghetti

Digging Deeper: Proverbs 19:21, Isaiah 52:7

Sunday, April 17

"For You said, 'I will surely prosper you and make your descendants as the sand of the sea, which is too great to be numbered.'" —Genesis 32:12 (NAS)

My friend Heidi and I walked from our hotel to the Vatican where we attended Mass at St. Peter's Basilica, the largest church in the world. Afterward, we waited outside with fifty thousand people in St. Peter's Square for Pope Francis to appear and speak to the crowd. I was astonished that so many people came. How joyfully they waited with balloons, musical instruments, and handmade signs for the pontiff to read.

I thought how easy it is to be a Christian at home and abroad as I celebrated with all those jubilant, faithful people. I remembered that on a cruise to the southern Caribbean, my husband and I and our friends Brenda and Paul had visited the oldest active synagogue in the Americas, Mikvé Israel-Emanuel in Curacao. The synagogue's floor was simply white sand for three reasons: to remind the members of the forty years of wandering in the desert from

Egypt to the Promised Land; to remember the "secret" Jews living in Spain and Portugal during the Inquisition, who put sand on the floor to muffle the sounds during their services so they wouldn't be discovered; to symbolize that God said to Abraham, "I will greatly multiply your seed as the stars of the heavens and as the sand which is on the seashore" (Genesis 22:17, NAS).

That Sunday as I squinted across St. Peter's Square for a glimpse of Pope Francis and listened to the roar of the crowd when he finally appeared, I understood that faith comes in different ways. Sometimes we cheer loudly; sometimes we walk quietly. And God listens, no matter how we approach.

Father, whether I express my faith quietly or with shouts of joy, thank You for listening. —Patricia Lorenz

Digging Deeper: Psalm 89:1–13, Galatians 3:23–29

Monday, April 18

Little children, let us stop just saying we love people; let us really love them, and show it by our actions. —1 John 3:18 (TLB)

I'm a great one for making lists. Every Monday morning I glance over my schedule for the week and set five goals for myself. They generally involve my work, exercise, a knitting project, and reading. Seeing that they were so often the same each week, I thought to mix things up and add something different.

I decided I'd do something special for my husband every day just to show him how much I love and appreciate him. Monday, I took the garbage all the way to the end of the driveway. Did Wayne notice? No.

Tuesday, I cooked his favorite dinner. No comment. And so it went day after day.

On Friday I got bad news. I'd booked a trip with one of my friends. Her husband had decided to join her, which meant I would end up being a third wheel. It seemed the only thing to do was cancel. To say I was disappointed would be an understatement. I told Wayne why I wouldn't be going and, without a pause, he looked up from the newspaper and said, "I'll go with you."

I was stunned. All week I'd assumed my extra effort to show him I loved him had gone unnoticed. Then, with four simple words, he let me know how much he treasured me.

Thank You, Lord, for my dear husband who teaches me what it means to love and be loved.

—Debbie Macomber

Digging Deeper: Ephesians 5:28

You surround me with songs of deliverance.
—Psalm 32:7 (NAS)

I need to focus on God, I thought. *But how? How do I tune out the pain and tune in to God?* It was almost two weeks post-op. I was beginning to feel better, but nighttime was difficult. I could no longer tolerate narcotic pain medicine, and muscle spasms attacked my leg.

I put on my headphones and closed my eyes to Andrea Bocelli singing "The Lord's Prayer." I let every word sink in. Bocelli's voice was like an angel's, its splendor and richness a taste of heaven. I played the song over and over; I let it consume me. "For thine is the kingdom and the power and the glory forever." Bocelli's voice crescendoed, and so did my love for God. Instead of thinking about my pain, I concentrated on God's magnificence. I felt bathed in His love, enveloped by His peace. I wanted nothing more than to praise Him. In the midst of my praise, my weary body relaxed and I slept.

The next night I found another song that, along with "The Lord's Prayer," carried me through my recovery. It was Melissa Greene's passionate rendition of "At Your Feet":

> *"Let the world fade away....*
> *Father find me now as I bow at your feet...."*

This centering on God became my replacement for pain medicine. Through these songs I abided in Him. As I did, not only the world but also my pain faded.

Thank You, Lord, for the peace You give.
May I always abide in You. —Kim Henry

Digging Deeper: Psalms 62:1–2, 145:1–3

Wednesday, April 20

"Therefore do not defile the land which you inhabit, in the midst of which I dwell...."
—Numbers 35:34 (NKJV)

Not again! I groaned. I'd just cleaned and swept the porch this morning. Every day it is a blessing to live on our family cattle ranch. I thank God that my "office" is surrounded by nature. But by afternoon I discovered that swallows had been at work, building their nests along the eaves of the house. Diligently, they were flying back and forth from the distant pond, packing mud in their tiny beaks.

Now what? Do I hose down the nests before they complete them? I love birds, but if I leave their nests alone, they will make an even bigger mess as they raise two or three batches of young during the summer. Country living means being among wild animals, but bunking with birds was taking it a bit far. Wasn't it?

Still, I didn't have the heart to destroy their hard work. After all, I reasoned, each swallow will eat three times its own weight in mosquitoes every day. When it came to dealing with mosquitoes, I could either spray them with chemicals or let the birds do what they lived for naturally. It was not such a tough choice after all.

"All I ask," I told the birds, "is to keep your nests away from doors and windows, and I'll know there are that many mosquitoes I don't have to swat."

Dear Lord, help me to work with the miraculous, intricate puzzle of Your creation, not needlessly battle against it. —Erika Bentsen

Digging Deeper: Psalms 24:1–2, 33:5

BEING RENEWED: Guided

"And the Lord shall guide thee continually...."
—Isaiah 58:11 (KJV)

After six days in the hospital, Gene moved to a brand-new rehab facility about twenty minutes from home. It looked more like a resort, but we knew the therapy would be hard. As we settled into his room at the Oaks of Athens, I prayed, "Father, please guide me now. I feel so inadequate to help Gene." I even sang, without making a sound, the words to an old hymn, "Guide me, O Thou great Jehovah."

As I was fussing about in Gene's room, arranging his personal items as though we were on vacation in a bed-and-breakfast, someone entered the room. "Good morning," a nurse's aide said. I looked up and saw a beautiful, statuesque woman with the most glorious smile I think I'd ever seen. My eyes settled on her generous lips painted a fascinating shade of pink. Her flawless skin was the color of coffee with lots of rich cream. The woman's dark hair moved when she talked; her curls bobbed around joyfully.

A name tag identified the woman, but I couldn't pronounce it: *Gida.* She helped me. "Guide-her."

"Oh, your mother must've given you that name so God would guide you through life!"

"I think so. I'm a minister, and God guides me moment by moment." I grabbed one of her hands and held on with both of mine tightly. She seemed to understand me, my concerns, my needs, even though Gene was the patient. "Pray, Gida. Pray for us—as a couple and for Gene's healing and…" She stood by Gene's bed, holding his hand and mine, and prayed earnestly to her Guide about us. After an *amen,* she announced, "He has it."

Lord, I'm willing to follow step by step.
—Marion Bond West

Digging Deeper: Psalms 25:9, 31:3, 32:8

And let them have dominion…over all the earth and over every creeping thing that creeps on the earth.
—Genesis 1:26 (ESV)

On Earth Day, established at the start of the environmental movement to promote care-taking of our earth, it's natural to think of the majesty of this country and this planet: the waterfalls and mountains, the oceans and prairies, the rainforests and deserts. I know I do. I think of the towering walnut tree in my boyhood backyard in New Haven, Connecticut, or the woods I used to hike in Maine. Sometimes it is easiest to feel our responsibility to God's creation when we look upon natural wonders.

I used to think my love of cities was at odds with my love for God's planet. What kind of environmentalist spends so little time actually *in* nature? Imagine my surprise then when I read an article making the case that New York City was the greenest place in America. How could an island packed with people, buildings, and trash be good for the environment? But when I read the story, it made sense. All those people living in such close quarters use up far less gasoline and electricity than if they were spread out over a big swath of the country. Cities help us preserve the beauty of the planet.

That doesn't mean, of course, that cities are any better than the country. It only means that God intends for us to use this earth in many ways, and we can be the stewards He commands us to be from the top of a skyscraper just as much as from the top of a mountain.

Thank You, Lord, for the beautiful and adaptable planet You have given us. —Sam Adriance

Digging Deeper: Matthew 5:14

Saturday, April 23

Cast thy burden upon Jehovah, and he will sustain thee.... —Psalm 55:22 (ASV)

I turned my pickup down Lou's driveway. The heavy roll of fencing wire, which was in back, slammed the tailgate. *God, that's how I feel. Like I've got a two-ton weight rolling around inside of me.*

The last few days my thoughts had been consumed by a friend whose feelings I'd accidentally hurt. I pulled up to the blue metal gate, stopped, and looked over at Lou. "Where do you want it?"

He pointed and said, "Let me open the gate."

I hopped out and lowered the tailgate. *What was I thinking? How are we going to get this out? It took a forklift to load it into my truck. If we roll it, it could easily fall on our feet and smash our toes.* Shaking my head, I climbed back into the truck.

After driving through the gate, I backed up toward the unloading spot. Then I had a crazy thought. I gunned the accelerator and raced toward it. Lou's eyes widened. Suddenly, I slammed on the brakes. The momentum launched the wire out of the truck and into the air. It rolled across the ground, stopping at the exact spot where we needed to unload it. Lou burst out laughing. "Wow, that was a great trick!"

I chuckled and said, "That's how cowgirls handle heavy weights—dump them quickly." As I said it, I felt in my spirit, *That's what I need to do with my broken friendship.*

Over the next couple of days, I wrestled to turn loose the burden. When I finally did, I prayed, "God, right now I choose to give the weight of it to You. Please mend my friendship." Miraculously, my friend called and asked if I'd like to go on a hike. Gradually, God helped us piece our friendship back together.

Lord, when I have a problem, remind me how cowgirls handle a heavy weight: by launching it to You. Amen. —Rebecca Ondov

Digging Deeper: 1 Peter 5:7

Sunday, April 24

Let what you heard from the beginning abide in you.
If what you heard from the beginning abides in you,
then you will abide in the Son and in the Father.
—1 John 2:24 (NRSV)

Abide is an old-fashioned word. I'd never used it
in everyday conversation and didn't understand its
meaning until I had the opportunity to pet-sit for a
friend.

"I'm going to change your name to Shadow," I
said with exasperation as Cinderella, the miniature
Boston terrier, trotted behind me. While I washed
dishes, she sat on the kitchen rug. As I ate lunch,
she jumped onto a chair. When I sat on the couch,
she scooted as near to me as possible. Pressed close
against my leg, she looked up at me with her puppy-
dog eyes and rested her head on my thigh.

Maybe this was standard behavior for a small,
indoor dog, or was Cinderella just missing her master?
It was a good thing she was cute. Otherwise, I might
not have put up with her constant craving for
togetherness.

But her dependence continued after that first
day. When I walked to the mailbox, she happily
followed at my heels. If I went into the bathroom,
she patiently waited outside the door. At night,
she crawled onto the bed and curled up at my feet.

She never whined when I walked away or when I pushed her aside to make some space between us.

The day before her owner returned, I was reading. Cinderella jumped into my lap and then climbed onto the arm of the chair. Pretending to ignore her, I watched as she gingerly put her front paws on my shoulder and leaned her head close to my neck. She rested her face against my cheek, sighed contentedly, and closed her eyes. All she wanted was to abide with me. I didn't understand her devotion, but the word *abide* became crystal clear.

Lord, like a dog yearns to be close to her master (or temporary master), help me to abide in You.
—Stephanie Thompson

Digging Deeper: 1 Chronicles 16:11, John 17:23, James 4:8

Monday, April 25

"Ask, and it shall be given you; seek, and ye shall find; knock, and it shall be opened unto you."
—Matthew 7:7 (KJV)

I was checking out at my neighborhood thrift store when a darling woman with curly silver hair hollered, "Roberta!" I must have looked perplexed because she added, "You don't remember me, do you?"

A second glance told me who she was: Patty. Summer. About five years ago. We prayed together on a porch at an estate sale. I'd never forget that hot August morning. She had tapped me on the shoulder while I was rummaging through a box of vintage glassware. "I'm a *Daily Guideposts* reader," she told me. "Aren't you Roberta Messner? When you say your prayers tonight, will you remember me? I'm having surgery for a brain tumor in the morning."

I'd immediately thought of *Daily Guideposts* writer Karen Barber, who founded the organization Prayer Igniters. Much of what I know about prayer, I've learned from her. One practical thing she taught me is to always seize the moment. So I asked Patty, "How about praying right now?" Then and there, even though I was a bit self-conscious, the two of us found a seat on that grungy porch banister and stormed the heavens on her behalf. And now she was telling me she couldn't be healthier.

Thank You for our amazing *Daily Guideposts* family, Lord Jesus, and for the power of prayer, which unites us all. —Roberta Messner

Digging Deeper: Matthew 21:22, Mark 11:24, John 14:13–14

Your statutes have been my songs in the house of my sojourning. I remember your name in the night, O Lord, and keep your law. —Psalm 119:54–55 (ESV)

I step outside to water my porch boxes. A young friend, now in grammar school, sees me and joins in the action. "Let's sing," she announces. "You choose," she suggests.

Selecting from our growing repertoire of Sunday school and camp songs, I break into "The Lord Is My Shepherd," and she joins in. Then we sing "All Night, All Day, Angels Watching over Me."

The tranquil landscape changes quickly when her toddler sister barges on to the scene. They start squabbling over toys and territory. I don't know quite how, but I get drawn into the drama. In an unmistakably sharp tone, I say, "Enough!"

When the squabble dies down, I remind the older girl that she is like a teacher. "Be careful what you say. You shouldn't call people names. Little sister hears you and learns from you."

She listens and quickly absolves herself. "But what will we do with the words that are already in her head?"

I hide a smile. Her quick logic renews my resolve to teach her more Scripture songs, more wholesome rhymes, and more encouraging words that I pray will stay in her mind, a lifelong repository of goodness and grace.

God, Your Spirit has so often brought spiritual songs and Scriptures to my mind. Help me to teach these gems to others of my own generation and the younger ones also. —Evelyn Bence

Digging Deeper: Psalm 1:1–2, 2 Timothy 3:14–17

Wednesday, April 27

"And God saw...." —Genesis 1:31 (KJV)

The rocky path was steep, and I was falling behind. I should have stopped and taken a breather, but my pride was pushing me to keep up with the group. Suddenly, I couldn't catch my breath. Panic seized me. *Am I having a heart attack? What if I fall and the others have to carry me miles to get help?* We were in the mountains of rural Zimbabwe, visiting recipients of a project we'd worked hard to create with the help of American donors.

"Pam, your face is really red," Ben, my son-in-law, said, alarmed.

"I think I'll go back and wait at the last place we visited," I answered. I was trying to sound casual, but I was terrified.

After convincing the others to go on, I walked back toward a little mud hut. *God, I came looking for You. Surely You didn't bring me here to die.*

Go slow. Breathe deep, He seemed to answer.

The little old woman who lived in the hut spotted me. Earlier she had shown us her chickens, her garden, her goats—all gifts from giving hearts back home. Now she offered me the only chair she owned. I sat gratefully. My breathing eased. My heart slowed. I smiled at her. Without speaking, she and I were in perfect communion. Other than the chickens pecking around the edges of her green garden, all was still.

Suddenly, there in the middle of a carefully swept dirt yard, sitting in a wooden chair, I found God. I'd missed Him in the hurrying. And now I saw what He wanted me to see all along: the beauty of His creation, majestic mountains and lush valleys that stretched as far as the eye could see. I smiled, resting in the quiet, feeling more alive than I'd ever been.

Father, I see You in all that's good. —Pam Kidd

Digging Deeper: Psalm 34:8, Ecclesiastes 3:11, John 11:40

Thursday, April 28

But the...Holy Ghost...he shall teach you all things, and bring all things to your remembrance.... —John 14:26 (KJV)

I was just thinking that everything that ever happened to me abideth in me somewhere, most of the time misfiled and misplaced in the most careless fashion. I mean, who was in charge of organization here, a newborn chipmunk? But inchoate and incoherent as it is in my memory, every wild, savory, painful, epic moment is there.

Here comes our daughter sliding out of the sea of her mother, followed seemingly moments later by her twin brothers. Here is my grandmother shrinking noticeably every day until she is a small dry stick and then a song we sing in Gaelic every year. Here is my oldest brother, a mountain of a man, and here he is during his last summer, half of what he was, but still grinning and making wry remarks as his voice failed and then the rest of him. Here is my mother riffling my crew cut and, fifty years later, here I am rubbing her shoulders, which are sore after a long day on the walker. Here are all my sins, squirming and sneering, though I have tried mightily to forget them and be shriven of them.

Everything that ever happened to you is inside of you, and a scent or a snippet of song or a voice in the distance or a sudden sparrow unlocks the door, and there you are, age five or fifty, weeping and giggling, inundated by miracles, admitting you have been a fool, delighted that sometimes you weren't. We forget nothing; we just forget the compartment number and the lock combination. Isn't this miraculous?

Lord, we hardly ever say thanks for the incredible moist computers on our shoulders, a million times cooler than any shiny machine that could ever be invented, for our wet machinery can handle love and joy and prayer and emotion and faith.... —Brian Doyle

Digging Deeper: 1 Corinthians 15:2

WHAT THE SAINTS HAVE TAUGHT ME
Catherine, Companion in Desperate Times

Now those who died by the plague were fourteen thousand seven hundred.... —Numbers 16:49 (RSV)

I met Catherine in her hometown, Siena, Italy. Her birthplace didn't tell me much: it was turned into an elaborate shrine five hundred years ago. There's nothing left of her father's dye shop with the family home above it. I could still walk down the same steep street, though, to the well at the foot of the hill, where she went each day for water after her parents turned her into the family drudge for refusing a well-to-do suitor. I could follow her struggling back up the slope with the heavy buckets.

It was only the first of the toils and conflicts that made up Catherine's life. This was the calamitous fourteenth century when the bubonic plague killed a third of Europe's population. Most people were terrified even to come near the hideously suffering victims. Catherine nursed them, consoled them, buried the dead with her own hands.

As her fame spread, Catherine was dragged into the venomous politics of the day. Italy's city-states waged savage war on one another, church factions battled, and she was called to mediate between the hostile groups. She traveled to Avignon in France to persuade the pope to return to Rome, only to see him followed by a pontiff so avaricious that cardinals held a second election, splitting Europe for decades between rival popes.

Brokenhearted over the failures of the church, Catherine fell ill with what may have been infantile paralysis, and after weeks of agony died at age thirty-three.

A tragic life? On the contrary, said Catherine, her life was heaven on earth! "All the way to heaven is heaven," she declared in the statement that I've kept for many years taped to my computer, "for He said, 'I am the Way.'"

Father, help me to see Jesus just ahead, even when the road is dark. —Elizabeth Sherrill

Digging Deeper: Deuteronomy 31:18

Saturday, April 30

Don't worry about anything; instead, pray about everything. Tell God what you need, and thank him for all he has done. —Philippians 4:6 (NLT)

There was a knock at the door at 7:00 AM, so I sprinted to see who was there. My neighbor Jack was trying to catch his breath.

"Bill, your water main sprung a leak! It's gushing down the hillside!"

I jumped into action. Our house sits on top of a hill, higher than the municipal water supply. A pump pushes the water uphill to our house. That pump sits about a block away, near the base of the hill and right above Jack's house. I could picture gushing water flooding his beautiful home.

My first *action* was to throw tools into my car. My first *reaction* was fear. *What if I can't fix it? What if the pump blew? What if it's expensive? What if I damage my neighbor's house? What if I don't know what to do?* I said an emergency prayer: "Lord, help!"

I arrived at the pump to see a massive flood from a cracked pipe. The good news was it was from the supply side, meaning my pump was okay. The bad news was I'd have to shut off my water to stop it.

Fortunately, my neighbor's house had no damage and I could fix the broken PVC pipes. I calmed down and figured out what I had to do and what parts I had to buy. After three trips to the hardware store and eight hours of digging, cutting, gluing, waiting, sweating, and praying, I turned the water main back on.

No leaks.

God treats me better than I deserve.

Thank You, Father, for strengthening me through life's stressful moments. —Bill Giovannetti

Digging Deeper: 1 Peter 5:7

GOD'S ABIDING LOVE

1 _____

2 _____

3 _____

4 _____

5 _____

6 _____

7 _____

8 _____

9 _____

10 _____

11 _____

12 _____

13 _____

14 _____

15 _____

16 _____

17 _____

18 _____

19 _____

20 _____

21 _____

22 _____

23 _____

24 _____

25 _____

26 _____

27 _____

28 _____

29 _____

30 _____

MAY

Anyone who loves their brother and sister lives in the light, and there is nothing in them to make them stumble.

—1 John 2:10 (NIV)

Kind words are like honey—sweet to the soul and healthy for the body. —Proverbs 16:24 (NLT)

My boys played in the living room as I coughed in bed. I lay there, useless, crumpled-up tissues scattered on the blanket, the humidifier with its steady stream of cool mist and the smell of menthol vapor rub in the air. I wanted a warm cup of soothing tea but didn't have the energy to get up and make it.

I retreated into my quilt, feeling a slight pang of single-mom self-pity. *Nobody takes care of me*, I thought. I ached for someone to fuss over me and make me feel better. Someone to make me a cup of chamomile like my father used to do or a concoction of lemon juice with honey like my mother always made. There was no hand to touch my forehead and check for fever, no one to say a small prayer like I do for my children.

As my sad little thoughts swirled, I could hear the boys clanking around in the kitchen. *What mess are they getting into now?* I thought. My aching body chose to ignore it.

Moments later, my four-year-old opened the door. "Close your eyes and count to six," he said. I shut my eyes and counted.

When I opened them, my six-year-old held out a spoon overflowing with honey. "Surprise!" he said proudly. "To make you better." It was the sweetest spoonful of honey I have ever tasted.

Lord, thank You for the sweetness of Your love and Your desire to take care of Your children. Thank You for showing us how to love others the same way.
—Karen Valentin

Digging Deeper: Romans 12:10

Monday, May 2

They are to do good, to be rich in good works, generous, and ready to share, thus storing up for themselves the treasure of a good foundation for the future, so that they may take hold of the life that really is life. —1 Timothy 6:18–19 (NRSV)

Union Theological Seminary in New York City had itself a predicament. A mallard had laid her eggs in the enclosed quad, unnoticed until they hatched. While the students took pictures and affectionately named the mother Hermeneuduck, the facilities and housing departments were left with the job of figuring out what to do. So far they had managed to keep the little family alive and well, but loads of people would be coming for commencement, as well as a wedding.

Arrangements were made for the mallard and her ducklings to be moved to a bird sanctuary until they could survive on their own, but the transfer didn't go well. Everyone—Hermeneuduck, ducklings, and humans—ended up stressed. The decision was made for them to stay two more days and then try again.

In the interim, the administration and staff put their heads together. Even with all of the activity in the quad, they told us, this would be the best environment for the ducks. The facility to which they would be moved was an infirmary type of space with no access to the outside and it would lower the ducklings' survival rate.

Union made a decision—one that I will never forget. It canceled the transfer and, instead, hired a security guard for the ducks.

God, let me never forget that all life is precious and the charge of earthly stewardship should stay in the forefront of my mind. Thank You for opportunities to see how to apply this in my everyday life. Amen. —Natalie Perkins

Digging Deeper: Genesis 1:31

Tuesday, May 3

Open your homes to each other without complaining. —1 Peter 4:9 (GNB)

Whenever I entertain, I get to worrying. *What should I cook? Will I be able to prepare it well? What if everything's not perfect?* These thoughts about the new neighbors we had invited over for dinner were going through my mind on my morning walk.

As I approached a curve in the road, I passed under a cherry tree in full bloom. I stopped to look up at the extravagant pink clusters of blossoms and recalled my girlhood days when an older couple had invited our family over with a simple yet wonderful invitation: "The weeping cherry tree in front of our house is in full bloom. We'd love for you to come over and see it." We drove up to their home and, indeed, the weeping cherry tree, as tall as their modest house, was a spectacular feast for the eyes against the deep blue sky. They pulled up kitchen chairs because they didn't have enough seats for all of us on their small sofa and served simple refreshments: cookies from a box and sweet iced tea in ruby red glasses. Dad took pictures of our gathering as if it were a huge celebration. What a charming, heartwarming memory!

Now I reached up and touched a cluster of soft blossoms, finding a few drops of water lingering after an overnight rain. I took the droplets and made the sign of the cross, so I wouldn't forget cherry-tree hospitality. It wasn't about perfection. It was only about welcoming others to share beautiful moments of connection and togetherness.

Dear God, help me to welcome others with the same love with which You welcome me. Amen. —Karen Barber

Digging Deeper: Luke 10:38–42, Romans 12:13

Wednesday, May 4

Greet those workers in the Lord, Tryphaena and Tryphosa. Greet the beloved Persis, who has worked hard in the Lord. —Romans 16:12 (NRSV)

I fall asleep every night around ten o'clock, and a few minutes after I've gotten into bed I hear it: a deep rumbly sound that starts loudly and then dissipates. It took me a while to figure out what it was, but eventually I did.

My neighbor, who lives around the corner, is a police officer who works the night shift. Each night when I'm ending my day, his is just beginning. I hear the sound of his engine, his car backing slowly down the driveway, and then turning and heading out of the neighborhood.

I've developed a kinship of sorts with his routine. A feeling of comfort and security sweeps over me the moment I hear his car start up. It inspires me to pray for him. *Lord, please watch over my neighbor who will be working tonight to keep me and my community safe.* It also inspires me to pray for all those—firefighters,

EMTs, police officers, doctors, nurses, and aides—who leave their homes to begin work when I'm about to end my day.

Lord, I continue, *bless the clerks at the grocery stores who are busy stocking the shelves tonight with all the items I'll need tomorrow. And don't forget the bakers who will rise up in the early morning hours to bake the cakes for all of the birthdays being celebrated. For these and others who work at night while I sleep, I pray.*

Lord, Who is always ever-vigilant and ever-present in my world, thank You for those who work while I rest. —Melody Bonnette Swang

Digging Deeper: Deuteronomy 15:10, Psalm 90:17

Thursday, May 5

For I do not do the good I want to do....
—Romans 7:19 (NIV)

I walked into the living room to find Kemo, our seven-year-old golden retriever, comfortably stretched out on the white love seat. "Kemo, what do you think you are doing?" I asked in amazement. Not because he was on the loveseat (this wasn't the first time) but because instead of jumping down at being discovered, he wagged his tail as if he was proud of himself.

I know this sounds weird—unless you are a dog person—but part of me wanted to laugh because I sometimes identify with him. The look on Kemo's face said, "I'm doing something I know you don't like, but I know you love me enough to forgive me."

I do that, too, especially with my husband. I show up late somewhere or continue looking at my laptop when he's talking to me or get annoyed with his slower walking pace. These are all things I know I shouldn't do, but I trust that Lynn loves me enough to forgive me again and again and again.

Lord, thank You for this reminder about taking someone's love and forgiveness for granted, including Yours. —Carol Kuykendall

Digging Deeper: Romans 7:14–25, 1 Corinthians 13:4–7

Friday, May 6

Those who hope in the Lord will renew their strength. They will soar on wings like eagles; they will run and not grow weary, they will walk and not be faint. —Isaiah 40:31 (NIV)

Just a couple of weeks after my hip-replacement surgery, I turned a corner. My leg eased its complaining. The swelling subsided. My strength began to return. With physical therapy, I was able to do more each day.

My body sensed when it was ready for advancement. I discovered, as Psalm 139 says, that I am "fearfully and wonderfully made." The way my body healed amazed me.

Gradually returning to life as normal felt fabulous. I switched from sweats to jeans and shirts. I cared enough to wear makeup. I savored every little thing: driving, dining with friends, walking, and working out. "Oh, normal day, what a treasure you are." That saying has always been one of my favorites. Now, going through times of trial has marked it indelibly on my heart.

My memory of my tough recovery period has faded. I feel better than I have in years. There's really nothing I can't do, although my doctor did tell me I shouldn't play football.

From the start, my hip-replacement prognosis was good. Even so, it was rough for a while. That experience has caused me to feel more compassion for those going through physical challenges, especially the ones who see no end to their trial. But God made all the difference for me, and I know He will make a difference for them.

Thank You, Lord, for the gift of healing and the treasure of You. —Kim Henry

Digging Deeper: Psalm 33:20–22, Hebrews 6:19, 1 Peter 5:10–11

"Consider how the wild flowers grow. They do not labor or spin." —Luke 12:27 (NIV)

When you live in the country, as I do, you can't help but be aware of the provisions of the season. Today, with winter waning and spring beginning, the cattle are thin, yet their long teeth scrape the yellow grass for greenness hidden beneath it. The birds at my feeder are roaming for tassels. Newborn calves butt their mamas' udders to let down milk. Little shoots stretch themselves toward the sunlight. The world, it seems, is aware of—and hungry for—the good things our Creator provides.

I'm rarely aware of God's provision except when I'm out in nature, out running, or gardening. Even in those moments, though, when every inch of existence around me demonstrates God's constancy and care, I often succumb to the oblivion of work and busyness. Other hungers—to get done, to get on with something else—squelch all awareness of the Provider and the provision.

My most acute hungers, most days, are for what I myself provide: a bag of microwave popcorn, a cold apple from the fridge, a cup of tea. Yet often, at the end of the day, I feel depleted, used up, worn-out—not hungry, exactly, but unfed.

I'm like the woeful little calf I saw bawling all alone in a field this morning. It had momentarily orphaned itself by wandering off from its mother, who was nevertheless alert to the problem and wailed back at it from two fences away, trying to get to her baby.

Stuck in the wrong field, I wail and fret, unaware that I've left God's side. That my Father's still there—providing, watching, determined to get my attention—escapes me. And, really, all I need to do is look up from time to time to see Him.

Nudge me, Lord. Remind me of Your presence. Help me rediscover, every moment, Your constant provision and care. —Patty Kirk

Digging Deeper: Matthew 6:25–34

Sunday, May 8

"Many women have done excellently, but you surpass them all." —Proverbs 31:29 (NRSV)

"You'll understand when you have a child of your own" was one of the things my mother would say when we disagreed. Since I had my daughter later in life, Mom was able to employ that line for several decades.

I never yearned for a baby like my mother, her sister, and her mother did. Unlike Mom and the women in her family, I didn't marry and have babies after high school. Being a mother seemed so ordinary. Instead, I earned a college degree, traveled the world, and worked in a career that fulfilled me.

Then at forty years old, I married the love of my life. Six weeks after our wedding, shock mixed with elation when I became pregnant.

Our daughter, Micah, was six months old when I first celebrated my very own Mother's Day. I invited Mom, Aunt Joyce, and Grandma Roma to brunch the Saturday before. They couldn't wait to take turns holding her. I had places set at the table for each of us, but we ended up bringing our plates to the living room since we preferred playing with the baby over eating food. We didn't talk about our lives or catch up on world events; all that the four of us wanted to do was entertain Micah.

After Mom opened her Mother's Day gift, I brought out three terra-cotta pots filled with pansies and handed one to Mom, one to Aunt Joyce, and one to Grandma Roma. "Well, I'm not your mother!" exclaimed my aunt with delight.

"But you're *a* mother," I said, "and you're all my role models."

Being a mother is the most important job I could hold. Yes, Mom, now that I have a child of my own, I finally understand.

Thank You, Lord, for the gift of mothers— especially mine! —Stephanie Thompson

Digging Deeper: Proverbs 22:6, 31:28; 1 Timothy 1:5

Monday, May 9

He who finds a wife finds what is good, gaining favor from the Lord. —Proverbs 18:22 (CEB)

I called Mom that morning to wish her a happy Mother's Day. She told me what the family would be doing and then asked, "Who's going to cook for Carol?"

"I guess I am," I said hesitantly. "I mean, Tim will be at church and Will's far away, so it's up to me."

"Honey, I'll do the cooking tonight," I announced to my wife more confidently than I felt.

"Great," she said. All I had to do was follow the directions on the recipe card. Carol had already bought all the ingredients: tuna, pasta, anchovies, salad, green beans.

The water started boiling, I minced garlic, heated the olive oil. *Oh no, too hot*—the garlic was turning brown. I glanced back at the recipe card. "Low heat," it read. *Darn!* Okay, wash the salad, cut the beans.

Just as I put the pasta on, Tim walked in the door. "Can I help?"

"No...I mean yes. Can you cut the rest of the beans?"

But the pasta needed to come out...now! And the beans needed to go into the microwave. A minute? Three minutes? "Dad," Tim said, "this colander is too small."

"Too late," I said, dumping in the pasta, watching it overflow.

"Dinner's ready!" I finally called. We sat at the table, and I said grace. The beans? Well, they were crunchy. And something was wrong with the pasta sauce. "Oh, honey, I forgot to add the anchovies."

Then I burst out laughing. "You know, Carol, maybe the point of Mother's Day is for you to know how much you're really, desperately needed." And I said the prayer all husbands must say: *Thanks for the thousands of things she does that I don't even know about.*

May I never underestimate, Lord, how much my loved ones do for me. —Rick Hamlin

Digging Deeper: Proverbs 31:28, 1 Corinthians 13:7

Tuesday, May 10

BEING RENEWED: Encouragement

"Encourage him...." —Deuteronomy 1:38 (KJV)

The encouragement Gene needed wasn't going to come from me. Long before his accident, he'd often told me, "I'm washed up. Old."

God, please send Your encouragement to Gene...for his hip and his emotions.

In the dining room, on his first full day at the Oaks, we were seated with a couple who were also new to the facility. Emmett, Daisy, and Gene were in their eighties, and I was in my seventies. They had been a tireless couple—farmers. Gene's dad also had been a farmer. Daisy explained matter-of-factly, "We have teeth, but we don't like 'em, so we don't wear 'em."

We smiled and nodded. Daisy and I discussed how we both put mayonnaise in our cornbread. She coughed frequently, placing her carefully folded white cloth napkin over her mouth. "I have congestive heart failure," she explained as though saying she had a hangnail. Sipping her sweet tea, she told us their son had died from a heart attack just weeks ago. Emmett looked down. "Emmett's a minister," Daisy offered joyfully. I told them Gene also had ministered at a rural church for twenty-eight years while he taught sociology at Oklahoma State University.

Conversation with them was easy. None of us could hear as we once did, so we leaned inward toward each other. Gene said we were all old, and there wasn't much to anticipate in life.

Emmett stretched way over, placed his hand firmly on Gene's arm, and looked directly into his eyes. "Young man, God's not through with you. He has a miracle for you. Hear me?" He spoke with amazing authority.

Gene nodded. So did Daisy. Me too.

Father, how I praise You for Your encouraging saints.
—Marion Bond West

Digging Deeper: Judges 20:22, 1 Samuel 30:6

"By day the Lord went ahead of them in a pillar of cloud to guide them on their way...." —Exodus 13:21 (NIV)

I was driving our fifteen-year-old van at seventy miles per hour on the interstate, worrying the whole way about what to do to help our son who was going through a divorce. This was uncharted territory for me, and everything seemed to be moving way too fast.

Suddenly, a strange, fast-clicking sound started vibrating in the dashboard. I glanced down to see that the speedometer needle was going haywire. I'd read that when you get used to the speed at which you're going, you can't truly gauge how fast you're going simply by how it feels. I couldn't wing it, so my only option was to find another vehicle in front of me that I felt was going the speed limit. I decided on a small car, followed it, and paced my own speed by it.

Just as my van needs a pace car, I thought, *I need one to navigate this difficult life situation with my son.* I vowed to pray and seek God's help and guidance, and when I got home I found a support group to help me along the way.

Dear Father, I am in uncharted territory today. I depend on You to set the pace and guide me about what to do. Amen. —Karen Barber

Digging Deeper: Nehemiah 9:19, Psalm 107:30

Thursday, May 12

Now the serpent was more crafty than any of the wild animals the Lord God had made.... —Genesis 3:1 (NIV)

Elizabeth, Stephen, and I were walking in the park when suddenly Elizabeth said, "Hey, look! A snake!" Sure enough, a step or two away on the pavement was a small, striped snake. It was perhaps fifteen inches long, as thin as a pencil. Another pace or two and one of us might have stepped on it.

We live in upper Manhattan, where the wildlife consists of people, groundhogs, skunks, hawks, and the occasional bald eagle. This was only the second snake I've seen in nearly two decades of living here. I was amazed. How was it that I hadn't seen it coming?

It was almost comically symbolic: the snake in plain sight that one doesn't see. I think of myself as someone who's alert to my surroundings, and yet, apparently, when walking in the city I only look out and around, not up and down. I guess there's a lot that I miss.

We watched the snake slither off into the grass, where it was quickly camouflaged and hard to follow. I sent up a quick prayer, thanking God for kids who don't freak out at snakes, for snakes in the city, and for reminding me that I have blind spots.

Lord, show me clearly the temptations I face that I'm not even seeing. —Julia Attaway

Digging Deeper: Psalm 27:7–8

WHAT THE SAINTS HAVE TAUGHT ME
Julian, Companion When You Need Hope

God is love. —1 John 4:8 (KJV)

All I knew about Julian of Norwich, before I stayed at the retreat house in her hometown in England, was that she was the first woman to have a book published in English…and that she had a cat.

Almost nothing is known about her life, not even her real name. All that's certain is that Julian lived from 1342 to 1416 and spent her last years in a cell attached to the Church of Saint Julian, an eighth-century bishop.

Though her cat was her only companion in the cell, Julian was anything but isolated. One window of her tiny room opened onto the church, the other onto the street, where thousands came over the years, seeking guidance and comfort in a despairing age.

In England, the black plague regularly wiped out entire villages. The Hundred Years' War brought further desolation, and the church, torn by internal quarrels, offered no consolation. It was to this hopeless world that Julian wrote her visions of God's love.

Because of the mother-images in her writing, many believe she was a mother who had lost her children in the plague that struck Norwich in 1361. "God is Mother as well as Father, who bears us in the womb of his love." While preachers thundered that calamity was God's punishment, Julian insisted on God's compassion. That she was fully aware of the horrors around her, her writing shows. Yet, summing up her lifelong communion with God, she wrote the words I've carried with me ever since my visit: "All shall be well, all shall be well, and all manner of things shall be well."

Father, let me, like Julian, look beyond the ills of our time to Your eternal goodness. —Elizabeth Sherrill

Digging Deeper: Psalm 9:18

Saturday, May 14

Do not remember the sins of my youth, nor my transgressions; according to Your mercy remember me, for Your goodness' sake, O Lord. —Psalm 25:7 (NKJV)

When I was young (read: stupid), my father and I worked on cars. I thought of myself as an expert by the time I was sixteen, so when I noticed a young woman standing beside her stalled Chevy, I asked what was wrong. "It won't start," she said.

I explained how the carburetor butterfly valve might be stuck or maybe the timing was off. She looked at me quietly; I thought she was considering my advice. Then she said, "My car has electronic ignition and fuel injection, so it's unlikely to be the timing. And it doesn't even have a carburetor. I think the dead battery is the obvious reason."

She was employing a scientific adage known as Occam's razor: the simplest explanation is the first one to try.

At sixteen, I didn't have much use for science or explanations . . . or razors, for that matter. Instead I relied on half-truths, wild guesses, and something I once saw some guy do on TV. That was my approach to everything. It did not serve me well.

And that is how we learn. I think of that often when I talk to college students. They sometimes mistake assumptions for knowledge, philosophy for faith, a passing relationship for a permanent romance. Their hurried decisions are exasperating and often wrong. We ask them—beg them—to explain what in the world they were thinking, but Occam tells us the answer: because they're just like us, just like we were once. We needed jumper cables and hard experience to shock our systems toward adulthood.

Youth isn't wasted on the young. Growing up—growing one's experiences, growing one's faith—takes time. It's really that simple.

Lord, remind us of the road we've traveled so we, like You, can show mercy rather than judgment.
—Mark Collins

Digging Deeper: Psalm 144:12–13, 1 Timothy 4:12

Sunday, May 15

"God is spirit, and those who worship him must worship in spirit and truth." —John 4:24 (ESV)

It was a Sunday in Berlin, Germany, and my wife and I wanted to go to church. But we'd just flown in, and the idea of dropping in at any church was daunting. I can't speak a word of German, and Carol, although she can read it pretty well, was intimidated by the idea of worshipping in a foreign tongue.

We were puttering around in our vacation rental, when I remembered a friend saying that the Berliner Dom, the massive neo–Baroque cathedral in the middle of town, offered simultaneous translations in English of their ten o'clock morning service.

We looked at our watches—9:15. Could we make it? We brushed our teeth, grabbed our maps, and dashed out. We arrived well after the opening hymn, but the usher heard Carol mutter, *"Sprechen Sie Englisch?"* and escorted us to the balcony for foreigners where a woman gave us headsets to hear the service in English.

My eyes scanned the magnificent interior, rebuilt after ruinous bombing during World War II. There were statues and mosaics of the apostles and Jesus, but also of saints of the Reformation. I looked at the program, the words to the hymn largely incomprehensible. Then the organist began playing it. Of course, I knew the tune well, one of those classics people have been singing for centuries. I joined in lustily.

The sermon was terrific, the prayers inspiring, and the opportunity to greet our brothers and sisters in Christ a blessing. Yes, I would have wished for the gifts the apostles had at Pentecost, hearing and understanding a foreign tongue, but now I had a notion of how that happens. When the pastor said, "The body of Christ," I looked around and saw how all of us were connected, despite the divisions of war and language.

God, how wonderful to worship You with Your children. —Rick Hamlin

Digging Deeper: Psalms 103:1, 105:1

Monday, May 16

For all who are led by the Spirit of God are children of God. —Romans 8:14 (NRSV)

I felt sad. We came to Seattle every year to visit Kate's parents, but this year we weren't staying with them.

Kate's dad was recovering from surgery, and her mom wasn't up to hosting our rambunctious family.

We deposited our bags in our friends' guest room and, tugging the kids away from a well-stocked playroom, got back in the car for the short drive to Kate's mom and dad's for dinner.

Kate's dad greeted us at the door, leaning on a cane. Her mom's hip was bothering her, shortening the daily morning walks she'd taken for as long as I could remember. I sighed, thinking about the cost of aging, the way it can gradually separate people from cherished routines and relationships.

I looked around for the kids; they were on the other side of the garden with Kate's dad. He'd had no trouble leading them to the playhouse he'd built for Kate when she was little. Frances and Benjamin were already inside, as delighted as they'd been in the other playroom.

Kate's mom pulled a casserole out of the oven, a recipe she always made when we came over, one I loved. The table was set. The house looked the same. Suddenly, I remembered something my own dad had said shortly before he died: "You know, on the inside, I feel no different than I did when I was a child. It's just the outside that changes."

We're all children, I thought, as Kate's mom carried plates to the table, *children of God. It's just the outside that changes.*

My life is in Your hands, Lord, from beginning to end. Thank You that I am Yours. —Jim Hinch

Digging Deeper: John 10:28, 1 Peter 1:23

Tuesday, May 17

The heavens are yours, and yours also the earth;
you founded the world and all that is in it.
—Psalm 89:11 (NIV)

I emerged from the subway on this glorious spring morning, the sky a screaming blue, wishing I could be a tourist rather than just another in the rush of workers headed for offices in lower Manhattan. Not a tourist in some faraway capital but a tourist in my own city. The narrow, occasionally cobbled streets of downtown were crowded with them...groups milling around the Stock Exchange, their leaders holding aloft color-coded pennants. People getting their pictures taken in front of the massive, fortresslike Federal Reserve. Throngs headed toward Trinity Church and the 9/11 Memorial or farther downtown to Battery Park to catch a ferry to the Statue of Liberty and Ellis Island, through which so many of our families came in search of this city, this country, this life, sacrificing everything.

I have a pang of nostalgia for the first time I, a young Midwesterner, experienced the raw energy of the city that runs through its history like a current. Now I barely glance at the new One World Trade Center, rising like a phoenix on the west side of the island. I defer my awe and quicken my step to try to beat the traffic light.

Occasionally, when I return to New York City after an extended time away, I experience an echo of that initial thrill, a fleeting vibration of discovery, a feeling quickly extinguished by worrying if there will be enough room to squeeze myself into the next rush-hour subway that rumbles into the station.

This morning I suddenly decide to sit for a few minutes in Chase Plaza. I watch the crowds—tourists and New Yorkers alike. All ages, all nationalities, laughing, texting, eating, jogging, pushing baby strollers for *three*. I let the panorama of life unspool before me. And I say a prayer:

Lord, let me see each day with new eyes, for it is the first time I discover the day that You have made.
—Edward Grinnan

Digging Deeper: John 14:27

Wednesday, May 18

FINDING REST: Practical Wisdom

But in the seventh year there shall be a sabbath of complete rest for the land, and a sabbath for the Lord: you shall not sow your field or prune your vineyard. You shall not reap.... —Leviticus 25:4-5 (NRSV)

The extreme weather of late has forced me to spend more of my daily walks on a treadmill in front of a TV. This less-than-ideal situation has gotten me thinking about the changes in our natural world: more and more severe storms, flooding, loss of farmland and homes. It seems the harder we strive to solve the problems of weather and overuse of the earth and the harder we work ourselves and the land, the worse things become.

I see more development and fewer open spaces, more build-up on the seacoast with no place for high tides or storm waves to go. The busier we get, the more rapidly we use up and even misuse God's gifts.

How wise God was to use Sabbath laws to protect the land and the people! How practical to teach us that both must have a rest to replenish themselves.

God's wisdom then was about more than compelling the Hebrews to obey the Sabbath rules of rest taught to them. Not only did they show them how to do what was good for themselves and the land, but they also showed them the wisdom of following the Creator's rules when it comes to creation.

Creator God, I rejoice in Your vast and practical wisdom, teaching us to rest and repair our minds and bodies and all that You've given us. Amen.
—Marci Alborghetti

Digging Deeper: Luke 6:1–2, 5

Thursday, May 19

"Ask the animals, and they will teach you...."
—Job 12:7 (NIV)

If I so much as look at his leash or glance at my shoes, our dog, Soda, gets up and waits by the door. So I lace my running shoes and he wags his tail and off we go.

The neighbors have grown used to seeing me at all times of day—dressed in pajamas, work clothes, and workout clothes, leash in hand—strolling with Soda. I have developed a keen eye for noticing small differences I never saw before: the briar bush where a rabbit has made a den; the squirrel nest on top of the tall dead tree; the repetitive *tap, tap, tap* of a nearby woodpecker. All of these things I would have missed were it not for Soda.

As we stroll on a lonely stretch over a footbridge that crosses a stream, I often find myself praying. Here, away from the houses, in the quiet of the woods, I work out things I'm worried about. I lift my arms and say, "Thank You! Thank You for this day!" and find myself saying the Lord's prayer to the rhythm of our steps.

Who knew my little scruffy mop of a dog, always ready and excited to take a faith walk, would make such a fantastic prayer partner?

Dear God, thank You for this blessing our rescue dog has brought to my life—the time we share together with You. —Sabra Ciancanelli

Digging Deeper: Genesis 1:29–31, Psalm 103:22

Friday, May 20

They promise them freedom, while they themselves are slaves of depravity—for "people are slaves to whatever has mastered them." —2 Peter 2:19 (NIV)

My friend Mollie told me I would love kickboxing class, that it would be a great way to exercise and to fit some social time into my week. Mollie was wrong.

I kicked and punched my way through five minutes before realizing *love* would never be the word I used to describe kickboxing. By the end of class, I had not only managed to pull a muscle, but I was incapable of figuring out the jab-cross-swing-uppercut sequence. I vowed never again.

Three days later, the memory (and soreness) started to wear off and I let Mollie talk me into going once more. It was slightly better than the first time. She talked me into it the next week too. By the end of three weeks, I had gotten the hang of how to jab-cross-swing-uppercut without injuring myself or others. While kickboxing class wasn't my favorite thing in the world, I started to enjoy the way I felt when I finished, as if I had accomplished something.

For too long I had become lackadaisical, getting caught up in the busyness of life and convincing myself that I didn't have the time or energy to exercise. That was untrue. I had time and energy. All it took was a few weeks of habit-breaking and sweat for the truth to come back.

Lord, reveal to me the areas of my life that so easily ensnare my time and energy, and help me to break those habits. Amen. —Erin MacPherson

Digging Deeper: Proverbs 4:10–17,
1 Corinthians 6:12

Saturday, May 21

A QUEST FOR BEAUTY: An Unexpected Turn

Casting all your anxiety on Him, because He cares for you. —1 Peter 5:7 (NAS)

The third weekend of May finally arrived; the Saturday my sister, Rebekkah, and I looked forward to all year long. It was time for the community-wide yard sale in a town two hundred miles away. We couldn't wait to start shopping for all of those bargains!

Part of the fun was visiting a huge bookstore that was open until 11:00 PM and staying at a favorite inn. When we arrived, I stacked the books I'd purchased on the edge of the bed and sat in one of the chairs. To my astonishment, it collapsed.

"How did *that* happen?" Rebekkah asked as she came out of the bathroom. She covered her mouth in an attempt to control her laughter. "I thought you lost ninety-two pounds."

This wasn't funny. A huge hematoma was forming on my face despite the fact that I'd barely brushed it on the mattress. The nurse in me panicked. "Quick, get some ice," I said.

Rebekkah pressed the washcloth packed with ice to the affected area and brushed the hair out of my eyes. But no matter what she did, the hematoma grew.

I was particularly concerned since the injury had occurred in the area where I have a longstanding tumor because of neurofibromatosis. I phoned my physician, a family friend. He assessed me over the phone and determined I wasn't having any pain or change in my vision. "I don't think you need to go to the emergency room," he said. "Just sit up tonight with the ice. I think you'll be fine."

All night long, I leaned my back against the headboard of the bed and prayed. An anxiety I couldn't name consumed me.

I'm so afraid of the unknown, Lord.
Please don't leave me. —Roberta Messner

Digging Deeper: Psalm 56:3, Isaiah 41:10, Philippians 4:6–7

Sunday, May 22

A QUEST FOR BEAUTY: Facing Stares
I will cry to God Most High...." —Psalm 57:2 (NAS)

The community-wide yard sale was in full swing the next morning. I fingered a lamp that wore the price tag from a design boutique. "Look, Rebekkah," I said. "This cost five hundred and fifty dollars new. They're only wanting forty for it."

"I love the crackled finish and the mustard paint," my sister said. "It's really a deal. I think it should go home with you."

A woman nearby spoke up. "I think you two should be more concerned with her face instead of a lamp. And in getting her out of that abusive relationship. Whoever did that to her doesn't love her, you know."

"But...but...," I stammered, trying to defend myself.

"Ignore her," Rebekkah said. "It's just people. You know how they can be."

Yes, I knew. When I was a teenager and the facial tumor caused by the neurofibromatosis first appeared, I went shopping. A stranger sauntered up to me. "Are you retarded or do you just look that way?"

I still recall the shame of that day. I felt like a freak of nature. My condition got so bad, the high school administration determined I could complete graduation requirements by restricting classes to mornings. "You'll never be college material," they concluded and placed me in a special program where I worked a menial job in the afternoons.

Today, I tried to act as normally as possible and have a good time, but the whispered accusations continued all day long.

Oh, Lord, I can't cope with the stares of strangers again. Please help me! —Roberta Messner

Digging Deeper: Psalms 50:15, 55:17; Jeremiah 33:3

A QUEST FOR BEAUTY: Trying to Trust

My times are in Your hand; deliver me from the hand of my enemies and from those who persecute me. —Psalm 31:15 (NAS)

On the Monday morning after my fall, I visited my primary care physician back home. He referred me to an eye specialist and a local plastic surgeon and telephoned my longtime craniofacial surgeon at the Cleveland Clinic. They all agreed to a wait-and-see approach and decided not to drain the large hematoma. "I think we should just let the blood reabsorb," the plastic surgeon advised. "I don't want to touch it with your history of the tumor there."

I normally wear only a little lipstick, but that was going to have to change—at least temporarily. I would have to return to work in a couple of days, so I decided to shop for some makeup. At a department store counter, the makeup artist demanded, "I want to know who punched you."

"No one." I stared at my feet. "I have a tumor, ma'am."

I left with a special brand of concealer they recommend for people after auto accidents, some new moisturizer to help the application of the concealer, and a foundation that was supposed to make it all look natural. I also stopped by a discount store and purchased a large magnifying mirror to help me with applying the makeup.

I wasn't prepared for what I would see. The disfigurement was beyond words, and with every passing day it didn't seem to be changing. I returned again to my physicians, but their only advice was to "give it time."

"A person's face is the first thing the world responds to," I agonized to my sister, Rebekkah. "What will I do if this doesn't get any better?"

Oh, Lord, I place my times in Your capable hands.
—Roberta Messner

Digging Deeper: Deuteronomy 31:6, Isaiah 41:10, Zephaniah 3:17

A QUEST FOR BEAUTY
What Really Matters

Your adornment must not be merely external...but
let it be the hidden person of the heart....
—1 Peter 3:3–4 (NAS)

I looked in the magnifying mirror, and my face didn't
look the same. It wasn't anything I could put my finger
on, but I telephoned my doctor. "Why don't you come
in this afternoon and we'll have a look?" he said.

The moment my doctor saw me, his demeanor
became frantic. "I'm wondering if maybe we should
have drained that hematoma in the beginning," he said.
"Sometimes things like this can cause a person's face to
disintegrate. I fear that's what is happening to you."

"Is it reversible?" I asked, my voice shaking, panicky.

"Not always."

Right away, I made plans to see my surgeon at
the Cleveland Clinic. "The trauma of your fall has
caused your tumor to return," he told me. "We can
only hope this won't progress with a vengeance."

"When can we remove the growth?" I demanded.

"We can't." He rubbed his cheek and then patted
my shoulder. "The new tumor is too close to the facial
nerve. We can't take a chance on severing it." His eyes
met mine. "But, really, your eyeglasses camouflage
most of the disfigurement."

His physician's assistant chimed in, "And you're quite beautiful, in spite of this. Inside and out."

Why couldn't I believe their words and the reassurances of friends who saw me?

Oh, Lord, let me seek the kind of beauty You desire!
—Roberta Messner

Digging Deeper: Genesis 1:31, Ezekiel 28:17, Matthew 23:27

Wednesday, May 25

A QUEST FOR BEAUTY: Giving Comfort

And God of all comfort, who comforts us in all our affliction so that we will be able to comfort those who are in any affliction with the comfort with which we ourselves are comforted by God.
—2 Corinthians 1:3–4 (NAS)

At the Cleveland Clinic, I encountered a tall, elegant woman whose bald head was visible under a paisley turban. She struggled just to make it to the entrance of the imposing building and garnered every ounce of strength to smile and hold the heavy glass door open for me.

That sole act of kindness astonished and transformed me. One moment I was furious at everyone and anyone over my own disfigured face, and the next I was pleading the heavens to make me more like this woman.

As the day wore on, I found myself seeking opportunities to comfort others. In the cafeteria, I noticed a mother with a child attached to an IV. They were finishing lunch. "Let me take your trays," I offered.

"That's the most helpful thing anybody has done since we've been here," the mother said. Then she added, "Did anyone ever tell you, you have an exquisite complexion. It's like a porcelain doll's."

Next, I gave an elderly man my seat in the waiting room and escorted a woman in a wheelchair to the restroom. As I continued to help others, I felt like myself again and noticed that people no longer seemed repulsed by my disfigurement. Instead, they took their cues from me and treated me with respect.

I could change others' reactions simply by the way I interacted with them. It was all up to me.

Teach me the beauty of comforting others, Lord.
—Roberta Messner

Digging Deeper: Psalms 46:1, 56:8, 71:20–21

Thursday, May 26

A QUEST FOR BEAUTY: God Sees the Heart

"For God sees not as man sees, for man looks at the outward appearance, but the Lord looks at the heart." —1 Samuel 16:7 (NAS)

My disfigurement was visible to most people only if I removed my eyeglasses. But still I was devastated. When I returned to my job at the Veterans Affairs Medical Center, I stayed in my office as much as possible and brought my lunch from home.

One afternoon, a young mother telephoned me. "I read in *Daily Guideposts* today that you have neurofibromatosis," she said, sobbing. "My little daughter is just like you. She has a tumor on her face. We're so scared."

I wanted to make certain I provided the woman with the most current information, so I looked up the disorder on the Internet. The worst pictures I'd ever seen appeared on my computer screen. One young man, a highly unusual case, had a facial tumor that hung in folds and completely engulfed his left eye.

As I answered the woman's questions, I surprised myself by ending the conversation with something my own mother always told me: "Don't forget, God sees the heart. Your little one is always beautiful in God's eyes. If you ever have any doubts, look in your Bible at 1 Samuel 16:7."

It was what *I* most needed to hear as well.

Thank You for Your reminder of true beauty, Lord.
—Roberta Messner

Digging Deeper: Psalm 34:5, Proverbs 31:30, 1 Peter 3:4–6

A QUEST FOR BEAUTY
God Is Ever Faithful

"You are altogether beautiful...and there is no blemish in you." —Song of Solomon 4:7 (NAS)

While shopping at an estate sale with my sister, I noticed a large gilded mirror with a cluster of flowers at the top. It was beyond beautiful, and the price had been unbelievably slashed.

"I think you should get it for your bathroom," Rebekkah said. "You've needed one for ages."

That was before the accident, I thought, noticing my larger-than-life reflection. My outfit showed off my ninety-two-pound weight loss, but did I dare look at my face? I glanced upward, first taking note of my new haircut, my tortoiseshell eyeglasses, and finally the blue-gray bulge where the tumor had returned.

Then the strangest thing happened. Instead of the unsightly blemish, I saw the fingerprint of God. His voice spoke to my heart: *When you thought I had forgotten you, I was protecting you. I've been holding your hand every minute.*

Rebekkah reached for my hand. "I know this year has been hard," she said, "but do you see the person you've become because of it? Your heart is bigger than ever." She wiped the tear that had dripped onto her chin. "You notice the pain that others are going through. It's like your heart has eyes."

Now when I look in that mirror, I have a ritual. Instead of anger and anxiety, my heart is filled with praise. In heaven, I'll have a perfect face. But until then, I will thank God every moment.

My quest for beauty has led me to You, Lord. Thank You. —Roberta Messner

Digging Deeper: Psalm 139:14, Ecclesiastes 3:11, Ephesians 2:10

Saturday, May 28

Two are better than one, because they have a good return for their labor. —Ecclesiastes 4:9 (NIV)

I was enjoying my vacation when my cell phone rang. "Hi. It's me. Richard." I thought back to how our journey had begun eight years ago when he asked me to be his mentor. Richard had wanted to get a seminary education, and I decided to support him in his journey.

We settled on weekly calls, laid out a plan for Richard to complete the undergraduate degree coursework and pursue his divinity degree, and discussed issues that weighed heavily on his mind.

"Hey, Richard. How are you doing?" I said now.

"I'm at seminary, getting ready to go home for the last time. I wanted to let you know I just finished my final class."

"Congratulations! You did it! You must be excited!" I said, beaming at his good news.

"I am. But before I leave the building, Pablo, there are a few things you need to hear. Thank you! You are my brother, my friend, and my mentor. You have been a true blessing in my life. You have helped me navigate this journey."

I was deeply humbled and honored by his words, and I realized that he wouldn't need our weekly meetings anymore. A feeling of loss accompanied my great joy, but I was comforted by the fact that our friendship wasn't ending. "Hey, you did all the work. Go celebrate," I said.

"I'm on my way," he replied, laughing. "I'm on my way."

Lord, thank You for allowing us to journey with our friends and to celebrate their achievements.
—Pablo Diaz

Digging Deeper: Proverbs 15:22, John 15:15

Sunday, May 29

Bear one another's burdens, and so fulfill the law of Christ. —Galatians 6:2 (ESV)

"Let the church pray for you," said my minister, Lee. I had confided in him what I'd been hiding for months: my fourteen-year marriage was ending.

"I'm too ashamed," I said. I rolled my aching shoulders, trying to remember when they hadn't been full of knots.

I was afraid of what the congregation would think of me, especially the older couples like the Boyds. They always sat in the pew behind me. For years, I'd admired their solid, abiding love for each other. How could I look them in the eye? In their day, marriage meant something—for better or worse. How would they react to my news? *This generation just doesn't honor the covenant of marriage. She should have tried harder.*

As humiliated as I felt, I asked for prayers that Sunday. After the service was over, I saw Mr. Boyd standing a few feet away. He looked me right in the eyes and made his way toward me. Before I knew it, he had enveloped me in a bear hug. He began sobbing, as though my pain were his own.

In that moment, I felt a burden lift from me. My shoulders, which had ached for months, suddenly felt lighter. The weight pressing down on them had transferred to Mr. Boyd's stronger, broader shoulders. We stood there for a long time, crying together. When he let go, he said, "We will pray for you every single day."

The days that followed weren't easy. But with my church family praying for me, each day I found that my shoulders ached a little less.

Father, thank You for the church and for these models of Christ's unfailing love. —Ginger Rue

Digging Deeper: Romans 15:1, Galatians 5:14

Monday, May 30

He being dead still speaks. —Hebrews 11:4 (NKJV)

My wife and I were visiting friends in Columbus, Mississippi. One afternoon they took us to see "Tales of the Crypt" at Friendship Cemetery, where college students role-play the life stories of those buried there.

The cemetery sits on a bluff overlooking the Tombigbee River. We arrived early, so I wandered around the burial ground, treading softly through the luxurious grass and stepping around the pink primroses that grow everywhere. I savored the warm spring air as I studied the touching epitaphs on the stones.

Suddenly I was confronted by the most striking tombstone I have ever seen: the legendary "Weeping Angel" memorial erected in honor of Thomas Teasdale, a compassionate preacher who organized an orphanage for children of fallen soldiers. A large stone angel is kneeling behind the monument, resting her head and arms on top of his stone, and weeping.

As I stared at it, I found myself blinking a lot. Allergies, probably, but I was thinking about God and the angels weeping over the orphans and widows of war and mourning the loss of fresh young men and women who forfeited their future to give us one. My chest felt heavy.

On Memorial Day there are many ways to remember our fallen heroes. Our neighbor, a veteran, puts a small American flag in every yard of our subdivision. We fly our big flag from the front porch. I go through old photo albums with my children and grandchildren, telling them stories of my uncles, Jimmy and John, who fought in World War II. Then we drive downtown to take in the parade.

But sometimes I just sit on the front porch steps under the flag and blink a lot.

Lord, these tears are for those who still speak to me, even though they are dead. —Daniel Schantz

Digging Deeper: Matthew 26:13, Revelation 7:17

Tuesday, May 31

In the morning, Lord, you hear my voice; in the morning I lay my requests before you and wait expectantly. —Psalm 5:3 (NIV)

Our greyhound, Sissy, is reserved in temperament. We adopted her when she retired from racing. She's gentle, timid, shy.

If one of our boys forgets to fill her bowl, Sissy stands by the cupboard and waits. If she has to go outside, she primly takes a quiet stance at the door. If she's in the mood for affection, she comes close and leans against our legs, but she never jumps, licks the boys' faces, or strikes us with a playful paw. All this changes, though, when the girl wants to run.

When we're out for a walk, Sissy's holding-back nature catches on the breeze. She plods along by my side for a moment and then lifts her tawny head and gives my hand a good, solid bump. She's respectful, but I get the message. It's time to run. The younger three boys, Sissy, and I become a wild pack, bolting down the tree-lined lane that winds behind our house. It doesn't matter how far we go or how breathless I become. I smile as we run. It makes me happy seeing Sissy be assertive.

It makes me wonder if it makes God happy when I'm assertive too. I'm reserved by nature, and in my prayer life I can hesitate to let my needs be known. *How can I ask for help with small things when others' needs are greater?* I'm embarrassed to share what's on my mind, even understanding that the Lord knows the quiet places of my heart.

But then there are the times when I remember that He paved the road for this relationship with the sacrifice of His Son, and I can speak to the Father with confidence, certain of His grace. My prayers can run bold, wild, fast, and free.

Thank You, Lord, for allowing me to share my true heart. Amen. —Shawnelle Eliasen

Digging Deeper: Psalm 6:9, Philippians 4:6, Colossians 4:2, Hebrews 4:16

GOD'S ABIDING LOVE

1 _____

2 _____

3 _____

4 _____

5 _____

6 _____

7 _____

8 _____

9 _____

10 _____

11 _____

12 _____

13 _____

14 _____

15 _____

16 _____

17 _____

18 _____

19 _____

20 _____

21 _____

22 _____

23 _____

24 _____

25 _____

26 _____

27 _____

28 _____

29 _____

30 _____

31 _____

JUNE

But I am like a green olive tree in the house of God.
I trust in the steadfast love of God forever and ever.

—Psalm 52:8 (ESV)

A man's heart plans his way, but the Lord directs his steps. —Proverbs 16:9 (NKJV)

"The outside of our home has never looked better," Margi said.

My wife was right. In anticipation of selling the house, we'd mulched, planted, weeded, and fertilized our landscape. For the first time in years, the beautiful, dark green, flawless lawn carpeted our yard without brown patches or weeds. "At least the landscaping won't turn off buyers," I said.

Soon afterward, our family enjoyed sixteen days of vacation. Before leaving, I made sure to adjust the sprinkler system to keep our lawn lush and green.

But when we returned my heart sank. Lush green had given way to a crackling straw-colored expanse. "What happened?" Margi asked.

I found the sprinkler controls set in the Off position; I had made the adjustments but forgotten to turn on the sprinkler.

My wife showed grace over my mistake. My kids teased me. I felt bad, not only for *my* failure but for what I considered to be God's too. I had taken such care and was so careful about setting the controls. I knew it was my fault, but couldn't God have intervened? Couldn't He have simply made me turn that control knob one more click?

"God knows what He's doing," Margi said.

I needed to hear that. Our house hasn't sold yet, but I know God has a plan and His ways are always better than mine.

Father, forgive me for blaming You.
—Bill Giovannetti

Digging Deeper: Jeremiah 10:23

Thursday, June 2

"Let them rise up to your help, and let them be a shield unto you!" —Deuteronomy 32:38 (JPS)

Anjin never barked. My husband, Keith, and I had been told not to expect a greyhound to be a watchdog, even though she was a sight hound. She had been raised to be sociable, not territorial or wary. She whined when she wanted to go out, desired attention, or needed to eat. She moaned contentedly when her neck was being scratched. She had "yipping" dreams, complete with twitching whiskers, rapidly blinking eyes, wagging tail, and jerking paws. But no barking—not even when she dropped her front quarters to the rug and demanded we toss her favorite stuffed toy so she could chase it.

Then, suddenly, Keith wasn't there and I was very alone.

In the beginning, Anjin seemed to be expecting him to come back at any moment. But over several weeks, she became more subdued and remained at my side. Whenever I left the house, separation anxiety kicked in and she would find ways to make her unhappiness known. I tried not to leave her for very long, which suited me because being at home among things that Keith and I had shared helped me to feel less lost.

It was several months before I became aware that Anjin was barking whenever she saw strangers through the windows or when she was outside in the yard. She began patrolling the perimeter, alert and protective. It was as if she were saying, "I know it's just us now, so I'll keep you safe."

Dear God, You will always find unexpected ways to uphold me. Thank You. —Rhoda Blecker

Digging Deeper: Micah 7:20

Friday, June 3

"For everyone who asks receives, and everyone who searches finds, and for everyone who knocks, the door will be opened." —Luke 11:10 (NRSV)

We were in Ashland, Oregon, stopping for a night on the drive home from a visit to Kate's family in Seattle. We'd looked forward to this stop. We love Ashland, with its pretty streets and parks, the cosmopolitan vibe of its Shakespeare festival. But a few days earlier, a wildfire had broken out in the mountains. A hot wind blew a haze of acrid smoke through the town. A layer of gray ash covered our car.

"So, no picnic?" the kids moaned as we checked into our motel. We'd planned to buy food at the market and eat at our favorite park.

"Sorry, guys," I said. "The smoke's too thick."

"Let's do what we can," said Kate. "We'll burn off some energy at the playground, then go to the market and eat our picnic in the motel room."

"Inside?" wailed the kids.

"Yes, inside," said Kate. "Sorry."

We managed fifteen minutes at the playground, then hurried to the store and bought fresh bread, cheese, fruit, vegetables, and some fancy chocolate. Inside the room, we tried to ignore the blaring air conditioner.

"I like the cheese, Mommy," said Frances, sounding like she was trying to convince herself.

"I like the grapes," said Benjamin, sounding more certain.

"Let's watch a movie while we eat our chocolate," said Kate.

"Yes!" cried the kids.

We don't have a TV at home, so this was a rare treat. We found a fun movie and settled back on the bed. Suddenly, the room felt cozy and reassuring. We'd forgotten to say grace at this hurried meal, so I silently said one now—a surprised and profound thank-you for God's inexhaustible ability to guide us to what was good, even when we were lost in our own disappointment.

Today I will look with Your eyes, God, seeing Your provision in all that I have. —Jim Hinch

Digging Deeper: Psalm 111:5, Jeremiah 31:25

Saturday, June 4

But I trust in your unfailing love....
—Psalm 13:5 (NIV)

I have a black eye. It looks like I stepped into the ring with George Foreman.

It was an innocent injury. Millie and I were down-hiking a steep but familiar section of the Appalachian Trail. My mind should have been concentrating on the scree that can make footing sketchy. But I was thinking about burgers for dinner: one medium-well for my wife (no bun, please), a miniburger, rare, for Millie (no bun for a golden retriever either), and medium-rare for me (definitely with a bun).

That's when my feet flew from under me. I pitched forward, threw up my hands, stopped my fall, but not before planting my face into a tree and falling in a heap. Millie looked at me reproachfully, as if to say, *If you would only go on all fours like the rest of us, this wouldn't happen!* I headed to the pharmacy for the biggest, darkest pair of red-carpet sunglasses I could get my hands on.

At the house I showed Julee my wound. She was more interested in the glasses. "They look great," she exclaimed, laughing, "on me!"

"I don't want people gawking at me."

"They'll definitely gawk if they see you in these glasses. But why do you care? Maybe they'll think you got it defending my honor or something. They probably won't notice at all. If we all went around noticing everyone else's flaws, that's all anyone would have time to do. Now don't burn the burgers."

I went to the grill where Millie was sitting patiently. Suddenly I felt greatly blessed that I had no more to show for my clumsiness than a black eye. It was the least of my flaws.

Father, You love me despite my many foibles and flaws. As Julee says, why should I care what anyone else thinks? But I do. It's a flaw—one I'm working on. —Edward Grinnan

Digging Deeper: Psalm 16:7–8

Sunday, June 5

And who is a rock, except our God, the God who girds me with strength and makes my way blameless? —Psalm 18:31–32 (NAS)

I ponder an unresolved issue while I wait in church for the passing of the Communion bread and cup. I believe Jesus offered His perfect life for my imperfect one, that He forgives my sins and makes me right with God. But I don't know what to do with my memories. Memories of wrongs I've committed and wrongs committed against me. Memories holding sadness or regret. They can show up suddenly. I am startled by their power to distract...to hurt.

I pray, *Lord, help me to understand these memories that I carry. They are part of me. I can't just change them.* A scene from the Bible comes to mind: Jesus, the night before He was crucified, taking a towel and basin of water and washing the disciples' feet. Simon Peter is aghast at such humble service from the Son of God. He cries, "Never shall You wash my feet!" (John 13:8). Jesus replies, "If I do not wash you, you have no part with Me" (John 13:8). Peter responds, "Lord, then wash not only my feet, but also my hands and my head" (John 13:9).

In this quiet Communion moment, Jesus speaks to my heart: *When I forgive you, when I heal you, all in you is made clean—even your memories. Don't be afraid of them.*

Relief floods me. His words ring true. I don't have to hide from God or myself in my memories. I don't have to dodge them. Jesus's love has reached even there.

"Thanks be to God, who always leads us in triumph in Christ" (2 Corinthians 2:14, NAS). —Carol Knapp

Digging Deeper: Acts 22:16; 2 Corinthians 3:4–6, 5:21; Galatians 5:1; 1 John 2:1–2

Monday, June 6

In all thy ways acknowledge him, and he shall direct thy paths. —Proverbs 3:6 (KJV)

I slapped a stamp on the envelope and tossed it in the Out of Town mailbox. Then I headed for the big double doors at the front of the post office. In my rush, I didn't notice the handwritten Use Other Door sign on the left one. I was going full speed when I ran into the heavy glass. *Smack!* Next thing I knew, I was on the floor in a daze. Anger rushed over me.

I was angry at the broken door. Angry that I was running late. Angry at the postal worker who was staring at me. Everything below my surface boiled over. My anger wasn't rational or reasonable; it was livid and pulsing.

It wasn't really about the door or the postal worker or that I was late. I was mad because last night I had finally asked out a young woman in whom I had been interested. I'm cautious, but from our conversations I was sure we had a connection. Still, it had taken me weeks to work up enough courage to ask for a date.

Her "no" felt like a slap in the face. Now that door was closed as tightly as the one I had just smacked into.

I shut my eyes and let the steam blow off. With a deep breath, I started to let go of my anger. I didn't understand why God left some doors open and closed others, and I didn't necessarily like the ones He chose. But I chose to trust that He would get me where I was supposed to go. Tentatively, I pushed open the door on the right.

Lord, You work in ways that I don't understand. Help me to trust Your judgment, even when it goes against mine. —Logan Eliasen

Digging Deeper: Psalm 32:8, Isaiah 30:21

Tuesday, June 7

Sovereign Lord, you are God! Your covenant is trustworthy, and you have promised these good things to your servant. —2 Samuel 7:28 (NIV)

"It must have poured last night," I said, shaking my husband awake.

He rolled over and blinked at me sleepily. "We weren't supposed to get any rain."

"Well, there are at least four inches of water in our driveway."

Suddenly, Cameron was wide-awake. He raced out the front door to find our front yard submerged in a giant pool of water. Our water main had broken overnight. The plumber charged five hundred dollars to stop the deluge.

A few days later, I noticed the light in the refrigerator was off. Seven hundred dollars and three days of eating food out of a cooler later, we learned that our main board had gone out. Next it was the dryer; four hundred dollars and two weeks of borrowing my mom's laundry facilities. Then it was the car battery... the natural gas tank... our son getting stitches in Urgent Care.

By the end of the month, we were three thousand dollars in the hole and not really sure how we were going to dig our way out. I panicked, chastising myself for not saving a bigger emergency fund and my husband for not knowing how to fix things. I fretted and worried and calculated.

Trust Me, God whispered. I ignored Him in my quest to find my own answers and worried some more, allowing my anxiety to nearly suffocate me.

Two days before the bills came due, my phone rang. It was our accountant. He had made a mistake on our taxes, and we were getting an unexpected refund for $3,033.00.

Lord, what an answer to prayer! But whatever outcome occurs, help me to learn to trust You. Amen.
—Erin MacPherson

Digging Deeper: Psalm 13:5, Proverbs 28:26

When I was at the end of my rope, he saved me.
—Psalm 116:6 (MSG)

Clinical depression undid me twenty years ago.
It's terrifying to lose yourself. Now, so many years
later, I couldn't deny the symptoms: loss of appetite,
insomnia, feeling hopeless. Just like before. Every
day I prayed the same desperate prayer: *Lord, I don't
want to return to that dark place. If I'm not better
tomorrow, I'll get help.*

One morning, I knew I couldn't go any lower. I
saw my doctor and began taking an antidepressant.
Two days later, Mother called. "Let's get some ice
cream," she said too eagerly. Her idea of going for
banana splits sounded as far-fetched as going on a
safari.

How could I say, "I'm afraid to leave my house
and ride five miles for a banana split?" Instead, I
mumbled, "I…I…I…"

"It'll be fun. Be there in twenty minutes."

She brought an old church hymnal and an
antique vase of pansies. And she was smiling. She
hugged me long and hard and began singing a few
lines of "Blessed Assurance" and "Only Trust Him,"
favorite songs from my childhood. She nudged me
until I joined in.

"Ready to get some ice cream?"

"Not really." But I went anyway.

The sun had warmed her car. When we walked inside, I noticed the aroma of food: french fries, hamburgers. I'd forgotten how to anticipate eating—or anything else. Mother ordered two banana splits. Slowly, I ate the cherry; it tasted good. So did the next bite. And the next. I almost smiled. Mother pretended not to notice.

"Thank you," I said. "I'd forgotten how good a banana split can be."

"Sometimes the way back is simpler than you think. You're gonna be okay."

I decided to believe her.

When I was dangling by a thread, Lord, You sent help: a kind doctor, my smiling mother, and a really good banana split. —Julie Garmon

Digging Deeper: Psalms 16, 18:2

Thursday, June 9

"My presence shall go with thee...."
—Exodus 33:14 (KJV)

Overnight the dogwood blossoms had disappeared. Wind and a quick rain had sent them fluttering to the ground. *Oh no,* I thought as I stepped into the kitchen's morning light, *I missed spring.*

I looked around. A number of cooking projects were laid out on the counters for the gathering we were hosting tonight. The floors needed to be cleaned. The sink was full of flowers, waiting to be arranged.

All week I had intended to go out and look for God in the springtime. I'd planned to meet Him in the woods, under the new green of trees. I'd find Him in the trillium popping up out of decaying leaves and in the purple violets tangled in the pine straw. But now it was too late. There was no time to go looking for God today.

I gathered vases for the flowers. I trimmed the stems and placed a tulip in the first vase—red petals, velvet black center. My eyes went deep into the flower and held there. A stillness settled around me. In that moment, then the next and the next, until the vases were filled and placed around the house, the Creator couldn't be denied.

Back in the kitchen a block of cheese waited. I grated it into long curly strips, added pimiento and mayonnaise. Crazy as it sounds, God was there with me, enjoying the process.

Dozens of tiny quiche came next. Then fruit salad, a tray of fresh vegetables. In everything, I stayed present. The silence of the kitchen with the sun falling across the counters felt holy. I didn't need to go looking for God in the woods. He was here now in my kitchen . . . found.

Father, You are as near as my breath. As long as I remember this, nothing can keep me from You.
—Pam Kidd

Digging Deeper: Matthew 1:23, Acts 17:27–28

Friday, June 10

"How often I have wanted to gather your children together as a hen gathers her chicks beneath her wings, but you wouldn't let me." —Matthew 23:37 (TLB)

I grew up on an Oklahoma farm where we produced part of our own food. My dad milked a cow, and we had a vegetable garden. Our flock of chickens provided plenty of eggs and meat. It was my job to feed and water the birds and gather the eggs—chores I hated! The roosters pecked my legs trying to get at the feed sack, and the hens pecked my hands when I reached in the nests. The chickens were smelly, and I had to replace the straw in their nests way too often.

My relationship with chickens caused me to notice a news article about a chicken sanctuary. The town's city council passed an ordinance allowing people to keep up to six chickens in their backyards, which created hundreds of instant farmers. But many knew nothing about chickens. They didn't know that roosters crow loudly every dawn or that they can inflict nasty wounds with their leg spurs. They were unprepared for the mess chickens make and the amount of care they require. So when unforeseen consequences outweighed the pleasure of fresh eggs, chickens were turned loose to fend for themselves. Thus the need for a chicken sanctuary.

The article prompted me to think about times when my lack of knowledge caused problems. Once I used a copier without reading the instructions and wasted a ream of paper before I got it shut off. Another time I took a chocolate cake to a family experiencing illness without realizing one person needed a gluten-free diet and two others were allergic to chocolate. Often I've spoken critical words, only to learn afterward that I had no understanding about a person's situation.

Only God has all knowledge. And with His help I am working hard to pray before I speak, think before I act.

Thank You, Lord, for lessons learned from chickens.
—Penney Schwab

Digging Deeper: Psalm 25:4–10, Proverbs 3:21–22, James 3:1–5

Saturday, June 11

"First the blade, then the ear, after that the full corn in the ear." —Mark 4:28 (KJV)

I slapped my pencil down, frustrated with a project that wouldn't come together. Physical labor relaxes me, so I trudged out back to my little orchard to tend some trees.

Our granddaughter Rossetti was visiting, and she wandered over to watch. "How come this apple tree doesn't have any apples?" she wanted to know.

"Well," I said, "it's a new tree. It takes three years for an apple tree to bear apples."

"Three whole years?"

"Yep, three years. God doesn't give it apples until the tree is able to bear them. See these branches? They are so skinny that the heavy apples would break them right off."

"It doesn't have many leaves," she observed.

"Right, and without lots of leaves to manufacture sugar, the apples would be sour."

I kicked the ground at the base of the tree. "And roots," I added. "Apples need water, but it takes time for roots to grow."

A teacher always learns more than his student, and the rest of the day I thought about the lesson in patience I had given my granddaughter. I decided to put my project aside for a while and work on other things.

Sunday morning I was singing in church when a solution to the project I had been working on suddenly became clear. By the end of the day, I had it finished.

I guess that harvesting apples is not so much about hard work as it is about being ready to receive the nurture that God gives in His own good time—this time with the help of a little angel named Rossetti.

I keep forgetting, God, that it's not all up to me.
My job is to be receptive to Your leading.
—Daniel Schantz

Digging Deeper: John 15:16, James 5:7

Sunday, June 12

O wretched man that I am! who shall deliver me from the body of this death? —Romans 7:24 (KJV)

I'm struggling to like someone. I can't say who; I can't even tell you the details of why I don't like her.

"To interest or engage or move a reader, you need to be specific," I'm always telling my creative writing students. "Give the details. Be concrete." But you can't be concrete if what you write might embarrass someone. You can't even be concrete about yourself on some topics.

Consider sin and temptation. Even among those who believe that we're all sinners, all tempted, only the tamest of sins and temptations (misspeaking, white lies, and minor covetousness, to name a few) are appropriate for open discussion. Some sins you can't even take up with your closest friends. Talking about specific sins or temptations reveals that I have them, and I generally like to pretend I don't.

I was thinking about this problem at church this morning as I read the prayer requests. All of them were for struggles unrelated to sin: sickness, grief, selling a house, safety of soldiers deploying, finding a job. Nobody requested prayer for an addiction or to be a better parent or spouse or for help loving a neighbor or, God forbid, an enemy.

The apostle Paul's writings reach me best when he speaks of his personal struggles. When he says he does what he shouldn't do and doesn't do what he should, for example. Or he mentions that thorn in his flesh. (He, too, was reluctant to specify.) Surely we all have thorns.

Perhaps, though, that's what the occasional "unspoken request" on the prayer list means. Just in case, I lifted up a heavy little prayer for them—and myself.

**Lord Jesus, Holy Father, have mercy upon me,
a sinner. —Patty Kirk**

Digging Deeper: 2 Corinthians 12:6–10

Uphold me according unto thy word, that I may live: and let me not be ashamed of my hope.
—Psalm 119:116 (KJV)

My hip that I injured exercising is talking to me, and it's not saying pleasant things. The anniversary of my father's death is coming up, and I'm feeling a little blue. A project I was enjoying was unexpectedly cancelled. On top of that, an opportunity that my son, Chase, was hoping for fell through, and a contract my daughter, Lanea, was counting on didn't materialize. All this means that I am trying to decide between paying the car insurance or the gas bill. I'm an optimistic person, but today is just not one of those "celebrate" days.

What I've learned, though, is I have to wash dishes when I don't feel like it, I have to exercise my aching hip when I don't feel like it, and I have to think good thoughts when I don't feel like it.

I'm tempted to feel ashamed; I don't want people to think I or God has failed to take care of my family and me. Instead, I have to trade my shame for hope. I choose to reminisce about my dad, which always makes me smile. I say thank you for my two children, who are beautiful, inside and out. And though I don't have hot water, I do have a roof over my head as well as my daily bread.

Pretty soon I'm smiling. I rub some liniment on my hip and happily limp to the kitchen for tea. It didn't start out as a great day, but since I am intentionally hopeful, trusting that God has good things ahead, I see the day getting brighter.

Lord, I trust You; I put my hope in You.
—Sharon Foster

Digging Deeper: Philippians 4:4, 6–8

Tuesday, June 14

"Stand at the crossroads and look; ask for the ancient paths, ask where the good way is, and walk in it, and you will find rest for your souls...." —Jeremiah 6:16 (NIV)

Recently I found a labyrinth in the courtyard of the Presbyterian church down the street. It was very peaceful amid the hedges and blue sky.

I followed the path to the center and stood there for a few minutes. *Thank You, God, for the joy of this discovery,* I thought. Now the labyrinth is a destination on my walking routes. At least once a week I go there to center myself.

I have walked the labyrinth so often I thought I'd memorized its path. Yet, at times, I find myself wondering which way I will turn next. The compact trail shifts back upon itself. Sometimes I am headed right to the center only to be led away and directed to the very outside. If I try to see where I'm headed, I'm often wrong. Yet I know if I stay on the path, I will make it to the center.

Trusting my steps to lead somewhere is easy when I'm walking in the labyrinth. It's a little harder to take that lesson with me when I'm not in it. With no clear path to follow, it's difficult to stay on course. This is when the other lesson of the labyrinth really comes in handy: pray on the path.

I do not hear God's voice, but I feel His presence and know we walk together. Sometimes I have a clear destination to aim for. Sometimes I cannot see which way I am going. I may take a detour, but I know God and I walk together.

Dear Father, walk with me and guide my steps today. Keep me on the path of Your choosing. Amen.
—Lisa Bogart

Digging Deeper: Judges 18:6, Isaiah 35:8–9

Wednesday, June 15

WHAT THE SAINTS HAVE TAUGHT ME
Bernard, Companion of Caregivers
I will search for the lost.... —Ezekiel 34:16 (NIV)

When I was a child, our neighbors owned a gigantic, gentle St. Bernard. I'd often be lifted onto his wide brown back to stroke the white stripe on his head.

So years later, when my husband and I were driving in the Alps, the name Great St. Bernard Pass on the map jumped out at me.

It was a spectacular trip through a perpendicular white landscape. At the highest point stood two stark-looking square buildings and the sign Great St. Bernard Hospice. Inside, a monk offered us a pamphlet about Saint Bernard. "He's patron saint of the Alps, you know"—the first time I'd actually noticed the "saint" in "St. Bernard."

"In 1049," the monk went on, "Bernard of Menthon built a hospice here for pilgrims bound for Rome. A traveler's greatest danger was the Alps' sudden blizzards. Time and again the saint and his followers set out through the snowdrifts to search for those stranded in a white wilderness."

"And the dogs?"

"Oh, they're still here." The monk led us to a large enclosed kennel where perhaps two dozen magnificent St. Bernards strolled, sat, or dozed. "We've brought them in because of avalanche danger, but ordinarily they're outdoors in the daytime." Nowadays, he added, helicopters have replaced the dogs for rescue work. "We keep them here to honor the men and dogs who for centuries risked their lives to save others."

**Help me respond swiftly, Father, to the need
I see today. —Elizabeth Sherrill**

Digging Deeper: Philippians 4:19

Bless the Lord, O my soul, and all that is within me, bless His holy name. —Psalm 103:1 (NAS)

Last summer I drove my mom and her neighbor Bubbles to dine with their friend Marybeth in her assisted-living community. Bubbles, at ninety, had vision impairment due to macular degeneration. Marybeth, at one hundred, shared the same problem. She asked Bubbles during our meal, "Do you ever get surprises when you eat?" Neither one of them could always tell what was on her plate.

Marybeth added something to our conversation that struck me so profoundly, it has rearranged my thinking. Commenting on her lost sight and all things lost—she'd been widowed twice—she remarked, "You can never be grateful enough until it's gone."

I try to be intentional about thanking God often for my blessings...to appreciate and savor them. But that day a dear person whose eyes were growing dim opened mine to a facet of gratitude I had never considered—grief. Far from distancing me from God or showing a lack of faith, grief is a deep expression of thanksgiving for something or someone I am missing.

James 1:17 (NAS) says, "Every good thing given and every perfect gift is from above, coming down from the Father of lights." When I grieve, I am acknowledging the "good thing given" and the One Who gave it.

Almost a year has passed since our luncheon. Marybeth is gone. Bubbles is gone. Mom and I miss them. But a wise centenarian who couldn't quite see her food has explained our sorrow in a clear and comforting way. We are expressing gratitude.

Accept my grief, Lord, as a thanksgiving offering.
—Carol Knapp

Digging Deeper: Lamentations 3:48–49, John 20:11–13, 1 Thessalonians 5:16–18

Friday, June 17

Jesus replied, "They do not need to go away. You give them something to eat." —Matthew 14:16 (NIV)

As my career has flourished, people have asked me if there was one defining moment when I knew I'd reached the pinnacle of success. Certainly, God has done for me above and beyond anything I could ever have hoped for or imagined, more than I'd ever dared to dream.

While I've had my novels hit the number-one slot on the *New York Times* best-seller list, those weren't the most significant moments for me. Actually, it happened on *Jeopardy!* I'm not smart enough to be a contestant on the TV game show, but my name and one of my book titles were an answer as a "Daily Double." I was excited and overwhelmed. I immediately phoned everyone in my contacts list to share the good news. "I was an answer on *Jeopardy!*"

The next morning, still gloating with delight, I heard about a member of our church who was in need. Right away I felt God talking to me: *Debbie, you can be her answer too*. That game I could play.

Lord, let me be the answer when You call.
—Debbie Macomber

Digging Deeper: Hebrews 13:6

Saturday, June 18

Don't forget to be kind to strangers, for some who have done this have entertained angels without realizing it! —Hebrews 13:2 (TLB)

As a frequent traveler, sometimes I worry about getting sick on a trip. One day I was talking to Mary Lou in Waukesha, Wisconsin. She told me about the time she and a friend flew to New Orleans for a cruise. Before they even boarded the ship, Mary Lou fell and broke her hip, which required an emergency room visit and surgery.

The ordeal could have been horrifying if it hadn't been for a few "God-moments," as Mary Lou put it. First, the emergency room doctor told her that his parents' best friends, Uncle Gene and Aunt Betsy, lived in the town she lived in. Mary Lou gasped. "I know them! Gene and Betsy are close friends of ours!" Later, the surgeon who replaced her hip told her she'd received her medical degree at Froedtert Hospital in Milwaukee, very near Mary Lou's home, which helped her relax.

Just three days later Mary Lou and her friend boarded the flight back home. Wouldn't you know? The woman sitting next to them just happened to be a nurse. When they changed planes in Atlanta, the woman in the seat in front of them was also a nurse. Both women helped Mary Lou get through the flights. "That whole experience taught me there are definite God-moments in life, and that week I saw one after another after another!" she exclaimed.

Now when I travel, I watch out for God-moments. I've discovered them in many places and in different faces: the woman who helped put my heavy bag in the overhead bin on the plane. The nurse who switched to a center seat, so she could sit next to a man who'd had a mild seizure. The pilot who walked the blind man to his seat. The train conductor in Rome who let me on even though my ticket had the wrong date.

Heavenly Father, You are with me everywhere I go. Thank You for the many God-moments You place in my path to remind me. —Patricia Lorenz

Digging Deeper: Ephesians 2:4–10, 2 Peter 1:5–11

Sunday, June 19

Honour thy father and thy mother, as the Lord thy God hath commanded thee....
—Deuteronomy 5:16 (KJV)

When God fitted me for math genes, apparently He was out of my size and gave me some that were a little short. My numerical incompetence has exasperated my father the engineer. Worse, my sister Cindy was a math whiz—and she was quadriplegic and had to do calculations in her head. My dad would look at her and then at me and think, *What went wrong?*

So I ended up as a writer and college adviser...and a person who trusts his gut, rarely measures before he cuts, and uses his smartphone calculator as an absolute crutch. This (lack of) approach irked my father—well, it added to a list of things about me that irked him.

Recently I had to take a certification class at the local community college, but first I had to pass an entry-level math test. Strangely, I crushed the test, missing one question.

Apparently years of figuring things out on my own had finally accomplished what three tries at trigonometry could not. When I told Dad, he shook my hand.

We have our differences, he and I; often we just don't understand each other. I wish he could appreciate the math I use, which measures life in terms of respect instead of accomplishment, decency rather than success, love above all else. My siblings and I fared well, mostly due to an amazing set of parents who bore tragedy with tenacity and grace.

I want to tell my father there is no calculus for a life such as this, yet he still figured out the correct result.

Lord, help me let my father know that gratitude can surpass all human understanding. —Mark Collins

Digging Deeper: Exodus 20:12, Proverbs 1:8

Monday, June 20

When they had finished eating, Jesus said to Simon Peter, "Simon son of John, do you love me more than these?" "Yes, Lord," he said, "you know that I love you." Jesus said, "Feed my lambs." —John 21:15 (NIV)

I have a young friend. She admitted to me a serious temptation she struggles with, and I agreed to hold her accountable.

A couple of stressful, busy months went by. Not only was I on a deadline, I was leading Bible study on Tuesday mornings, going to a small group on Tuesday nights, doing junior high ministry on Wednesday nights, and serving at church on the weekends. Add to that a husband and a son, and I had zero margin in my life.

So when I opened up a message from my young friend, calling me out for not being there for her, I had a thousand excuses. Only none of them would cut it.

I could hear the words Jesus spoke to Simon Peter: "Feed my sheep." God had put one of His sheep into my path, to serve and love and disciple, but in saying yes to so many ministries, I no longer had time for other people. How could I let Jesus be Lord of my schedule or how could I say yes to His opportunities if my days were already jam-packed and laid out?

Instead of giving my friend a list of excuses, I apologized. She graciously forgave, and I'm in the process of simplifying. Because even good things can get in the way of God's best.

Lord, please never let me overlook or ignore the sheep You have given me to feed. Forgive those times I let my schedule get so busy, I don't leave room for what You cherish most—people. —Katie Ganshert

Digging Deeper: Matthew 25:35–40, 1 John 3:17

Tuesday, June 21

Praise the Lord from the earth, you creatures of the ocean depths. Mountains and all hills, fruit trees and all cedars, wild animals and all livestock, small scurrying animals.... —Psalm 148:7, 9–10 (NLT)

In the last few days, the seventeen-year cicadas have emerged. The ground is crawling with beetles looking for a tall place to climb, so they can shed their hard skin.

Yesterday when I went outside, I noticed hundreds of them walking on top of one another with mangled wings. A quick search online blamed manicured lawns. The cicadas couldn't find a tall blade of grass or tree to climb, so their fragile wings dried in a deformed position.

"We can't cut the lawn," I told my husband, Tony. Then I got the stick idea. As the sun went down, I gathered branches from our compost pile and stuck them in the ground all over our yard. Early the next morning, my impromptu trees were covered with cicadas transforming. By my flower garden I found cicadas that had shed their skin but fallen off the Saint Francis statue. Carefully, I carried them to our picnic table where they climbed to the edge and slowly opened their wings. Morning after morning I helped the ones that had fallen.

"Why are you wasting so much time on bugs, Mom?" Solomon asked.

"If you had to spend seventeen years in darkness and finally managed to come above ground to fly, wouldn't you want someone to help you spread your wings?"

"They're bugs," he said.

So I took him outside and showed him the cicadas on the picnic table with beautiful gossamer wings stretched and hardening. Then I searched the ground and showed him one with twisted wings that will never fly.

"Can I help?" he asked.

Dear God, thank You for the amazing creatures that give us pause. Teach us to love and nurture the wonders of Your creation. —Sabra Ciancanelli

Digging Deeper: Psalms 50:10–11, 103:22, 150:6

Wednesday, June 22

If one member suffers, all suffer together; if one member is honored, all rejoice together.
—1 Corinthians 12:26 (ESV)

I fell in love with soccer when the sport was not popular in America. Where I'd always found lots of people who loved to talk basketball or baseball, I was often the only person who seemed to care about soccer. This was sometimes isolating but I liked it: my separateness.

At World Cup 2014, soccer became a global phenomenon. Everyone talked about the United States' chances in its "group of death." At first, I resented this enthusiasm. I heard so many uninformed things about soccer, the kinds of things new fans would say. There was nothing wrong with them, but I didn't like the intrusion on this love that was mine alone!

I knew I was being crazy, but I was resistant anyway—until I watched the USA-Portugal match at a crowded restaurant with my friend. Abby had never seen a game but was so excited. I explained what I needed to and watched along with her and the building full of fans.

As we all cheered after Clint Dempsey scored the go-ahead goal and then groaned when Silvestre Varela tied the game at the very last moment, I finally let go of my resistance. If loving sports was consistent with God's plan for me, then it was not for private enjoyment but for the ability to connect, in some small way, with others.

Thank You, Lord, for always giving me more chances to grow closer to the rest of humanity.
—Sam Adriance

Digging Deeper: Hebrews 10:24–25

Thursday, June 23

Enjoy the good of all his labour that he taketh under the sun all the days of his life, which God giveth him.... —Ecclesiastes 5:18 (KJV)

Thistles—*ugh!* I scanned the field with dismay. They were everywhere. In the two years since I'd hurt my back fighting a wildfire on our family ranch, I hadn't been able to keep up with the weeds. *Lord, how am I ever going to beat this mess?*

Sure, a thousand-mile journey begins with a single step, but how was I going to tackle thousands and thousands of thistles?

Change you before changing this field. The words filled my heart with a warm glow, and I struggled to understand. Change my perspective? How? What good could I find in the most boring of all ranch work?

Suddenly, the thought hit me. Even if I couldn't ride a horse yet, I could still "saddle up" the four-wheeler to spray those weeds. Riding the ATV uses the same muscles as riding horseback, but it wasn't going to spook unexpectedly and injure me. I could use the time to gradually and carefully rebuild my strength, so that maybe I could saddle up for real once more.

Another plus? This is the land I love: the mountains in the distance; the green valleys; the pine-and-juniper-studded buttes; cattle, birds, deer, and antelope all around me. Even if the job could be monotonous, the view was not.

Praise You, Lord, for showing me the way to find the joy and the good in my least favorite labor. You can turn a weedy field into a cathedral of worship. —Erika Bentsen

Digging Deeper: Romans 8:18, Titus 3:14

Friday, June 24

FINDING REST: Volunteering

"If you return to me and keep my commandments and do them, though your outcasts are under the farthest skies, I will gather them from there and bring them to the place at which I have chosen to establish my name." —Nehemiah 1:9 (NRSV)

Over the past few years, my husband, Charlie, and I have traveled a bit. We've spent extended time in Key West, Florida, and in different cities in California, Baltimore, and New England. The first thing I look for when we arrive in a new place is a church that might be a good fit for us. Sometimes it takes a visit or two to different churches to find the right one. Once in a while, we volunteer with a church-based program. But for the most part, we rest during these times away. Quite often we don't even realize how much we need to rest and repair from our responsibilities at home.

It is always interesting for us to see how other churches work. From a Saint Vincent DePaul group near San Francisco, we learned how to listen to people express their needs. From a Key West soup kitchen, we learned how to serve a huge meal with very few resources. From a hospitality park on the grounds of a Baltimore church, we learned why Jesus taught us to spend time with the poor and disenfranchised.

We bring all of our experiences home to New London, Connecticut, every time we return from "resting" in a different place.

Father, please act in and through me even as You give me rest from the work that You've blessed me with. Amen. —Marci Alborghetti

Digging Deeper: Jeremiah 15:19

Saturday, June 25

As for me, far be it from me that I should sin against the Lord by failing to pray for you. —1 Samuel 12:23 (NIV)

John graduated from high school yesterday. There were thirty-four students in his class at the therapeutic school. Most had been in the residential program. These are kids who have been hospitalized for clinical depression and other mental illnesses. Many have experienced major trauma, struggled with learning disabilities, and had to overcome poor coping skills.

I looked at the expectant families. What struck me was that every single person in that room had known deep suffering. We'd all been in rough places most people don't have to go. We'd all learned to be intensely grateful for things that others take for granted—like the mere fact that our children are still alive. Graduation probably wouldn't mean an end to difficult times for anyone there. It would, however, provide a landmark that allowed us to pause and remember what we and our children had survived.

"Pomp and Circumstance" began to play, and we stood up. Someone started clapping, and the applause continued long and hard and loud. The graduates stood tall, proud, and pleased. More than one mom or dad needed a tissue.

As the students received their diplomas, cheers went up from parents and siblings and relatives and social workers and kitchen staff and teachers and even maintenance men who were honoring the hard, hard work each youngster had done to become a healthier human being.

I kept the program, not as a keepsake, but as a prayer list. There are thirty-four kids and their families whose needs I must lift up to the Lord.

Jesus, let every hurt in my heart be turned into prayer.
—Julia Attaway

Digging Deeper: Romans 5:3, 8:18

Sunday, June 26

"He has risen from the dead.... Now I have told you." —Matthew 28:7 (NIV)

I went into the kitchen after a restless night, thinking about a friend recently diagnosed with a brain tumor considered terminal, and turned on the morning news. A man had just hijacked a car with a four-year-old boy inside. Police were chasing the driver through the streets of Denver in rush-hour traffic. A helicopter was filming the pursuit live, showing the car going eighty miles per hour through red lights and busy intersections.

I watched in horror, waiting for the accident that was sure to happen. Amazingly, this car kept missing others. The chase went on for ten minutes with dangerous maneuvers across an open field to access another busy highway, where the man drove the wrong way. Finally, he got a flat tire and the car spun to a stop. The suspect jumped out and started running, but police surrounded him. The chase was over. I felt exhausted but relieved that it ended safely, especially for the child in the backseat.

Later, I watched a rerun of the shocking events with my husband but was surprised to find that it was a totally different emotional experience for me. I felt no fear because I knew the end of the story.

I kept thinking about the parallel of the car chase to my friend's cancer diagnosis. Even as her story unfolds with frightening unknowns, I know the ultimate ending. God promises us eternal life. My friend knows that promise, too, and I can pray she keeps receiving comfort in believing.

Lord, You have already written the ending, which gives us hope while still living in the middle of our stories.
—Carol Kuykendall

Digging Deeper: Matthew 28:1–9, Luke 24:1–8

Monday, June 27

"Truly I tell you, anyone who will not receive the kingdom of God like a little child will never enter it."
—Luke 18:17 (NIV)

As I applied lotion after a hot shower, I thought of *loshie,* the word one of my four children used as a toddler for "lotion." Each of my kids had his or her own collection of mispronunciations and homemade words. I often smile when I think of one, but sometimes the memory brings a few tears. I miss those days; my babies are now ages six to eighteen.

I miss the 5:00 AM feedings and cuddle fests during those quiet, sacred mornings; the sweet coos and the tiny hands wrapping tightly around my index finger; when my biggest worries were if my child would overcome his separation anxiety or if she'd ever master potty training. As I prepare to send my children back to school and survey the college brochures that daily fill our mailbox, I find myself sighing and wondering, *Where did the time go?*

In the same breath, my eyes twinkle when my seven-year-old reads from a level-two reader, cover to cover, sounding out big-girl words like *amazing*. My heart skips a beat when I discover my nine-year-old has written "Live by faith" with chalk on our driveway. I burst with pride to see my thirteen-year-old run with agility on the football field and continue to earn awesome grades. I marvel over my eighteen-year-old whom I literally look up to and who nurtures and cares for his younger siblings with never a complaint.

I am grateful for this healthy, wild, and rambunctious clan and for the memories of the precious babies they were. But I am learning to shed fewer tears, knowing it's never loss but only gain to grow.

Father, may I treasure the memories of yesterday while embracing the joys of today. —Carla Hendricks

Digging Deeper: Matthew 18:1–5, 19:13–15

BEING RENEWED: Laughter Is Good Medicine

"God will let you laugh again...." —Job 8:21 (MSG)

Gene continued to heal physically with the excellent care and therapy he received. I should've been content with that. But I wasn't. I wanted us to laugh again, have fun. Sometimes when Gene was sleeping or watching a basketball game, I'd hear some of the nurses' aides laughing in the hall. I wanted to run out and beg, "Tell me what's funny. Let me laugh too."

I didn't.

"Guess what Girl Friend's doing?" I asked Gene one gray, gloomy day—all ready to laugh about the antics of our cat. He looked straight ahead at the TV and didn't answer. I pretended he had. I pretended a lot. "She's sleeping on all those tax returns you left scattered over the dining room table after you fell." I leaned around him and gazed into his eyes, but he remained grim.

Give up, Marion. Stop trying. Let him be.

I sat back down in the comfortable recliner by his bed. Gene broke the long silence. "Will you put on my shoes? It's almost time for lunch."

I struggled with them, being careful with his injured left side. *Whew!* Finally I had them on. Gene sat upright. "You've got them on the wrong feet!"

Surely I hadn't. Who could be so dumb?

As Gene glared at me laughter erupted. Tears plopped onto his clean white sheet. My stomach hurt, I laughed so hard. His slow chuckles were like a train starting up.

For a few glorious moments, we weren't in rehab but had been zapped back together in our long-distance courtship.

Oh, Father, how I praise You for knowing humankind would need to laugh. —Marion Bond West

Digging Deeper: Psalm 126:2, Ecclesiastes 3:4

Wednesday, June 29

This is the day which the Lord hath made; we will rejoice and be glad in it. —Psalm 118:24 (KJV)

Stephen was lying on the living room floor, looking up at the ceiling while I looked at him. My little boy wouldn't be a little boy much longer. "How do you like being ten?" I asked him.

"I don't," Stephen said, sighing. "Seven was my golden year."

I was startled by such a wistful reflection from a fifth-grader. Weary glances back into the past are more the province of geezers like me. "Why do you say that?" I asked.

"A lot of reasons. But mostly because Maggie was only ten then. She liked to play imagining games with the stuffed animals. I still like that, but she doesn't. Now that she's thirteen, she doesn't have time for me."

"It's hard when you feel that your big sister is growing up and away from you," I said. "But it's only natural for her to need some space for herself. She still loves you."

Stephen didn't seem convinced.

My son can look ahead to many more years, and I pray that a lot of them will be golden. I've got a whole lot more behind me than I do in front, and when the mood is on me, my looks back are more at what I haven't done and my looks ahead are more about what I won't have the time to do. But today I'm here with my not-so-little boy, and we can read comic strips, go out to the schoolyard, watch cartoons, or take a walk to get some frozen yogurt. There's no reason I can't start making a golden year right now.

Lord, help me to see in what I do today a little glimmer of the golden streets where I will walk with You forever. —Andrew Attaway

Digging Deeper: Psalm 127:3, 2 Corinthians 6:2

Thursday, June 30

Look to the Lord and his strength; seek his face always. —Psalm 105:4 (NIV)

I lay awake. The dream had pulled me from sleep. In my slumber, my teenage son was a little boy again. His eyes were a shining blue. His smile held a line-up of baby teeth. And he laughed. It had been so long since I'd heard that sweet sound.

The past months had been tough. His father and I were weary from wading through deep waters of teen turbulence. We laid boundaries in a foundation of love, but the boundaries left us on one side of a chasm, our son on the other. The longing for a restored relationship was a physical ache in my chest.

I tossed and turned, wrestling with fears that came close in the night. I didn't want to wake my husband, Lonny. He hadn't been sleeping well either. I swung my legs over the side of the bed and hoped the sofa would offer rest, but the living room was void and vast. Our grandfather clock ticked into the emptiness. Emotion, thick as the dark, filled me. I moved to the rug, sat in the center, curled my arms over my knees, and cried.

"What are you doing?" came a voice from the darkness. In a moment, Lonny was close, his breath warm on my neck. His arms wrapped around mine and he cradled me tight. "When you're hurting," he whispered, "please stay beside me. Don't leave. You don't have to hurt alone."

We sat for a long while in the shadow of night, in the center of our worn wool rug. As Lonny held me, I began to feel God's arms wrap around me, too, and was reminded of an even greater truth: the Lord was always with me. I didn't have to hurt alone.

Lord, thank You for holding me. Amen.
—Shawnelle Eliasen

Digging Deeper: Psalm 139:7–10; Isaiah 9:12, 41:10;
Romans 8:38–39

GOD'S ABIDING LOVE

1 _____

2 _____

3 _____

4 _____

5 _____

6 _____

7 _____

8 _____

9 _____

10 _____

11 _____

12 _____

13 _____

14 _____

15 _____

16 _____

17 _____

18 _____

19 _____

20 _____

21 _____

22 _____

23 _____

24 _____

25 _____

26 _____

27 _____

28 _____

29 _____

30 _____

JULY

May the God of hope fill you with all joy and peace in believing, so that by the power of the Holy Spirit you may abound in hope.

—Romans 15:13 (ESV)

"Be strong and courageous. Do not be afraid...
for the Lord your God goes with you...."
—Deuteronomy 31:6 (NIV)

"Oma, say yes, please!" I could hear the voices of my
four granddaughters when my son called, urging me
to join them on an overnight camping trip.

I hesitated. Camping always sounds like more fun
than it really is. It involves lots of packing, cooking
and cleaning, dirt, cold water, and long nights lying
in a tent, vividly remembering every "Bear Mauls
Camper" story.

"Oma, it would be an *adventure*!" the girls
chorused into the phone.

That one got me. They know I love adventures,
and we'd never been camping together. How could
I say anything but yes?

So I packed my warmest sweatshirt, wore my
already dirty jeans, kissed my husband good-bye,
and drove off to meet them at the campsite.

Guess what? It was lots of work and lots of dirt
and ants and some rain. I volunteered to spend
the night alone in the tent with the girls, so their
mommy and daddy could sleep outside under the
stars. I'm pretty sure I didn't sleep at all because I had
the same vivid image of animals prowling around
outside the tent. I was thankful to finally see the

first fingers of dawn, and then revived by a cup of lukewarm coffee, the beauty of the morning, and the enthusiasm of the kids.

Maybe I was just proud of myself for doing something I wasn't sure I'd enjoy, but as I drove down the mountain that afternoon, I savored the new memory of an adventure with my grandchildren.

Lord, may I always say yes to invitations to adventure because with You, I can do more than I think I can. —Carol Kuykendall

Digging Deeper: Psalm 119:148, Isaiah 55:12

Saturday, July 2

Pray every way you know how, for everyone you know.... —1 Timothy 2:1 (MSG)

For the past few years, my husband and I have started each day sitting on the front porch together. Our five porch-party rules are simple:
1. No nagging or criticizing.
2. Avoid discussing problems.
3. Notice something beautiful in our surroundings or each other.
4. Say only positive things.
5. Ask for prayer.

One morning, I plopped into my rocking chair with a heavy heart. Family concerns pulled at me from all directions: Katie, our daughter, was going through a divorce. Gene, my stepfather, was in the hospital; he'd broken his femur and hip. My mother-in-law was recuperating from a quadruple bypass. One of my brothers was living in a homeless shelter. The list seemed endless, so I let out a long sigh.

"What's the matter?" Rick asked.

"Oh, nothing. I just have a lot on my mind."

After thirty-five years together, he probably knew what I was thinking. We sat quietly for a few minutes, sipping coffee and rocking. "Want me to pray?" he asked.

"Would you? I'd love that."

We hadn't prayed together for a while, though I'm not sure why. We bowed our heads, and Rick offered prayers for each person on my heart. Then, he paused, giving me a chance to pray.

To my surprise, my spoken words to God bubbled up quickly, effortlessly, authentically. The first thing I praised God for was a praying husband who led the way.

Forgive me, Lord. Pride and fear nearly kept me from one of the sweetest times of spiritual intimacy I've ever known—praying for others with my husband. —Julie Garmon

Digging Deeper: Job 42:10, Ephesians 6:18, 1 Timothy 2:1

Sunday, July 3

"For you are standing on holy ground."
—Exodus 3:5 (NLT)

My church embarked on a major building campaign, and the pastor offered everyone a unique opportunity. "The foundation has been laid, but it's time we put down the true foundation. We want our church to be built upon the love, prayers, and commitment of *you*, so come next Sunday to write down your prayers, blessings, and hopes on the concrete slab."

The next week my family and I walked through the cordoned off areas of the new church. There were hundreds of people excitedly pointing to the worship space, the children's wing, the coffee shop, and the bookstore. We found our perfect spot in the sanctuary and knelt down to write on the exposed concrete floor. Using colored markers, we wrote our hopes and prayers for ourselves and for future generations. When I finished, I stood up and looked around, completely humbled by this simple, yet profoundly powerful, act.

Loved ones were gathered together, down on their knees, with Bibles and notebooks in hand, intent on inscribing their names, prayers, and Scriptures that they'd encircled with big hearts. George Herbert, an Anglican priest in the 1600s, wrote that "things of ordinary use" could be made to "serve for lights even of heavenly truths." Without a doubt, I was bearing witness to this today.

The new carpet would be put down shortly and would cover over our sentiments. But not to worry, for I was quite sure that the messages, hopes, and dreams had been lifted up to heaven already.

Lord, the church's true foundation is not concrete but Your Word. This, above all else, is what I choose to stand upon. Amen. —Melody Bonnette Swang

Digging Deeper: 1 Corinthians 3:10, Ephesians 2:20

Monday, July 4

I will lead the blind by ways they have not known, along unfamiliar paths I will guide them; I will turn the darkness into light before them and make the rough places smooth.... —Isaiah 42:16 (NIV)

It was the first Fourth of July after my divorce. My ex-husband had the girls for an eleven-day stretch. I wasn't sure I could make it through my annual family reunion in Mississippi, an hour away from my home in Alabama. I missed my girls too much. All of my cousins' children would be there—fishing, swimming, playing baseball. Seeing them all together would make my heart ache even more.

But at my cousin Bryan's urging, I attended the reunion, not planning to stay long—just enough to make an appearance before I went home to have a good cry. Much to my surprise, I remained until right before dark. I still missed my girls, but being with my family—even watching the other children play—brought me a sense of calm I hadn't expected.

After I said my good-byes, I climbed into my car and followed Bryan, who lives in the same town as I do, just in case I had any car trouble on the way back. Bryan's path home was different from the one I knew. We were the only two cars on curvy back roads as the darkness fell quickly around us. I kept my eyes glued to his taillights. *Please don't let me lose sight of him, Lord*, I prayed.

Eventually, those curvy back roads led to the highway I knew. I waved at my cousin as he took his turn and I continued on my path, safely to my home where I would welcome my girls soon.

Father, help me to remember that You know the way even when I don't. —Ginger Rue

Digging Deeper: Psalm 119:35, Proverbs 3:6

Tuesday, July 5

"I am the Lord your God, who brought you out of the land of Egypt, out of the house of bondage. You shall have no other gods before Me."
—Exodus 20:2–3 (NKJV)

The sun beat down on my back as I shoveled sand and concrete mix into the cement mixer. I dumped the latest batch into the pump and wiped cement spatter from my forehead. Then I heard my boss Matt's voice over the din of the machinery: "Hey, shut everything down! Something's plugging up the tubes!"

I nodded, then switched off the equipment. All I could think about was the one warning Matt had given me a hundred times: "Watch out for rocks in the sand. If they make it into the mix, they'll jam the whole rig."

By the time I reached Matt, he was already taking apart sections of tubing, looking for the telltale plug. An hour later, he held up the sinister piece of gravel. It wasn't huge, just big enough to catch in the pipes. "I know these are hard to spot when you're shoveling the sand," Matt told me, "but the small rocks are the ones that sneak in and cause all sorts of problems."

It was kind of like idols. They had a way of worming into my life when I wasn't looking: like the relationship I wanted so badly, or the new phone I was saving for, or the GPA I was carefully maintaining. They seemed like such small desires that they had slipped into my life unnoticed. But now they were plugging up my relationship with God, taking my focus off of Him, and causing all sorts of problems.

"Well, I guess we'd better start putting things back together," Matt said.

I nodded. "I guess we'd better."

Heavenly Father, help me to recognize the idols that try to slip into my life and remove the ones that I already have. —Logan Eliasen

Digging Deeper: Leviticus 26:1, 1 Corinthians 10:14, Colossians 3:5

Wednesday, July 6

"Keep these words that I am commanding you today in your heart." —Deuteronomy 6:6 (NRSV)

This Lent I challenged myself to discuss Scripture at least once daily. I was impossibly regimented about it, as I typically am with self-improvement projects. It couldn't be just any Bible passage; it had to be from where I was currently reading: namely, reconstructing Jesus's life chronologically by skipping around the Gospels.

I made up my mind to "talk" online about Scripture to spur dialogue. The result was a Lent-long conversation with my brother Larry, the only person who reliably read what I posted and took time to comment.

In retrospect, the project seems silly. As with dieting and daily Bible reading, I beat myself up on days I failed. And sometimes I didn't have much to say about the passage I'd read, so posting seemed an empty ritual.

The project did have one valuable result though. Throughout Lent, my brother and I chatted about worthy things. Larry lives in Colorado and I in Oklahoma, so we rarely see each other. Occasionally we talk on the phone. For forty days, though, we were branches of the same vine, linked daily by God's words.

After Lent, I didn't post for months though I thought often of the Scriptures I'd discussed online. When I did post again, though, Larry was quick to reply: "Yay! You're back!" Still later, after seeing an owl photo I'd posted, he mourned, "Your brother misses you."

I miss him too.

Thank You, Lord, for the gift of family who spur us on to love You more. —Patty Kirk

Digging Deeper: 2 Timothy 3:14–17

Thursday, July 7

See to it that no one fail to obtain the grace of God; that no "root of bitterness" spring up and cause trouble.... —Hebrews 12:15 (RSV)

Twice a month I drive twelve miles to a nursing home to visit a friend, a kind and generous former neighbor. As a younger woman, she took pride in her immaculate home and personal appearance. There was never a hair out of place—standards far beyond mine, though she rarely commented. After retirement, even if she had no plans to go out, she put on makeup.

Circumstances have changed. Her gnarled arthritic fingers don't work well enough for her to apply lipstick. After helping her bathe, an aide runs a comb through her thin, untrimmed hair. Her earrings never leave the drawer. Though she's suffered memory loss, she still has a sense of what ought to be. And in her powerless frustration, she lashes out at me. "Your hair looks terrible. You need a cut." "Pull in your stomach." "Put on some lipstick." "Quit biting your nails!" "Quit mumbling!"

More than once I've walked to my car crying, worn down by her anger. But I've responded better since attending a class about parenting. The advice? When challenged, smile and take a deep breath. These physical actions help me keep my cool; my body tells my brain to resist the negativity, set aside the personal gibes. Recently I've been praying with my friend at the nursing home before I leave. It gives both of us a focus beyond ourselves. I can remind her of God's presence in her restricted world. I can draw out a smile. I can drive away asking God to strengthen her faith. At a stop sign, I glance in the mirror. Maybe a haircut *is* overdue.

Lord, help me see ways to deflect any fiery verbal darts that others throw toward me so that we might all experience Your abounding grace.
—Evelyn Bence

Digging Deeper: Galatians 5:25, 6:18

Friday, July 8

Blessed be God, who didn't turn away when I was praying and didn't refuse me his kindness and love.
—Psalm 66:20 (TLB)

My hunka-hunka-burnin'-love likes his vacations to involve cruising to various Caribbean islands. Cruising is easy. Get on the ship, unpack your clothes, eat, sleep, watch entertainment, eat, swim, play games, eat, take a tour on an island for a couple hours, eat, get back on the ship, sleep, eat, and go home. Jack loves it. Me? Not so much.

I travel for many reasons. I travel to visit my four children in California, Wisconsin, and Ohio; my dad and Bev in Illinois; my brother in Kentucky; and various friends scattered around the country. I also give speeches in various states, and I travel to see the world and experience a wider range of cultures. I've been to twenty-eight countries so far. However, twelve of those are in the Caribbean because I try to be a good wife.

Jack and I definitely have two different paths and ways to travel. But I go on cruises with him and he comes on adventures with me.

It's just like prayer: many ways, same result. Some of my prayers are fast and easy. Some are slow and deliberate. Sometimes I can pray for twenty people in five minutes. Other times I can ponder their needs and pray for an hour. Sometimes my prayers are interesting as I focus on lots of details about the person I'm praying for. Sometimes I pray that Jack won't suggest another cruise. But whatever it is, I'm sure God hears and answers every prayer in His time and His way.

Father, help me to keep my prayer life vibrant, interesting, and faithful. Thank You for answering all prayers, no matter how they're said. And thanks, Lord, for a husband who's willing to compromise.
—Patricia Lorenz

Digging Deeper: 1 Corinthians 7:32–39, Jude 20

Saturday, July 9

And whoever receives one such child in My name receives Me. —Matthew 18:5 (NAS)

One summer night out by our fire pit with my grandson Ian, two years old, I carried him in the dark while we played "Peekaboo Moon." He wriggled with excitement each time the bright orb appeared between the trees. It was such fun to acquaint him with the moon in a way I hoped he might remember.

Six months later my husband and I were in the moving process. Our daughter and her children came over for one more family time in our home. We heard a little voice call to us from upstairs to come see the moon. Sure enough, Ian stood at the bedroom window, looking up at a glowing full moon.

He and his sister had been playing fort in the empty closet. Ian was holding the flashlight I'd let them use. He turned from the window and shined it on the bare wall. It made a small circle of light in the darkened room. Recalling our imaginative summer Peekaboo Moon play, I exclaimed, "How did that moon get in here?"

Oh, the sheer joy in that boy as he shined the moon all around the room and the rest of us tried to catch it! Another unforgettable moon memory.

The day Jesus took the children in His arms and blessed them, saying, "Permit the children to come to Me; do not hinder them; for the kingdom of God belongs to such as these" (Mark 10:14, NAS) must have been a memory-maker for those boys and girls. The delightful acceptance He conveyed . . . the playfulness . . . the welcome!

Throughout the Gospels Jesus is portrayed as thoroughly enjoying the presence of children. Perhaps some nights He was out making moon memories with them.

You, Lord, were once a child and never forgot it.
Make each child precious in my sight.
—Carol Knapp

Digging Deeper: Matthew 18:1–6, 21:15–16;
Mark 5:22–24, 35–42

Sunday, July 10

Long time therefore abode they speaking boldly in
the Lord, which gave testimony unto the word of his
grace.... —Acts 14:3 (KJV)

I taught Sunday school for two years, and the moment
I remember best was this one: a moppet, age eight,
asking me, with some exasperation, if I had ever seen
miracles, because I was going on interminably about
how miracles are everywhere and every moment is
filled with miracles if we pay close enough attention.
I blurted out the answer that rocketed from my heart
straight to my lips without running through the tact
filter, and my answer was as follows:

Heavens, yes, I have seen miracles. I saw people
come out of my wife. There were people living
inside a woman I really loved! It was like she was an
apartment building, and there were people living
in there without paying any rent, and finally they
emerged slowly, all looking like wet Yodas, and after
that everyone lay there moaning. It was awful.

Also during all these miracles I was exhausted, and all I wanted to do was go to sleep, but my wife kept insisting that I stay awake for some reason, as if watching people come out of your wife is a fun experience. It is not a fun experience! It is…well, stunning and holy and amazing and the most moving thing I ever saw in my life and it is a miracle, that's for sure. I mean, you can talk about embryonic cell mitosis all you want, but the fact is that new life is a miracle and, yes, that will be on the test, Joey.

Well, you can imagine the startled faces of my students that day. But as my pastor has wryly observed, they'll never forget that definition of a miracle, nor that life is holy.

Lord, we don't thank You enough for the greatest gift of all, which is even better than clean water and music and basketball—kids. Thanks. Best gift ever.
—Brian Doyle

Digging Deeper: Psalm 139:13–16

Monday, July 11

Do not be conformed to this world, but be transformed by the renewal of your mind….—Romans 12:2 (ESV)

I had a unique undergraduate experience at St. John's College. Focusing entirely on the great books of Western civilization, I spent four years thinking about the biggest questions in life: what it means to be human, our place in the universe, and God's role in that.

When I graduated, I dropped those questions and concentrated on the practical as I struggled for money and studied for the LSAT. I stopped thinking about Plato and started worrying about a job and paying the rent. At first, I was happy and played up my desire to "get out of the clouds" in my personal statements for law school. It was a good thing. My laserlike focus on which steps I needed to take seemed like an overdue change.

I continued that way for a few years until my dad asked me how I was. I said "fine" instead of my usual "good."

"Is there something bothering you?" he asked.

Almost without knowing what I was going to say, I answered, "I don't believe in magic anymore. And I don't like it."

I'd become more cynical about nearly everything, from miracles to the value of classroom learning. I did almost everything by thinking only about what it could get me, without paying attention to the bigger questions. I knew I had to make changes. I had to open up my mind again or I would end up a lonely middle-aged man with no joy in his life.

It may be hard to find a job with a humanities degree, but it's even harder to live without reflecting on the questions that make one human.

Thank You, Lord, for reminding me of the miracles of Your truth. —Sam Adriance

Digging Deeper: Mark 9:24

Let all things be done decently and in order.
—1 Corinthians 14:40 (KJV)

Writer Kurt Vonnegut told this story about his brother who worked for General Electric. Bernard Vonnegut was a brilliant scientist, but his dramatically messy laboratory alarmed the safety officials at GE. When confronted with their concerns, Bernard tapped the side of his head and said, "If you think this laboratory is bad, you should see what it's like in here."

I have used that line to describe my own office, which has all of the chaos but none of the brilliance. Imagine a Jackson Pollack painting—oceans of paper thrown helter-skelter without sense or logic. Every morning I sigh and swear that I'll clean it up someday. Sometimes I just swear. I know why I'm reluctant to fix this problem: to create order out of such bedlam requires time and an ability to prioritize... not to mention a very good memory. (Is there a reason I am saving an "after-hours campus parking" memo from 2009?)

Sadly, my prayer life is equally untidy—frenzied requests for help, for solace, for more time. They aren't the orderly invocations of my youth ("Hail Mary, full of grace..."), but frantic, half-mumbled entreaties that are decidedly not full of grace and loaded with promises I know I will never keep.

I don't know what God's office looks like. I hope the Almighty's to-do list has room for cleaning up the multiple messes that I've created, things done and left undone...which sounds eerily similar to the last prayer I sent. Something about needing help for all I need to do that I cannot, cannot, cannot do alone.

Lord, somewhere among these piles of paper with legs, let me know You are near. —Mark Collins

Digging Deeper: 1 Kings 8:28, Colossians 2:5

Wednesday, July 13

I will declare your name to my brothers and sisters; I will praise you in the very center of the congregation! —Psalm 22:22 (CEB)

I wasn't sure why George e-mailed me. We hadn't seen each other in a couple of years. We had served together on a committee, representing our respective organizations. I had tremendous respect for him, and our occasional lunches were full of laughter. But that was then. This was now.

"I'd love to see you," he wrote. "Let's have lunch someday."

The invitation was open-ended enough that I could just let that "someday" spin off into a well-intentioned "someday but not soon." Still, there was some reason he wanted to get in touch.

We picked a date and met at a midtown diner. The conversation ranged along work, movies, books, food, mutual friends, but I could tell there was more that George wanted to talk about. We plowed through our burgers and then it came out: he wanted to talk about faith. He'd struggled for a long time with belief, while also struggling with alcoholism. For a year now he'd been going to a twelve-step group, and not only was he sober, but God had come alive to him.

"My life is tougher than it's ever been and the future more uncertain, yet I've never felt more positive that everything will turn out all right," George said.

Earlier that day, I'd been praying through Psalms and I'd come to this passage (22:22): "I will declare your name to my brothers and sisters; I will praise your name in the very center of the congregation," and wondered what that meant in my life.

At once it seemed clear. George wanted to share his newfound faith and was looking for someone with whom he could praise God's name "in the very center

of the congregation," or in this case, a midtown diner.
I'm glad it got to be me.

**God, send me to those who need You as much as
I need You. Together, we find You.** —Rick Hamlin

Digging Deeper: Romans 12:10, Colossians 3:16

Thursday, July 14

WHAT THE SAINTS HAVE TAUGHT ME
Joseph, Companion of Fathers

Joseph her husband was a righteous man.
—Matthew 1:19 (CEB)

When I thank God, on Father's Day, for all the
wonderful fathers in my life—my own father, my
husband, John, in his fathering of our children,
our sons with their families—I always include the
adoptive father of Jesus.

We don't know much about Joseph, but every
glimpse we get points to a father that any of us would
cherish. We meet him first as he's confronted with
shocking news: his beloved young fiancée is pregnant!
Many men of that time would have called for the
customary penalty: death by stoning. Joseph rejects
such a horror. He will not even shame Mary by public
divorce but will end the engagement quietly.

Next we glimpse his faith. When, in a dream,
God tells him that Mary is innocent, Joseph does

not question the impossible. He names the newborn baby Jesus as God instructs, takes mother and child to Jerusalem to perform the required temple ritual, and raises the boy as his own.

Joseph performs the fatherly roles of provider and protector. On his woodworker's income, he feeds, clothes, and educates Mary's son, seeing that Jesus receives schooling in Scripture, doubtless far more thorough than his own.

For me, though, Joseph's fathering shines most clearly in Jesus's favorite name for God: *Father*. When I hear the man Jesus cry, "*Abba! Daddy!*" I see a little boy running to the father who will take him in his lap to soothe a skinned knee and come at bedtime, no matter how long his workday, to hear the prayers of his son.

Heavenly Father, bless fathers everywhere, that all people may hear in Your name the echo of a loving parent. —Elizabeth Sherrill

Digging Deeper: Matthew 7:11

Friday, July 15

"At that moment Jesus' disciples returned, and they were greatly surprised to find him talking with a woman...." —John 4:27 (TEV)

On our anniversary trip to London, my wife and I were charmed by the taxi drivers who actually took an interest in us. "What brings you here?" the first one asked.

"We are celebrating our fiftieth anniversary."

"Quite lovely! Not many couples make it that far. Are you religious then?"

"Yes. We live in Missouri, the heart of the Bible Belt."

"I've always thought there must be a Creator," the driver said, pointing to the massive London plane trees that line the streets. "All these beautiful things...But then I see how people treat each other and I wonder. You know?"

I gave the driver an extralarge tip and then, to my surprise, I found myself using his technique with people we met all day long, like the waitress at our hotel.

"Is Monday a hard day for you?" I asked her.

"Oh, Monday is a madhouse. No one's in a good mood on Monday."

"How do you stay calm?"

Her eyes twinkled. "I just keep smiling. It always gets to them. You know?"

Fascinating people seemed to come out of the woodwork the rest of the day because I was taking an interest in them. I thought of a line I once read in a book on manners, something like, "The most interesting person in the world is the person who is interested in me."

As I lay in bed that night, I thought about Jesus and all the conversations He had with people, like the woman at the well and Nicodemus and Zacchaeus. No wonder people loved Jesus; He paid attention to them. I'll bet He smiled a lot too.

It gets lonely down here, Lord. Help me to be everyone's friend today. —Daniel Schantz

Digging Deeper: Proverbs 17:17, Luke 7:34

Saturday, July 16

O Lord, you are so good, so ready to forgive, so full of unfailing love for all who ask for your help. —Psalm 86:5 (NLT)

I am standing in the second oldest house in New York State, watching a small group of people from the historical society reenact a typical funeral from the seventeenth century. Candles dimly light us, the pretend-mourners in the main room.

As we stand around a shrouded mannequin with a bouquet of fresh flowers nearby, the sin-eater comes through the narrow door. The sin-eater, a narrator explains, was a very poor person, often an outcast with a drinking problem or mental illness, who was paid a small fee to consume the deceased's sin along with some stale bread and flat beer and then was beaten out of town.

For the rest of the mock-funeral my mind is stuck on the sin-eater, burdened by the weight of another's transgressions. Questions fill my head: *Did they have a drinking problem before they took on this job or after? Did they really believe they were taking on the sins of the dead or were they scam artists? Why would they do it?*

Sin. The word itself gives me a bad feeling. Sin is anything that separates us from God, and I think I feel that distance even in the word. I can barely handle my own wrongdoings; I can't imagine consuming someone else's.

As I drive home, I think about my faith and the beauty in knowing that Jesus is the ultimate sin-eater. He sacrificed His life for our sins and offers us the priceless gift of forgiveness.

Lord, when my heart is burdened with regret and I turn to You, You cleanse me of guilt and make me feel pure again. —Sabra Ciancanelli

Digging Deeper: Matthew 6:14–15, Luke 7:47

Sunday, July 17

Contribute to the needs of the saints and seek to show hospitality. —Romans 12:13 (ESV)

"What are you doing after church?" I asked my friend Beth. Sunday school had wrapped up early, and we had a few moments before service.

"We're having neighbors over for lunch," she said. Her blue eyes twinkled with excitement.

I wondered what Beth would be serving—something lovely, for certain. She was a classy lady. She was always sharply dressed, lived in a beautifully restored Victorian, was polished, and radiated quality. I imagined a breakfast soufflé, stuffed French toast, a delicate chicken salad with nuts and sweet grapes. "What are you serving?" I asked.

"Scrambled eggs, buttered toast."

"Scrambled eggs? Toast?"

Beth picked up on my surprise. "Kal and I love to have people over, and I learned long ago that it's best for me to keep the meals simple. That way my focus is on what's around the table instead of what's on top of it."

I admired my friend. Her smile was easy, inviting—just like the way she'd chosen to open her home. When I invited people over, fretting was a precursor. The food had to be just so. The house had to be in perfect order. It was exhausting. I smiled.

"What?" Beth asked.

"I've learned something just now," I said, "and I'm going to try things your way."

"What's that?" she asked.

"Serving simple hospitality . . . and maybe a side dish of eggs."

Lord, let the heart-focus of my hospitality be people. Amen. —Shawnelle Eliasen

Digging Deeper: 1 Peter 4:9, 3 John 1:8

Monday, July 18

A man without self-control is like a city broken into and left without walls. —Proverbs 25:28 (ESV)

A drunken man staggered into our subway car during rush hour. I exchanged looks of irritation with other tired commuters as he verbally terrorized us. A few stops later, he held the door open as it repeatedly tried to close.

"Come on, guy," a young man said, "let it close!" That request resulted in a fury of filthy words as the drunken man leaned into him.

I braced myself to witness a messy fight. The young man was tall, well-built, and could clearly have taken on the man if it got physical, but to my surprise the young man kept his cool. He looked away, biting his tongue, though I could see in his eyes, in his heavy breath and clenched fists, that he wanted to react. Finally, the doors opened at the next stop and the drunken man left.

Everyone breathed a sigh of relief, but it was obvious the young guy was still upset. I hesitated to say anything. Then, before I got off at the next stop, I knew I had to tell him how I felt.

"You handled yourself really well by not engaging with his stupidity," I said. "You made a good choice, and I'm proud of you." The anger in his face melted into a smile, and he thanked me.

It was an awkward thing to say to a stranger on a train, but I was happy I'd listened to that overwhelming nudge in my soul to speak up. With so much focus on the bad choices that youth make, I wanted to recognize and affirm the right choice this young man had just made.

Lord, help me to be brave and speak up not only for the injustices of this world, but also for the good choices that honor You. —Karen Valentin

Digging Deeper: Proverbs 16:32

FINDING REST: Sufficient unto the Day

"So do not worry about tomorrow, for tomorrow will bring worries of its own. Today's trouble is enough for today." —Matthew 6:34 (NRSV)

Beth, my friend and spiritual adviser, listened as I cataloged all my woes. "I've been sick off and on for fourteen months with this stupid infection, and the doctors don't know what's causing it. My insurance deductible is so high, I might as well have thrown the money into the river for all the help I've gotten. I've been sick through two Christmases in a row! My favorite time of the year ruined. Oh, and speaking of insurance? The flood insurance on our building has skyrocketed. Two owners have had their units repossessed by the banks, and that means the values on the rest of our apartments are plummeting. I get depressed just thinking about what's coming next."

"Then don't."

I paused. "Believe me, I'd love to stop thinking about the future, if only I could."

Beth paraphrased Jesus: "Sufficient for tomorrow are its own troubles."

"Gee, that's a big help!" I snapped.

"Seriously," Beth persisted, "don't you have enough on your plate? How are you going to give all that to Jesus if you're already worrying about what you'll be adding to the burden tomorrow? Isn't it time to give it a rest?"

I tried to get angry at her, but the tears stinging my eyes wouldn't let me. They were tears of release . . . and relief.

Lord Jesus, when I feel overwhelmed by the troubles and distractions and tomorrows of my life, gently lead me to rest my burdens and myself in You. Amen. —Marci Alborghetti

Digging Deeper: Psalm 78:38–39, Luke 21:34

Wednesday, July 20

Shout aloud and sing for joy, people of Zion, for great is the Holy One of Israel among you. —Isaiah 12:6 (NIV)

She doesn't remember that we talked just five minutes ago, that she told me it had been raining all day and she was enjoying a cup of tea by the fire. So we have the conversation again, raindrops beating against the window, providing a calming cadence to soothe my anxious heart.

"Well, good-bye, Erin. We'll talk again soon."

"Good-bye, Grandma. I love you!" I hang up the phone, a lump catching in my throat at the sound of my name. At least she still remembers me...for now.

Tears come, and I remember the good times: mornings on her cattle ranch, helping her toss hay out of the tractor; long afternoons picking buckets of blueberries in the sunshine; comforting hugs; gentle prayers. They are a spiritual heritage I am grateful for to this day.

The phone's ring jerks me out of my reverie. "Oh, hi, Grandma!"

"Erin, how are you? It's raining here, but I'm still having a lovely day...."

"Oh, Grandma, I'm so glad."

She pauses. "Erin, God is just filling me with His presence today, as if the only thing that can bring me contentment is Him."

There it was: something different, something real, a glimmer of the person she once was. Yes, she is slowly and terribly losing her mind and the memories that had taken a lifetime to build, but God isn't letting go. Instead, He clings to her and fills her with blessed contentment even when all else is gone.

Lord Jesus, fill my soul with the joy that can come only from You until the very end of my days. Amen.
—Erin MacPherson

Digging Deeper: Psalm 27:6, John 16:22

Thursday, July 21

And let the peace of Christ rule in your hearts, to which indeed you were called in one body. And be thankful. —Colossians 3:15 (ESV)

It was a hot afternoon, and the gym stank. I sat off to one side, laptop on my knees, while Frances bounced through gymnastics practice with her teammates. There was no air-conditioning, so everyone sweated, including me and the other parents perched on metal folding chairs.

How I dreaded these practices. I knew they were good for Frances. She loved being on the team, and Kate and I noticed how much more grown up she was since embarking on a sport. She was more assured, more attuned to other people, learning to cope with failure.

Still, that didn't mean I liked driving her to practice several times a week, sweltering in the gym while trying to eke out a couple hours' worth of work. There was something depressingly symbolic about it all. Was this a sign that my attempt to combine parenthood with a freelance career was a failure? Did real writers work in sweaty gyms like this, trying to tune out the sugary pop songs on the sound system?

I looked up from the computer and happened to catch Frances in midtwirl on the parallel bars. She executed a complex maneuver and landed confidently on the mat. She looked over to see if I was watching. When she saw my face, hers lit up.

Her smile demolished my complaining. Suddenly, I felt stupid and selfish. So what if I had to work in this hot gym? I was blessed to have work at all. I was even more blessed to have work that allowed me to witness these fleeting moments of Frances's growing up.

I watched another maneuver on the bars and another. Then I got back to work. It was hot and the gym stank and the music was loud. I was happy.

Today I will rejoice in all the gifts You give, Lord, no matter how small. —Jim Hinch

Digging Deeper: Psalm 31:15, John 15:12

Friday, July 22

But do not forget this one thing, dear friends: With the Lord a day is like a thousand years, and a thousand years are like a day. —2 Peter 3:8 (NIV)

"Your room is not ready yet, *signore*. Maybe an hour."

I had just gotten to my hotel in Rome, jet-lagged and out of sorts. This was not what I wanted to hear, especially at the beginning of a ten-day tour of sacred sites. Then again, I was on "Italian time."

The desk clerk sensed my exasperation. "Why don't you go see the statue?" He pointed across the street to the ancient stairway of a modest basilica I'd never heard of, San Pietro in Vincoli. I had no idea what statue he was talking about, but I dropped my bags and did as he suggested, after stopping for a double espresso.

A few minutes later I was standing in a nearly empty sanctuary, staring at one of the most magnificent sculptures I'd ever seen. I read the plaque: *Moses* by Michelangelo Buonarroti.

The Michelangelo? I was awestruck. The billowing beard and flowing hair, the stone tablets resting in Moses's muscled right arm, an expression I couldn't quite interpret. Maybe that's how the great sculptor wanted it: inscrutable, open to the perceptions of the observer. Possibly Moses felt all of those things, but for an artist to capture them seemed impossible.

Yet here in this little church was perhaps the truest depiction of one of the most dramatic moments in the Old Testament. I felt as if I were seeing what the Israelites had seen when Moses came down from that holy ground. I was looking at a man who had met God.

I stayed for more than an hour, sitting in a pew, studying the statue. Only the Almighty could have granted such vision to the great sculptor. And just possibly I had been led there to remind me that I, too, was on holy ground. The sculpture was five hundred years old. My room was an hour late. Maybe I was on Italian time, but I was also on God's.

Lord, I have never been a patient person. Help me remember that I live in Your time, come what may. —Edward Grinnan

Digging Deeper: Psalm 90:4

Saturday, July 23

Purge me with hyssop, and I shall be clean; wash me, and I shall be whiter than snow. —Psalm 51:7 (NKJV)

Colonel Ken, Guideposts' retired military liaison, and I met with a young chaplain during our visit at a military base. "I served in Afghanistan with my unit," the chaplain shared with us, "but it was my experience with a soldier prior to and during my deployment that impacted me.

"There was a young man who came to me and said, 'Chaplain, I'm afraid to deploy. I feel that I'm going to die.' I offered spiritual support to the soldier, yet he still went AWOL (absent without leave). I tracked him down at his mother's home and got him to return to his unit. Two weeks into his deployment, the soldier was killed in action. He was the first casualty of their unit."

I could see the pain in the chaplain's face and hear it in his voice. The military have a phrase for the conflict they feel when confronted with death and misery in their line of work: *moral injury.*

"May we pray with you?" the colonel asked. The chaplain nodded, and Ken prayed, "Lord, thank You for the service and sacrifice of Your servant. Comfort him and make him strong. Give him peace."

In all walks of life we can experience moral injury—an injury that is cured only by God's grace.

Lord, heal and teach us to forgive ourselves.
—Pablo Diaz

Digging Deeper: Job 2:11–13,
Lamentations 3:21–22

Sunday, July 24

Yet you brought me out of the womb; you made me trust in you, even at my mother's breast.
—Psalm 22:9 (NIV)

"God never gives you more than you can handle."

Ooph! How many times have we said that to the mother with a house full of sick kids? To the cancer patient undergoing chemotherapy? To the road-weary churchgoer brave enough to confess his doubt in overwhelming circumstances? But do we really think God believes we can keep standing on our own after the death of a spouse, the loss of a home, or the terror of a life-threatening illness?

If you're feeling guilty about repeating that quasi-comforting phrase to those who are hurting, then you're not alone. I'm guilty too. I've said it to friends with long to-do lists, neighbors with water damage, and old college buddies with life-changing decisions to make. Such an empty reply to what was clearly a cry for prayers and help.

Now I don't say it anymore. Instead, I believe that God does allow us to be given more than we can handle. He watches as we're loaded to the brim with finals, job stress, trials, and personal conflicts. It's not about punishing or testing us, but rather one single lesson: if God didn't do this, how would we ever learn that we need Him—and His grace—so desperately?

Looking back on times when I felt completely overwhelmed, it was then that I leaped into God's arms, clawing my way to find a better place in Him.

From now on, I'm rewriting the old saying to make this new version: God allows us to be given more than we can handle. But when we put our hope in Him, trust Him, and seek His help, He gives us the tools we need to handle those seemingly impossible situations.

Lord, thank You for giving me the opportunity
to have to trust in You in the difficult times.
Amen. —Ashley Kappel

Digging Deeper: Psalm 44:5–7, Jeremiah 39:17–18

Monday, July 25

"And know...." —Psalm 46:10 (KJV)

For several days I'd noticed a tattoo on our
contractor's arm. I recognized it as a Latin phrase
but had no idea what it meant. He had come to us,
highly recommended, to make some repairs on our
house. He was a fine craftsman, meticulous in his
work. Finally, on a morning break, I gathered the
nerve to ask, "So what does the tattoo say?"

"*Tabula Rasa*...clean slate," he answered.

Clean slate. I smiled, remembering when Brock
was a fifth-grader with a bad case of being "all boy."
I would tuck him in each night with the same
reassurance: "Tomorrow's a new day. The slate is
wiped clean."

Some of us are fortunate. Our past infractions
aren't bad enough to put us in jail or require
extensive rehabilitation. Some of us have experienced
pain, discouragement, and hurt so severe we have
succumbed to drugs or alcohol or violence. But
there's one thing we all have in common. If we look

for God, even in our darkest times, we'll find He's very near...already busy wiping our slates clean.

I went out on the deck to think about the tattoo. The day was clear. A cardinal was singing on a nearby tree. I had a sense that looking for God and knowing He's near wasn't quite enough. I had to do my part by meeting Him. The clean slate was just the beginning.

As I stood in the cool of the day, with the sun warming my skin, I felt all of my "if onlys" and "I should haves" melting away. Not only does God deliver a clean slate anytime we ask, He follows up by offering the profound peace of the present moment: "Stop. Be still. Know Me."

**I find You in the stillness, Father.
Somehow I know You are there.** —Pam Kidd

Digging Deeper: Psalm 119:18; Isaiah 40:28, 41:10

Tuesday, July 26

Oh, the depth of the riches both of the wisdom and knowledge of God! How unsearchable are His judgments and unfathomable His ways! —Romans 11:33 (NAS)

"All God's acts are done in perfect wisdom, first for His own glory, and then for the highest good of the greatest number for the longest time." I read these words by A. W. Tozer as part of a Bible study.

So far I had studied God's goodness, sovereignty, and holiness. I didn't have problems with any of those attributes. In fact, up until that point, the study had been deepening my intimacy with my Savior.

Then I reached the chapter on God's wisdom, and it was as if a giant wall had gone up in my heart. I had no trouble with the first part: "All God's acts are done in perfect wisdom." It was the second part that had me crying foul: "for the highest good of the greatest number for the longest time." I couldn't see it.

I'd just returned from the Congo, one of the poorest countries in the world, where thousands of children die of preventable diseases every day. How did this fit into Tozer's definition of God's wisdom?

As I wrestled with this question, I found myself standing at the crossroads of faith. Would I trust that God is Who He says He is, despite the circumstances?

I wish I could say that God took away my doubt; He didn't. I still struggle with His wisdom. But do you know what? He's God. He doesn't answer to me. I am not His judge. It's a truth that brings freedom.

Lord, I don't understand Your wisdom. Sometimes I even doubt it. Help me to rest in You, even when I don't comprehend Your ways. —Katie Ganshert

Digging Deeper: Job 38, Ecclesiastes 3:11, Isaiah 45:9

Now faith is the substance of things hoped for, the evidence of things not seen. —Hebrews 11:1 (KJV)

I called Mom and found her in the greenhouse. She was sitting in the sunlight among numerous pots of soil, the day after planting.

"What are you doing in there?" I asked. The thought of sitting around a bunch of barren flowerpots sounded depressing.

"Oh no, it's beautiful," she replied. "I'm imagining what they will be. You could say I'm dreaming in flowers."

Her words resounded in me. I had been a cattle rancher, but a back injury put an end to my career. I shriveled up, mired in devastation, not sure who I was anymore, not sure what I should be doing. But God saw me as more than my profession and over time miraculously led me to a richer, fuller life. Still in the country surrounded by the animals I loved, I watched God throw open doors for me that I thought were closed when I was working on the ranch, like getting married to my best friend and devoting more time to my writing.

God filled my life after ranching with joy, not sorrow. As I put my trust in Him and began to follow His path, I began to see my grievous back injury as a blessing. Because of it, the Master Gardener has helped me grow beyond anything I could ever have dreamed of, and I know He isn't finished with me yet.

Dear Lord, please nurture me into becoming the flower You planted. I want to lift up my face to You and shine with all of the love You have given me.
—Erika Bentsen

Digging Deeper: Jeremiah 1:5

Thursday, July 28

He which testifieth these things saith, Surely I come quickly. Amen. Even so, come, Lord Jesus.
—Revelation 22:20 (KJV)

"One day," said a preacher I heard in a midtown Manhattan church, "a man came up to me, handed me a tract, and said, 'Repent! The end is coming!' 'That's great,' I said. 'I'm a New Yorker. It couldn't come soon enough.'"

Well, I'm a lifelong New Yorker and I have to say, I know what that preacher meant. I love the city and wouldn't want to live anywhere else, but there are days when hearing the last trumpet would be music to my ears.

Now, don't get me wrong, I think the brusqueness of New Yorkers is greatly exaggerated but, nonetheless, the city can be wearing. The other day I was in a hurry and got stuck behind a woman in the center of the sidewalk with a cell phone pressed to her ear. And there's something about the subway that brings out the worst in people. Yesterday as I was trying to exit, there were people standing in both sides of the doorway who wouldn't get out of the way and a line of people pushing past me to get in. I was eager to push back, elbows first.

I tried not to, not only because I was afraid of starting a fight, but because I didn't know how many of those folks were exhausted or were having a really bad day and needed the comfort of a door to lean on or a place to sit. So I gritted my teeth, tried to smile sincerely, said "Excuse me," and exited the car as unobtrusively as I could.

And you know what? A big, burly, angry-looking guy smiled back at me and moved out of the way.

I love my city, Lord, but I thank You for the glorious hope of living in a city not made with human hands, where You live and reign forever.
—Andrew Attaway

Digging Deeper: Proverbs 15:1, Revelation 21:2

Friday, July 29

"And there will be no more night; they need no light of lamp or sun, for the Lord God will be their light...."
—Revelation 22:5 (NRSV)

The Walker Art Center in Minneapolis, Minnesota, is a gem of a museum. My favorite part is the outdoor Minneapolis Sculpture Garden, and my favorite piece is by the American artist Dan Graham called *Two-Way Mirror Punched Steel Hedge Labyrinth*. It is an arrangement of mirrored glass, stainless steel, and arborvitae (a fancy way of saying live greenery).

When my friend and I saw it, this beguiling work struck me as a wonderful picture of what it's like to be in relationship with God. One is compelled to walk around it, to see how it looks from this side or that. From any given angle, we can only catch glimpses, shadows, refractions of ourselves and of the divine. But each snippet encourages us to search for more, to circle, to see how things appear from various perspectives, none the same. The goal is to try to take in as much of the beautiful, challenging, awe-inspiring whole as you can.

As we wandered around it, I was taken by how each person absorbs it through different eyes. The entire thing was about the movement and play of light, but my friend was seeing distinct things—a ray here, a reflection there. And as we talked, it became clear to me how, together, we got more than we did or could separately. We, too, were lenses for each other.

Does art imitate life? In this case, it reflects and amplifies it, light begetting light. As sisters and brothers in a collective faith, do we do the same for one another?

Lord, let us walk this labyrinth of life together.
Help me reflect Your light to all I meet. —Jeff Chu

Digging Deeper: Matthew 4:14–16, Luke 11:33–36

Saturday, July 30

"The eyes of the Lord run to and fro throughout the whole earth...." —2 Chronicles 16:9 (KJV)

Being as quiet as a ten-year-old boy could be, I wiggled out of my sleeping bag and crawled toward the door of my grandparents' room. I could almost touch my fishing rod, waiting on the front step of our family cabin.

"Where do you think you're going, Brockwell?" It was the voice of my grandmother Bebe. Busted!

Bebe started the day with a reading from *Daily Guideposts* and expected me to join her before I went outside. But for a boy thinking only of hooking a largemouth bass, those devotions seemed like a very slow, very long walk.

Many years later, at Bebe's urging, I entered the Guideposts Young Writers Contest. I didn't miss the irony, but I had a story and was looking for ways to earn extra money for college. When I was awarded second prize, a scholarship, and a brand-new typewriter, no one was prouder than Bebe.

She was prouder still when I was asked to try out for *Daily Guideposts*. Through college and after I landed my first job, my life was enhanced by letters and calls of encouragement from loyal readers. And now as I consider the publication's fortieth year, I think of all who said, "I feel like I know you." These are the people who reached out and cheered me through the rough patches of life, each one a reminder that God is near.

"Where do you think you're going, Brockwell?" my grandmother's voice floats over the decades. Well, thanks to her, the support and prayers of *Daily Guideposts* readers, and God's grace, I can't help but feel I'm headed in the right direction.

God, thank You for those who help lead us forward into Your world. —Brock Kidd

Digging Deeper: Job 28:24, Psalm 139:2

Sunday, July 31

Whatever your hand finds to do, do it with all your might.... —Ecclesiastes 9:10 (NIV)

That Sunday morning as we rushed to get ready for church, my daughter was still at it, driving me nuts about the pug dogs. "Why can't we help them and get one?" she challenged.

Micah and I had spent the previous day at Puggerfest, a fund-raising event for Homeward Bound Pug Rescue. I'd noticed the event's flyer when

I took our pug, Princess, to the groomer earlier that week. I'd never heard of the organization, but it sounded like fun.

Princess frolicked in the fenced area of a park with two hundred other pugs while Micah played with the ones available for adoption.

"Please, Mommy, please!" she begged. "They need us!"

I laughed at her determination. I didn't want another pet, even though the agency was desperate for foster families. To ease my conscience, I wrote a check and thought that was that.

But twenty-four hours later, my child was still as tenacious as a bulldog. "We really need to get one of those dogs," Micah persisted as we jumped in the car and headed to church.

"We made a contribution," I reminded her and then tried to change the subject. "Say your memory verse to me."

"All right, but I don't understand it. 'Ecclesiastes 9:10: Whatever your hand finds to do, do it with all your might.'"

Silence fell over me. Micah might not have understood the verse, but I did. Was it possible I'd found the flyer because we were destined to help homeless dogs?

The next week, we applied to be a foster home. Over the years, we've loved several pugs until they've found forever-families, thanks to a flyer that made its way into my hands and my daughter's heart.

Father, help me to remember that I'm Your hands here on earth. —Stephanie Thompson

Digging Deeper: Ephesians 6:7–8, Colossians 3:23

GOD'S ABIDING LOVE

1 _____

2 _____

3 _____

4 _____

5 _____

6 _____

7 _____

8 _____

9 _____

10 _____

11 _____

12 _____

13 _____

14 _____

15 _____

16 _____

17 _____

18 _____

19 _____

20 _____

21 _____

22 _____

23 _____

24 _____

25 _____

26 _____

27 _____

28 _____

29 _____

30 _____

31 _____

AUGUST

"For you shall go out in joy and
be led forth in peace. . . ."

—Isaiah 55:12 (ESV)

He himself is before all things, and in him all things hold together. —Colossians 1:17 (NRSV)

This summer I helped lead a children's musical theater camp. I taught voice to first- through third-graders and music-directed *The Wiz* for fourth- through sixth-graders. The theater was under construction, so the camp met and performed in the sanctuary of a nearby church.

One day I sat in on a dance rehearsal that the director was running. She was reblocking a song with the children. The rehearsal process was quick, and the kids were having trouble remembering what they were supposed to be doing and when. Over and over the director had them run this particular piece. Over and over she respaced and returned them to their proper positions. Over and over the children ended up in the wrong place, just off center. Finally, she pointed behind her and yelled out in frustration, "Kids, Jesus is center!"

I got up from my seat to see where she was pointing. Sure enough, there, smack-dab in the middle behind the pulpit, was a stained-glass window with an artist's depiction of Jesus. I broke into uncontrollable giggles. The director turned to me, winked, and said, "Well, it's true, isn't it?"

"Amen!" I said and made a mental note to check and realign my life with Jesus at the center of it as well.

God, thank You for making Your presence known so that we may follow a path that is centered on You. Oh, and thanks for the laughs. —Natalie Perkins

Digging Deeper: 1 Peter 1:13–16

Tuesday, August 2

Great are the works of the Lord; they are pondered by all who delight in them. —Psalm 111:2 (NIV)

A neighbor had just moved in and stopped by for some advice about which flowers to plant in her garden. With glasses of ice tea in hand, we strolled through my yard. "These pink knockout roses and azaleas are always good choices," I advised. "And don't forget the annuals, like dianthus and impatiens. They'll keep your yard full of color."

We walked to the backyard garden, where she admired the combination of purple agapanthus mixed in with bright yellow lantana. She pointed to a spot in the corner where four-foot-high green stalks were planted. They were bare, except for a few small leaves. "What happened?" she asked.

"Oh, that's my milkweed," I replied.

She looked closer. "Oh no," she exclaimed, "there are some striped caterpillars eating it!"

"I know," I said, laughing.

"Don't you mind?" she asked.

"No," I answered. "They're monarch caterpillars. The monarch butterflies lay their eggs on the milkweed, and these caterpillars that hatched eat the plant in order to survive. They'll cocoon and eventually become beautiful butterflies."

"But they've eaten off all the leaves and flowers," she said. "That's not very pretty."

"Oh, I think it's beautiful," I replied, still laughing. "You see, every flower in my garden is a gift from God, and planting milkweed in order to help sustain the monarch butterfly population is the best way I know to pay His gift forward."

Lord, fill my heart with appreciation for Your never-ceasing gifts. Please give me the creativity to find meaningful ways to pay Your gifts forward.
—Melody Bonnette Swang

Digging Deeper: Matthew 10:8, 2 Corinthians 9:7

Wednesday, August 3

WHAT THE SAINTS HAVE TAUGHT ME
Lydia, Companion of Mold-Breakers

The Lord opened her heart to respond to Paul's message. —Acts 16:14 (NIV)

Lydia is the first known convert to Christianity in Europe. She was a path forger, in fact, in many ways: a successful businesswoman in an age when few women had careers outside the home; a Gentile who worshipped the Hebrew God rather than the state-sponsored gods of the Roman Empire.

At a time when most people lived and died in the place where they were born, Lydia moved from Thyatira, a small town in today's Turkey, to the booming Roman colony of Philippi in Greece. Thyatira was known for the purple dye extracted from a tiny snail and used in the manufacture of purple cloth so expensive that only the very rich could afford it. Lydia must have decided this costly cloth would find a better market in thriving Philippi. Once there, she began worshipping with the small Jewish community, which is how she came to hear a traveling missionary named Paul. Persuaded by his preaching, she asked to be baptized and, as was the custom when the head of a household was converted, her children and servants and workers were baptized too.

For Lydia, it was a total conversion of heart, mind, and fortune. Her house became a second home to Paul and Silas. After the two missionaries departed, Lydia welcomed, fed, and nurtured new converts. Her home became the meeting place of the fledgling community to which Paul would one day write, "I thank my God every time I remember you!"

An unconventional woman making her own way in a patriarchal society had found, in the convention-shattering figure of Jesus, the truth to which she would devote the rest of her life.

Give me the courage, Father, to find my unique life path. —Elizabeth Sherrill

Digging Deeper: Luke 24:45

"But wisdom is proved right by her deeds."
—Matthew 11:19 (NIV)

I did something stupid today.

If my grandchildren heard me say that, they would correct me. "Oma, you can't say *stupid!*" But that word fits the foolish thing I did.

Running late and rushing to one of their soccer games, I entered the parking lot and drove over a small concrete barrier that I didn't see and got a flat tire. My husband, Lynn, didn't tell me it was stupid, but I know that's what he was thinking. Because here's another detail: I was texting "*we r here*" to my son when it happened. And Lynn always tells me never to reach for my phone when I'm driving. He's right.

So the flat tire was totally my fault, and it changed our day. Instead of hurrying to the soccer game, we stood in the parking lot while Lynn called for help, which took forever. And we missed the whole first half of the game. At the tire store to replace the flat, the man told Lynn, "Can't do that. In order to safely balance your car, you need matching tires." So Lynn bought four new tires.

When he got home, he didn't say anything about the cost of my mistake. Instead he said, "Probably about time we replaced those tires. Now I know you'll be safe when you're driving that car."

He knew that *I* knew I'd made a stupid mistake. His example helped me learn a sweet lesson about love, patience, forgiveness, and, yes, never texting while driving.

Lord, I'm grateful that You redeem my foolish mistakes. —Carol Kuykendall

Digging Deeper: Proverbs 15:1–2, James 1:5

Friday, August 5

But as for you...pursue righteousness, holy living, faithfulness, love, endurance, and gentleness.
—1 Timothy 6:11 (CEB)

I teach at a seminary. To get a degree in one of the programs I oversee, the doctor of ministry, students must complete a major project. It's a formidable task involving significant research, planning, implementation, and evaluation related to their particular place of ministry. For some students, it takes years to accomplish.

"Why such an involved project?" my friend Bill asked recently. "Why not just give them a final exam like other programs?"

I thought for a minute. "Because," I said, "the goal of our program is not to measure whether you've read the books. The goal is to see if you can apply what you've read...and that means using it."

"Oh," Bill said, his face brightening, "sort of like the Bible and faith. It's not just a matter of repeating what it says. It's actually having it affect your actions."

Bill was right. When it comes to faith, it isn't enough simply to know what the book says. To have it make a difference for yourself and those around you, you need to apply it in daily living.

I can't award you an academic degree for making the application of the Bible your life's work, as I can for my students, but you can discover the same kind of deep satisfaction and meaning that they experience when they complete their projects and see the same kind of positive impact. The key for them, and for you and me, is exactly the same: it's not simply knowing what the book says; it's applying what you know to guide you every single day.

Guide me, O God, in making the inspired words of Scripture my life's project, that I might bring Your hope to the world. Amen. —Jeff Japinga

Digging Deeper: Ruth 1:6–18, Matthew 9:1–17

Saturday, August 6

"You shall teach them diligently to your children, and shall talk of them when you sit in your house, when you walk by the way, when you lie down, and when you rise up." —Deuteronomy 6:7 (NKJV)

We drifted in the rusty rowboat across the placid pond. A few geese squawked their disapproval. Cattle lowing in the distance and crickets starting their song were the only other sounds besides our lures hitting the water. My twelve-year-old son, J.D., was taken by the beauty. "Look at this, Dad. It's like a postcard."

He was right. A sweeping vista of rolling hills stretched into the golden sunset. A gentle breeze lifted the scent of water and ranch, of cattle and grasslands. The pond on my friend's ranch offered an angler's dream of untouched waters.

"It *is* like a postcard," I said.

J.D. insisted on using a bait-caster, one of the toughest fishing reels to master. I watched the concentration on his face. His tongue sticking out. His adrenaline rising. His minor fury as he fought the four-pound bass into the boat. I saw the smile of satisfaction and the gleam of accomplishment in his eyes. He lifted the flopping fish by its lower lip. Triumph.

Moments later, J.D. slid the fish back into the water. "Well," he said, "our family wouldn't have been hungry today—if we needed the fish, that is."

"That's right," I said. "We're surrounded by abundance."

"Hey, Dad. May I have your phone? I want to take a picture."

He did—not of his big bass but of God's handiwork all around.

Thank You, Lord, for teachable moments with my son. —Bill Giovannetti

Digging Deeper: Psalm 19:1

Sunday, August 7

"I have loved you with an everlasting love...."
—Jeremiah 31:3 (NIV)

"I rummaged through hundreds of family photos in boxes and picture albums. My mother and father were about to celebrate their forty-fifth wedding anniversary, and I was making a video of their journey together. The first pictures were frail black-and-whites of a nervous bride and groom, the exchange of rings, and smiles near a tall wedding cake. The honeymoon followed, and they looked like movie stars.

I scanned each picture, focusing only on the two of them. They had the same look of love in their eyes in each one. I couldn't contain my emotion as I completed the video and played it over and over. The music in the background vowed "I will be here" as I watched my parents grow old together in less than four minutes.

Their testament to love and commitment has been remarkable. Though it's beautiful, it pales in comparison to the greater love God has promised to me, to all of us. It also helped me to understand an even greater love. Through the years of joy and pain since I said yes to the Lord, His promise of "I will be here" has never faltered. It's one I can count on for a lifetime.

Lord, thank You for Your promises and Your sustaining love and for those who demonstrate that kind of love with each other as an example of Your own. —Karen Valentin

Digging Deeper: Ephesians 5:25

Monday, August 8

Thou art my portion, O Lord: I have said that I would keep thy words. —Psalm 119:57 (KJV)

I'm a visiting leader at the Bible Witness Camp in Pembroke, Illinois. There are games, crafts, loads of activities and skits, chapel, and learning memory verses. And every day there is a theme word. Today it was *integrity*.

After an exhausting day, another leader, Marshelle, from Chicago, and I stumbled into the cabin we shared. We were ravenous, looking for a quick bite before retiring to our beds. Searching through the fridge, I spotted a pot of chicken vegetable soup I'd thrown together. Because I was not at home, I'd made use of spices I don't normally put in soup and it was surprisingly delicious.

"I could have soup," I said to Marshelle.

Half-teasing, she reminded me, "But you promised that soup to the other leaders."

I looked longingly at the pot. *The others have probably forgotten about it by now, right?* Then I remembered the word of the day. "I guess I wouldn't be behaving with *integrity* if I ate it," I said to Marshelle, sighing.

Her smile broadened. "That soup was promised."

"Promised soup." I nodded in agreement. Lack of sleep was making us silly.

"Soup of Promise," she said, chuckling.

At a potluck gathering the next day, I brought the soup. It was a hit! Marshelle was right: the soup was tastier when shared as promised.

Lord, help me to keep my promises, even small ones.
—Sharon Foster

Digging Deeper: Isaiah 38:6–8, Luke 1:45, Acts 2:39

Tuesday, August 9

"Come to me, all you that are weary and are carrying heavy burdens, and I will give you rest."
—Matthew 11:28 (NRSV)

Kids in bed. House quiet. My favorite part of the day. Not because I'm glad for a moment's peace, though I am grateful for that. It's the sense of deepening holiness as the evening advances.

Dinner is a jumble of conversation in our family. Then the hassle of pajamas and tooth-brushing gives way to the calm of bedtime stories and prayers. We sit on the sofa, a child on either side, reading a few books.

I love the twilight of their rooms, their sleepily murmured prayers and good-nights. Then I return to the sofa, prayer book in hand, for *Compline*. It's an ancient monastic prayer service said at the close of day. It has some of the most beautiful, most reassuring language I know. It begins: "The Lord Almighty grant us a peaceful night and a perfect end. Our help is in the Name of the Lord. The maker of heaven and earth."

From where I sit on the sofa, I can look outside to the backyard, the garden, and the moon and stars hanging in the sky.

The service continues: "Into your hands I commend my spirit, for you have redeemed me, O Lord, O God of truth." On nights when Kate is home, we sometimes say Compline together. When she's at a meeting, I say it alone, sometimes from memory in the dark.

My favorite part: "Guide us waking, O Lord, and guard us sleeping; that awake we may watch with Christ, and asleep we may rest in peace." I sometimes wonder whether God lets our lives be tiring just to wear us out enough to stop and listen. I always hear Him in this evening silence. He speaks in the words of the prayers.

The service ends: "The Almighty and merciful Lord, Father, Son, and Holy Spirit, bless us and keep us. Amen."

No matter how hard today is, I will find my rest in You, Lord. —Jim Hinch

Digging Deeper: Isaiah 26:3–4, Hebrews 4:10–11

Wednesday, August 10

And thine ears shall hear a word behind thee, saying, This is the way, walk ye in it.... —Isaiah 30:21 (KJV)

The Coherent Mercy, as a dear friend of mine calls the One, presented my lovely bride and me with three children over the past twenty years, and remarkable beings they are, headlong and rude and hilarious and surly and foolish and brilliant. When they were small, we were exhausted from the physical labor and the mental strain of keeping them safe from rabid badgers and careless drivers. But then when they lurched snarling into their teenage years, our work grew incalculably harder, for now they were wild of will, disrespectful of advice and counsel, dismissive of reason and caution. But there was one moment, with one of them, I will treasure all my life.

He was setting off to college, this one, on his own, and we were all proud and sad and bereft and delighted. And he and I went for a walk, and this he said to me: "I'll always have your voice in my heart, Pop. I trust your voice. I know what to do even when I think I don't know. You're not always right, but you're never wrong. If I am quiet enough I can hear what you would say. That's a good thing, Pop. You did a good job. So did Mom. But I hear your voice inside. I feel Mom's hand when I am hurting or scared, but I hear your voice when I am confused. Be proud of that, Pop. You gave me a compass, and it will always be in there."

I wept. Sure, I did. You would weep too. And I wept again when I opened my trusty old King James Bible the next morning, at dawn, and read this: "I am the vine, ye are the branches: he that abideth in me, and I in him, the same bringeth forth much fruit: for without me ye can do nothing" (John 15:5, KJV). And I thought, not for the first time, *Thank You, Mercy, thank You.*

Lord, if ever there was a guy who didn't deserve the miraculous grace of children, it is selfish, silly me. But You were merciful and showered them upon us, and I will be grateful until my last breath. —Brian Doyle

Digging Deeper: 1 John 2:27

Thursday, August 11

Many are the plans in the mind of a man, but it is the purpose of the Lord that will stand.
—Proverbs 19:21 (ESV)

My wife, Emily, and I have had our cat, Crookshanks, for a little more than three years now. Crookshanks is a joy, at times full of energy and eager to do backflips in pursuit of her toys, and at other times happy to curl up in one of our laps. We don't have children yet, so caring and taking on the responsibility for her is the closest I've come to knowing the unconditional love that parents must feel for their children.

The hardest part is attending to Crookshanks's health. At the vet's office, all she sees is a new and scary place with new and scary people who hold her down and stick needles in her.

Pills are scarcely better. Last year she got a skin infection, and the vet prescribed a pill to stop the itching. Crookshanks wouldn't take it, so we wrapped it inside a treat. This worked for a while, but eventually she was too crafty for that. We finally had to give her the pill and hold her mouth closed until she swallowed it. I hated doing this because she was clearly unhappy, but it was the right thing to do.

I think that I am often in Crookshanks's position in relation to God. For whatever reasons, I don't and can't understand. I fight against what is happening and have no idea what might be best for me in the big picture. Unlike Crookshanks, maybe I can learn to stop fighting and just take my medicine.

Lord, help me always to accept Your will even when things don't go as planned. —Sam Adriance

Digging Deeper: Proverbs 3:5

Friday, August 12

BEING RENEWED: Finding Wholeness
Husbands, go all out in your love for your wives.... —Ephesians 5:25 (MSG)

Gene had a phone right by his bed, but he refused to take any calls. However, he welcomed visitors.

When I asked him to phone me, he said flatly, "No. I'm not answering or calling anyone."

Silently, I gathered his clothes to be laundered, got ice in his giant Oklahoma State University mug, and filled it with soda.

"Thanks. I'm ready to get back into bed." He punched a button and a nurse's aide came to help him from the wheelchair to the bed. I sat on the side of the bed and squeezed Gene's hand. He squeezed back. I should have been content. But I'm greedy. I longed to experience again that first burst of long-distance love we'd known. It had happened on the phone before we met in 1987 and was almost electric. At fifty, he'd made me feel twenty.

The sun was setting when I leaned over and gently kissed him. "I love you."

"Love you too," he murmured.

I'd been home two hours. It was nine thirty—the time of the nightly phone call he'd make from Oklahoma even though we'd never met in person. Now a sudden desperation and loneliness settled in my heart and house.

The phone rang. "Hello," I said.

"Hey, there," a sweetly familiar voice said.

"You called! At the old time." My heart thumped joyfully.

"I knew you needed me to. Besides, I wanted to hear your voice. I love you," he said, his tone now sprinkled with joy and anticipation. "How early will you be here in the morning? I want to see you."

My heart flipped over as I fell in love again on the phone.

Father, You didn't cause Gene's broken hip but used it to make whole again our somewhat fractured marriage. —Marion Bond West

Digging Deeper: Judges 19:3

Saturday, August 13

Then make my joy complete by being like-minded, having the same love, being one in spirit and of one mind. —Philippians 2:2 (NIV)

The perfect day, I thought. Lonny, our five sons, and I cruised the Mississippi River's main channel. The sun pressed on our shoulders. Brown water churned behind our boat in a frothy trail. My summer-bronze sons were all together for an afternoon of fun.

"Anyone want to water-ski?" Lonny asked.

The boys cheered. Lonny steered into the backwaters. The bigger guys gathered equipment. The little guys waved their arms in the air. I didn't know when I'd been so happy.

Then our boat struck a sandbar. We stopped short. The older boys lunged and grabbed the younger ones. My knees buckled. Lonny moved quickly and found that everyone was okay.

"I checked the map," he said. "The water's supposed to be deep here." Stranded on a sandbar wasn't what we'd expected.

"Let's push," our oldest said. He jumped in and stood in water knee-deep. We followed. Lonny and the bigger boys shoved while the rest of us encouraged them. Soon the little boys waded over, pressed their hands on fiberglass, and pushed too.

"We're working together!" five-year-old Isaiah said.

Before long, we dislodged and were puttering slowly back to the dock. It wasn't the family day we'd planned, but we'd come together in an unexpected way: to help, to share a burden, to make things better. Tough times are always lighter when we share the load.

Thank You, God, for the help of others. Let me be a ready helper too. Amen. —Shawnelle Eliasen

Digging Deeper: Exodus 17:12, Galatians 6:2, Philippians 2:4

Sunday, August 14

Now I know in part; then I shall know fully, even as I am fully known. —1 Corinthians 13:12 (NIV)

My husband and I moved our family to the small town of Port Orchard, Washington, at a time that was difficult for us all. The three older children were young teens, and the youngest was in fifth grade.

One of our first tasks was to find a church home where we could worship as a family. It wasn't long after we settled in that the hunt began. Because I'm a list-maker, I mapped out an extensive catalog of wants. Vitally important was a thriving teen group for our three oldest and a strong youth program for our youngest. Naturally, I sought a women's group and a Bible study. A choir was another plus and, if possible, a talented music director.

Weeks passed as we bounced from church to church. After each service, I'd check my list and sadly shake my head. There was always something lacking. My feelings of discouragement grew.

Then one morning, I spread out my list and asked God to guide us to the church that would give our family what we needed and wanted. As I was praying, I felt the Lord speak to my heart: *Debbie, that list you have—that's heaven. Ask Me to guide you to the church I have chosen for you.*

I did, and within a month we found a church where our children thrived and Wayne and I grew in the Lord. It wasn't perfect. No church is. But as the Lord assured me: the perfect church is heaven.

Dear Lord, may my expectations be met in You and may the joy that comes with worship be an added blessing to an already full heart.
—Debbie Macomber

Digging Deeper: Psalm 16:11

"Now if you are ready when you hear the sound of the horn, pipe, lyre, trigon, harp, bagpipe, and every kind of music, to fall down and worship the image that I have made, well and good." —Daniel 3:15 (ESV)

Solomon puts down his trumpet. "Of all the composers, I like Bach best," he says.

I think back to the months before my son was born, when I was excitedly preparing the nursery. I searched online for a specific mobile I'd read about, one that swirled brightly colored shapes to the melodies of classical music.

When the mobile came in the mail, I set it above Solomon's crib and climbed in his little bed to experience what he would see. Would he get a thrill when he kicked his teeny-tiny feet to the sounds of Mozart, Beethoven, and Bach? What kind of little person would he grow to be? Would he play an instrument?

"Why do you like Bach best?" I ask.

"I just do," he says. I fold the laundry, and he goes back to playing the first few bars of "Louie Louie" for what seems like the hundredth time.

I think about all the musicians and the moms and dads who encouraged them, who listened to scales played incorrectly, notes off-key, repetitive bars of "Louie Louie," and then I think about the mobile and how I wanted him to love music. *Maybe it was the mobile that did it. Maybe it planted a seed of harmony in his heart.*

"Mom?" Solomon asks. "There's one thing I don't understand. I just don't get how Bach and Chewbacca are related."

"Chewbacca? The hairy *Star Wars* character?" I ask.

"Yeah," he says. "That's why I like Bach—because of Chewbacca."

Dear God, thank You for the unique and funny ways You inspire the music-makers.
—Sabra Ciancanelli

Digging Deeper: Nehemiah 11:23, Psalm 100:1–5

Tuesday, August 16

The sabbath was made for man....
—Mark 2:27 (KJV)

I was approaching a busy intersection, but when I stepped on the brake pedal, it dropped to the floorboards and I rolled onward. "Look out, everybody! I'm coming through!"

Fortunately I got through safely, turned on to a side street, and stopped with the hand brake. When I looked under the car, I found that a brake hose had ruptured and the fluid had leaked out. It's a terrifying experience when brakes fail. Suddenly my wheels became a four-thousand-pound asteroid looking for a place to crash and burn.

Like my car, I, too, need to slow down and stop, but that's easier said than done. I love to work, especially outdoors. I can work from sunrise till dark, but my wife, Sharon, is my brake. "Danny, it's time to come in. You have been working all day. You are going to be sick, and your joints will be killing you tomorrow."

"I know, I know. Just let me finish planting this tree…"

When I listen to her and slow down, I actually enjoy work more and make fewer mistakes. I also sleep better, and my joints don't complain.

I used to think God was a killjoy, asking us to rest one day a week. What a waste of time, just sitting around, when I could be doing something productive! Now I can see that God is actually trying to increase my joy by restoring my energies.

Whether I take off a whole day, a couple of hours every day, or just go to bed a bit earlier, I need to use my brakes if I want to avoid a crash.

Father, forgive me when I think I am wiser than You. I can see now that You know what's best for me. —Daniel Schantz

Digging Deeper: Psalms 23:2, 55:6

Wednesday, August 17

Be happy about it! Be very glad! For a tremendous reward awaits you up in heaven. —Matthew 5:12 (TLB)

I decide to clean up my e-mail address book by eliminating correspondents I no longer write to. As I go down the list, I'm dismayed to see that three of my friends have died in the previous months. It was hard to press the Delete button, knowing I'd probably never see their names on my computer again.

Then I went through my handwritten address book, the one I'd purchased twenty years earlier. I found twenty-six people who had died in recent years.

At my fiftieth high school reunion, we were all shocked to discover that more than one-third of our class had died. The next year when we celebrated my dad's ninety-fifth birthday, I realized he was one of only a couple of people left from his high school class.

This year I said good-bye to a number of seniors in my neighborhood. I began to ponder the fact that the older I get, the smaller my circle of friends, loved ones, and acquaintances gets.

But that's when my faith comes in handy. Death doesn't bother me the way I've seen it destroy some people. That's because as believers we don't have to worry. We abide in Christ, even after we've been deleted from everyone else's address book. Life goes on, and so will we...only in a much better place. I love the comfort of that.

Father, it's so hard to say good-bye to loved ones, so when it happens, please remind me of what's waiting, after death, for all of us. —Patricia Lorenz

Digging Deeper: Psalm 116:3–9, Ecclesiastes 7:1–4, John 3:1–21

Thursday, August 18

In every situation, by prayer and petition, with thanksgiving, present your requests to God. —Philippians 4:6 (NIV)

I heard that whenever Billy Graham had to give a talk on radio or TV and was asked to check the sound on his microphone, instead of saying, "Testing, testing, one, two, three," he would recite, "For God so loved the world, He gave His only begotten Son."

I thought of that story when I was making a short video on prayer in our office, waiting for my colleague Doug to check the sound on the mic attached to my lapel. All afternoon the phone in my pocket had been vibrating with messages between family members. My nephew's wife, Kathleen, had checked in to the hospital that morning to give birth to her first child.

"Okay, Rick," Doug said, "let's check the mic."

I thought of Kathleen, her husband, Charlie, the excitement in the hospital, the good news we hoped for. "I'd like to say a prayer for Kathleen and Charlie," I said into the mic. "That they have a healthy baby and that all goes smoothly for the newborn and mom."

"Sounds good," Doug responded from behind the camera. "We're good to go."

"Praying for others is at the heart of prayer," I said, getting back on script. "Just look at the words of the Lord's Prayer. It's in the first-person plural because even if we pray alone, we're including others. We pray for people who suffer from ill health, job losses, marriage struggles, financial distress. Right now I'm praying for my niece…"

I did one more take and then we were done. My phone vibrated. I took it out and looked at the text message. "Lucy Patricia was born today at 12:28. Mother and daughter doing very well."

Time for a prayer of thanksgiving, not just a test.

I give thanks, Lord, for every moment of prayer.
—Rick Hamlin

Digging Deeper: Matthew 6:6

Friday, August 19

"For if you forgive others for their transgressions, your heavenly Father will also forgive you."
—Matthew 6:14 (NAS)

A friend betrayed me. I told myself I'd forgiven her and forgotten the incident, but the memory of it wouldn't leave me. We never had words, but I had nothing to do with her again.

Then, one day, I ran into her. "Losing your friendship is the hardest thing that's ever happened to me," she said through tears. "Is there any way you can let me back into your life?"

It was with considerable reluctance that I agreed to do so. Trust was a key issue. But as I prayed, God helped me to see the error of my own ways, and I offered my friend the gift of a clean slate. Over the next few years, our relationship became stronger and lovelier than ever, and my friend gave her heart to God because of it.

This past year, my friend was diagnosed with cancer. She passed away less than a week later. Her family asked me to give the eulogy at her funeral, and at the close of my talk I shared the story of my friend's conversion. I'll be forever grateful that our friendship was restored.

Precious Savior, I almost failed to forgive my friend. Help me to never withhold what You've so freely given to me.
—Roberta Messner

Digging Deeper: Luke 23:43, Galatians 6:1–2, Ephesians 4:31–32

Saturday, August 20

The heart of man plans his way, but the Lord establishes his steps. —Proverbs 16:9 (ESV)

My siblings and their spouses, thirteen now, spread across three time zones, gathered for an infrequent reunion. In the yard, after the meal, I tentatively announced my intention: "I'd like to have prayer before we leave." I inhaled deeply. I really didn't want the traveling-mercies, God-bless-you-all benediction modeled by our deceased dad. But I was tongue-tied until my brother-in-law, Bob, filled the void.

"This year I've been going to Quaker-style meetings, where anyone's free to share a thought or a prayer. Or we just sit and reflect in silence. I'll start with a thanksgiving." He was effusive; his college-age granddaughter had discovered the extended family she barely knew.

Others followed with personal thanksgivings, worries, even confessions. Were we talking to one another or to God? It wasn't clear, though occasionally in the pause between speakers—silences no longer awkward—I reverently said, "Lord, hear our prayer."

The next twenty minutes were exactly what I'd hoped for. Feeling heart-bound to these natural and spiritual brothers and sisters, impulsively I raised a song, with all joining in: "The Lord bless you and keep you." I was grateful that the Spirit had prompted Bob to introduce a beautiful communal prayer form that I'll suggest we use again.

Lord, sometimes I have a vision but not a plan. Help me to be open to and grateful for suggestions that draw me and others toward blessing.
—Evelyn Bence

Digging Deeper: Numbers 6:24–26; Isaiah 30:15, 18

FINDING REST: Sabbath Is More Than Sundays

The Pharisees watched him to see whether he would cure on the sabbath, so that they might find an accusation against him.... Jesus said... "Is it lawful to do good or to do harm on the sabbath, to save life or to destroy it?" —Luke 6:7, 9 (NRSV)

In Charles Dickens's *The Christmas Carol*, the ever-shrewd businessman Scrooge accuses the Ghost of Christmas Present of taking away the opportunity for the common person to earn a living every seventh day of the week. Of course, this is Dickens taking a shot at the Church of England, and the ghost accordingly responds indignantly that he would never rob people of their livelihood and that just because church and government leaders say they are acting in the name of God's law doesn't make it so.

In an ideal world, I believe people should not work on the Sabbath. But if working on Sunday means a parent can feed her child or pay his rent or save a little for college, should this be prevented? Are the churches and pastors who advocate for workless Sabbaths willing to provide the income the poor and the working class must sacrifice? Is it not possible for people to rest in the Lord on a day other than Sunday? Where should the line be drawn?

When someone we love needs medical attention on Sunday, don't we thank God when we see the ambulance crew and the doctor? If volunteers did not staff shelters and soup kitchens on Sunday, what would happen to the homeless and hungry who need, and rely on, these services?

One thing Jesus has taught me: just when I think I have an answer, I don't. God's law is not black and white. And that's as it should be because God is not limited the way I am.

Jesus, teach me Your compassion so that I do not judge others or presume to know how and when they rest in You. Amen. —Marci Alborghetti

Digging Deeper: Psalm 116:6–7, Luke 9:58

To them God has chosen to make known among the Gentiles the glorious riches of this mystery, which is Christ in you, the hope of glory. —Colossians 1:27 (NIV)

My mood soured as grains of dirt and grime stuck to the bottoms of my feet. Hadn't I just swept the kitchen floor? I had, but with three kids and a golden retriever, a twice-daily sweeping is the norm.

I pulled out the broom, snarling at my poor dog who was lazing on the floor in a patch of sunlight, unaware that he was the cause of my angst. I shooed him outside and looked longingly out the window, wishing I could be playing with my kids, enjoying the sunshine and the warm Texas breeze. Instead, I began to sweep crumbs from last night's couscous into the dustpan, grumbling to myself about the endless chores that come with being a mom.

Maybe some praise music will ease my mood, I thought. I clicked on Spotify and selected "Top Praise Music List"; Matt Redman's "Here for You" came on. I took a deep breath and continued sweeping, closing my eyes and letting the lyrics speak to my soul.

I may not be doing the most exciting things with my days, but in the middle of those highs and lows and downright monotonous chores, one thing remains true: I am here for a purpose—on a mission, if you will. And that mission is to glorify God in all I do, in all I say, and even in every crumb I sweep.

Lord Jesus, give me grace and joy in my everyday life so that I can fulfill Your purposes for me. Amen.
—Erin MacPherson

Digging Deeper: Galatians 2:20, Colossians 2:6, 1 John 2:28

Tuesday, August 23

A friend loves at all times, and a brother is born for a time of adversity. —Proverbs 17:17 (NIV)

My phone is ringing, but my first instinct is to ignore it. I've had a cold all week and still don't feel well. The last thing I want to do is slap on my everything's-okay voice. But by the fourth or fifth ring, I pick up. "Hello?"

"Hey, Logan, it's Matt. How are you doing?" Matt's my buddy from college. Normally, I would love to catch up with him. Today, not so much.

"I'm doing pretty well." I try to make it sound convincing. I'm usually rather good at that, but Matt doesn't respond the way I expect him to.

"How are *you* doing?" he asks again.

"I already told you, I'm good." A little irritation slips into my voice. I regret picking up the phone now. I don't have time for this.

"No, how are you *really* doing?"

The gates I've been manning bust open. "I'm terrible. I haven't had a good night's rest in days. I have a paper due tomorrow that I haven't even started. I'm coughing, sneezing, and shivering. I'm running on coffee and decongestants. I'm not doing great at all."

Matt chuckles. "Yep, I knew you weren't. Doesn't it feel better to let it out?"

I pause to think about what he said. I still feel shaky and cold. My head still throbs. I still have 150 things on my to-do list. But having a friend who cares enough to call my bluff, to pull off my mask, and to share my problems makes a world of difference.

"You know, I do feel better."

Heavenly Father, thank You for putting friends in my life who share both the burdens and the joys.
—Logan Eliasen

Digging Deeper: Ruth 1:16–17

Wednesday, August 24

"No one can come to me unless the Father who sent me draws them, and I will raise them up at the last day."
—John 6:44 (NIV)

I was chatting with a friend when my daughter Lulu phoned for the first time in weeks.

"Let me call you back," I told my friend.

Turns out Lulu wanted her dad, the family computer-fixer. In faraway Massachusetts, her computer had crashed. I tried to eke out a conversation anyway, but her voice was tight with college-student stress. Papers due. Drafts surely lost. "If I don't post my Italian homework by tonight, I won't get credit. No, of course I didn't save it on a USB! Why would I?"

Every word echoed the looming despair of my own students' similar crises. Emergencies that clumped together and sank some of them. Dire in the moment, forgotten when resolved. There was no help I could offer Lulu, no better comfort than the weak, "Don't worry. It'll be okay," with which I try to calm my frantic students. Then she was gone.

But her trouble stayed with me. I knew I'd wake and worry about it during the night. So I decided to do what the sleep book I'm reading recommends: schedule some worry time before sleeping.

Why not right now? I thought. So I worried about Lulu's problem and my helplessness to fix it, reminding myself that it was her problem, not mine. That learning to solve her own problems was an important part of growing up.

Before long, that little worry swelled into my ever-present worry for my girls (*Will God be in their lives?*), and my worry session swelled into prayer: "This is Your problem, God, not mine. Anyway, I can't make it happen, but You can."

When I went to bed, I was able to sleep through the night.

Draw my loved ones and me, Lord, into Your rest.
—Patty Kirk

Digging Deeper: Psalm 91

Thursday, August 25

"When you pray, don't pour out a flood of empty words...." —Matthew 6:7 (CEB)

"I don't add everyone with concerns to my prayer list," my pastor friend said.

"You don't?" I was shocked. "How can you not pray for people who ask?"

"I pray for every person and request at the time of immediate need," she explained. "But when my prayer list tops six or seven pages, I can't pray in depth. It really isn't prayer when I'm just reciting names."

I've kept a prayer list for years. It's invaluable in remembering to pray for people who ask me to pray for them as well as for groups of people (government leaders, military personnel, and teachers). But last year I found myself experiencing what my friend had: praying in a preoccupied fashion, asking God for general blessings instead of addressing specific needs.

When the new year began, I tried something different. I chose a Scripture to help guide my prayer time: "I led them with bands of human kindness, with cords of love" (Hosea 11:4, CEB). This passage helped me focus on God's constant love and guidance. I was reminded that the Holy Spirit is present with me and with those for whom I pray, even in the most difficult circumstances.

After asking God for discernment, I removed a number of old requests. Then I noted specific needs by each name: a family adopting a heroin-addicted infant; a friend with Alzheimer's disease and her caregivers; a woman desperate for a full-time job.

I've added and removed names through the year. I have no idea whether my intercessory prayers have made a difference in other people's lives, but the act of praying intentionally, from the heart, has certainly made a difference in mine.

Holy One, know our needs and lead us with cords of love. Thank You. —Penney Schwab

Digging Deeper: Ephesians 6:18–20, 2 Thessalonians 3:1–5

Friday, August 26

"Well done...enter thou into the joy of thy lord." —Matthew 25:21 (KJV)

"Abby, what was the best thing that happened to you today?" I asked my granddaughter.

Our family was in Zimbabwe at Village Hope, the little farm where we, along with a caring network of friends, take in children orphaned by AIDS. There, a loving local couple transforms castaways into some of the finest youngsters you will ever meet. Abby's life in Nashville, Tennessee, is a far cry from the lives of her African brothers and sisters, and it's always enlightening to hear her observations.

"Washing socks," she answered without hesitation.

"Washing socks?" I said, laughing.

"I'm serious, Mimi. It was Chepo's turn to wash the socks, and she let me help. It was so fun! We put water in this big pot and heated it over the fire. Then we put some water in another pot and added the socks. We scrubbed with this big, long chunk of soap, got some clean water and rinsed them, and hung them out in the sun on a long line. They were clean and pure white!"

Never had I seen more delight in a child.

"You know, Abby," I said, "God would call that serving. How did that make you feel?"

"When I looked back and saw all those socks hanging on the line, Mimi, I felt happy."

Father, give me the wisdom of a child, smart enough to find Your joy as I work beside You...even if it's hand-washing socks! —Pam Kidd

Digging Deeper: John 13:17, 1 John 3:18

Saturday, August 27

And offer every part of yourself to him [God] as an instrument of righteousness. —Romans 6:13 (NIV)

Left-hander David Price is one of the best, most consistent pitchers in Major League Baseball, so as a New York Yankees fan I didn't relish the fact that my team would be facing him on the mound, pitching for the Detroit Tigers that day. He was in the midst of another great season, even a possible second Cy Young Award. But an amazing thing happened. In the second inning, the Yankees, who were mired in a terrible batting slump, got nine straight hits off Price, tying a long-held MLB record, and scored eight runs, driving the shell-shocked hurler to an early shower.

I'd like to think the Bombers' bats got hot, but the truth was, this all-star pitcher just didn't have his stuff that day. In fact, he had never failed so miserably in his entire career. I probably could have gotten a hit off him. Usually a pitcher of Price's prowess guts out a start when he doesn't have his best stuff, laboring to do what's necessary to keep his team in the game. They call it "grinding."

There are days when I feel like I'm grinding, when I don't have my best stuff, when my faith falters a little—until I remind myself that those are the days when I need faith the most. And then there are those days, like the one Price had, when out of the blue your whole game just goes to pieces. Nothing seems to work…good, bad, or otherwise.

Somewhere in Price's historic failure there was a lesson for me. That remarkable game reminded me there will be days when I can't seem to get anything right, when even my best efforts are for naught. All God asks of me then is that I trust Him, even with my failures, and believe that the next day will be better.

FYI: Five days later Price took the hill again and pitched a shutout.

Father, today and every day I offer all my efforts—good, bad, or otherwise—to You. —Edward Grinnan

Digging Deeper: Ecclesiastes 9:7

Sunday, August 28

Honor the Lord with your wealth and with the best part of everything.… —Proverbs 3:9 (NLT)

I'm not proud of this, but I can be stingy.

Someone announced a shoe drive for the following week in church. Those who wanted to participate could bring their used shoes to donate to Soles4Souls, a nonprofit organization helping to fight global poverty. On my way out, I grabbed several plastic bags and planned to fill them at home. I left the bags on the kitchen counter for a whole week. I meant to gather my shoes, but I didn't.

The truth is I like all of my shoes. I didn't want to give them away, so I pretended not to notice the empty bags. *Other people will bring shoes. They don't need mine,* I reasoned.

The next Sunday, one of the pastors walked onto the platform wearing flip-flops. He explained where to place our donated shoes and added, "For those of you who forgot your shoes, you can donate the ones you're wearing. We have flip-flops available, so you don't have to go home barefooted."

I glanced at my cute wedges with black straps. I imagined how wonderful it might feel to say *yes* and give them away, but I didn't. I wanted them for myself. All the way home, I tried to ignore my heavy heart.

Two hours later, my son called. He'd attended the next service. "Mom, my truck's broken down in the church parking lot. Can Dad come back and help me get it started?"

It's not over, I thought. *I have another chance to give.* Kneeling on the floor of my closet, I knew exactly what I was supposed to do.

Lord, help me remember the joy in surrendering everything. —Julie Garmon

Digging Deeper: Deuteronomy 15:10, Proverbs 3:27

When the poor and needy seek water, and there is none, and their tongue faileth for thirst, I the Lord will hear them, I the God of Israel will not forsake them. I will open rivers in high places, and fountains in the midst of the valleys: I will make the wilderness a pool of water, and the dry land springs of water. —Isaiah 41:17–18 (KJV)

I started the pump on the family ranch and limped down to the empty pond to wait for the water. Tomorrow we would rotate the cattle into this pasture. I sat on the bank in the hot sun, staring absently at the cracked, dry mud at the bottom of the water hole, pockmarked with old hoofprints. *My faith is like this dried up water hole*, I thought. Long after I'd had back surgery, my healing hit a plateau, painfully teetering between walking and using a walker. I was physically and spiritually exhausted. I knew God was with me, but right now I felt a bit lifeless and hollow.

Half an hour later the water began fingering its way into the pond and trickled into the first hoofprint. The indentation filled. Then the water spilled over into the next, and on and on. Suddenly, the water in the first hoofprint began to bubble up, almost as if it were boiling. The next pocket of water splashed with fervor. I couldn't tell what was happening until I got on my knees and studied it closely. It was completely filled with writhing, vibrant, one-inch-long fish.

When the pond dried out in the spring, these tiny fish had crowded into the last of the water trapped in the hoofprints and eventually burrowed into the relative safety of the mud. With the return of the water, they were instantly reawakened and rejuvenated. I needed to hang on to this image to get myself through this dry spell.

Dear Lord, when my faith is stagnant, help me remember the fish—dormant, not dead—awaiting the life-giving water. I trust that I, too, will be refreshed. —Erika Bentsen

Digging Deeper: Psalm 36:9, John 7:37–38, Romans 15:13

Tuesday, August 30

So then, my beloved brethren, let every man be swift to hear, slow to speak, slow to wrath. —James 1:19 (NKJV)

As a journalist, I often write about faith. I'm grateful for the opportunities to talk about—and with—God, to ask uncomfortable questions and receive profound answers. Thanks to my work, I've lately gotten more invitations to speak at conferences, colleges, churches. This has meant plenty of planes-trains-and-automobiles days—seemingly endless journeys during which

I occasionally ask myself, *Is it Tuesday? Am I in Cleveland? Did I eat breakfast already? Or was that yesterday?* Recently, I realized that God isn't just the frequent subject of my work; He's also the only consistent traveling Companion I have.

Early one morning, I was en route from Washington, DC, where I'd spoken at a church, to Newark Airport in New Jersey, where I'd board a flight to my next stop in Texas. As the train zipped northward, I rattled off assignments I hadn't completed and calls I hadn't made. I was exhausted, but my mind was abuzz: *What next? What will this article be about? What will that speech convey?*

Suddenly, it occurred to me that I was sitting by the window, yet I hadn't once looked outside. When I did, I saw placid, slate-colored waters and a layer of fog hovering above. And inside me, I heard familiar words: *Be still. Be slow. Be sure.*

Amid life's bustle, I often forget the importance of putting down my pen and opening my eyes, of closing my mouth and opening my ears. God is with me always, yes. But what kind of travel companion am *I* if I don't pause to listen to what He has to say?

Lord, thank You for being my constant Companion in the journey of life. —Jeff Chu

Digging Deeper: Deuteronomy 31:1–8, Psalm 119:132–133

Wednesday, August 31

And we know that in all things God works for the good of those who love him, who have been called according to his purpose. —Romans 8:28 (NIV)

I sat in the pediatrician's office with my big seventh-grader, Christian, waiting to follow the nurse to the examination room. Christian was due for a checkup before starting football.

My mind wandered back to our first visit to the doctor's office, just a week after we'd finalized Christian's adoption and brought him home from Russia. At age two, Christian wasn't cooperative. He cried when he saw the doctor approach, scrambling away whenever he could. When the nurse stuck a needle in Christian's arm to administer immunizations, he screamed at the top of his lungs.

As a toddler, Christian couldn't understand why these strangers were hurting him. He couldn't appreciate the benefit of their medical care. He didn't comprehend the purpose for his pain. But I understood the purpose in his pain, and I've learned to see the purpose in mine.

Some time ago when I experienced two miscarriages in the same year, I couldn't find any purpose in losing those babies. Well-meaning family and friends tried to comfort me. Though I appreciated their love and care, their words did nothing to bandage my wounded soul. Then, slowly, my pain led me to hear God's voice again.

I knew that only He could heal me, and He even gave me a new dream: adoption.

I can't imagine life without our funny, sweet seventh-grader. Our family is far richer because Christian is part of us.

Lord, may I seek You, find You, and love You in the midst of my pain, knowing that in all things, You work it out for good. —Carla Hendricks

Digging Deeper: Romans 8:18, 1 Peter 5:10

GOD'S ABIDING LOVE

1 _____

2 _____

3 _____

4 _____

5 _____

6 _____

7 _____

8 _____

9 _____

10 _____

11 _____

12 _____

13 _____

14 _____

15 _____

16 _____

17 _____

18 _____

19 _____

20 _____

21 _____

22 _____

23 _____

24 _____

25 _____

26 _____

27 _____

28 _____

29 _____

30 _____

31 _____

SEPTEMBER

*Every worthwhile gift, every genuine benefit
comes from above, descending from
the Creator of the heavenly luminaries. . . .*

—James 1:17 (TIB)

Thursday, September 1

Hope in the Lord! Be strong! Let your heart take courage! Hope in the Lord! —Psalm 27:14 (CEB)

Students and faculty gathered around the coffeepot following our weekly worship service. We got to debating the definition of *courage*. My son had just jumped out of an airplane for the first time, I said. Someone mentioned Clint Dempsey, the great American soccer player who stayed on the pitch despite a bloodied, broken nose and scored the winning goal. A coworker brought up a nephew who had just completed a coast-to-coast bicycle ride; another relative had hiked the Appalachian Trail alone.

Which of these actions, we wondered, had taken the most courage?

"My great-aunt Sadie," came a small voice from the far edge of the conversation. It was one of the quieter students. "Her neighborhood has had a lot of kids getting shot. She organized the people in that neighborhood, even after the gang doing the shootings had threatened her." She paused. "She is ninety-two."

Aunt Sadie reminded me of the writer Henri Nouwen, whose writings I'd read just that morning in my own devotions. We usually think about the kind of courage that is "connected with taking risks, the desire to test our physical limits." Nouwen went on to say, "Spiritual courage is something completely different. It is following the deepest desires of our hearts. It asks of us the willingness to lose our temporal lives in order to gain eternal life."

I'd never seen myself as all that courageous, but after that conversation I began to redefine my courage. It's less about whether I have the courage to jump out of an airplane and more about the courage I have to live a life focused fully on God. The latter is a lot more demanding, but it's the kind of courage I hope I'll be remembered for someday.

God, "Grant us wisdom, grant us courage, for the living of these days; for the living of these days."
—Jeff Japinga

Digging Deeper: 2 Samuel 7:18–29, Acts 13:44–52

Friday, September 2

It is good to praise the Lord . . . proclaiming your love in the morning and your faithfulness at night.
—Psalm 92:1–2 (NIV)

The car keys rattled as I hung them on the rack. I plopped my purse on the table and puttered into the kitchen. It was Friday night, and everyone at work was doing something fun with their spouses or children. That is, everyone except me. I didn't want to get cleaned up and go out, yet I didn't want to stay home alone.

After dishing up my meal, I set my plate on the table and dropped into a chair. Poking my food with a fork, I thought of all the friends I needed to call and catch up with but didn't have the energy to. I glanced at the Bible, which I had propped at an angle above my place mat, and read the verse in Psalm 92 about proclaiming God's faithfulness at night. *What a great idea! What if I make tonight an evening with God?*

After washing dishes, I turned on a worship CD and snuggled into my prayer chair in the living room. Over the next hour I shared with God the wonderful parts of my day, instead of my trials and tribulations. And you know what? It was a fun Friday night.

Lord, when I get caught up in the complexities of life, remind me to recount Your great deeds. Amen.
—Rebecca Ondov

Digging Deeper: Zephaniah 3:17

Saturday, September 3

"Out in the world the master sits at the table and is served by his servants. But not here! For I am your servant." —Luke 22:27 (TLB)

The topic of servants came up in a recent conversation, and it led me to think about the fact that my life is easier and more enjoyable because of all the people who serve. Not a day passes without someone else adding value to my life through their service.

Many of these people I'll never meet. This summer I will grow my own green beans, but for today's lunch I zipped open a package that had been grown, harvested, stemmed, and flash-frozen by many different workers. An assembly line of people made my washer and dryer; the machines save time and my clothes aren't torn to shreds by the Kansas wind. A voice on the telephone helped to solve my computer problems.

I am grateful for these anonymous services, but my attitude toward those who serve me face-to-face needs adjustment. There was the young woman in the restaurant: "Hi, I'm—! What can I get you to drink?" When she brought my coffee three minutes later, I'd already forgotten her name. A trio of skilled carpet layers spent several days at my house. We chatted while I microwaved their lunches, but I never bothered to learn their names or ask about their families. It's the same with the "oil-change guy" who services my car and the two men who haul off my trash.

Jesus came among us as a servant. What if I looked into the eyes of each person who served me and saw our Lord? What if I made the effort to know their names and thank them for their work?

Sunday, September 4

In him the whole building is joined together and rises to become a holy temple in the Lord. And in him you too are being built together to become a dwelling in which God lives by his Spirit.
—Ephesians 2:21–22 (NIV)

My alarm goes off, piercing the silence with its electronic shriek. I let out a groan while I fumble around for the snooze button. My face is pressed deep into my pillow where the light can't reach me. How can it be 8:30 AM already?

It's been a long week of studying and working the graveyard shift at the library. I don't want to get out of bed for church. I could easily just roll over and go back to sleep.

I should feel guilty for wanting to play hooky, but I'm too groggy to care. Besides, I'll read my Bible later. I'm sure God will understand. He told His people to rest, right?

But as hard as I try to persuade myself, I know that if I don't go, I won't really feel rested. My spiritual tank will run empty. I might make it through most of the day or even the week, but eventually my engine will start sputtering. I'll be spiritually exhausted.

I'd like to be able to check off my God time with a cup of tea and some Psalms, but we're not meant to be lone believers. There's something special about the way God fills the church with His presence, and I won't get that from my reading chair.

So I roll over and let the sun blind me awake. I dangle my feet over the side of my bed for just a moment. Then I get ready for God to top off my tank.

Jesus, thank You for providing a place where we can worship You as brothers and sisters. And thank You for filling Your temple with Your Spirit. —Logan Eliasen

Digging Deeper: Matthew 18:20, Acts 4:31

Monday, September 5

The sleep of a labouring man is sweet....
—Ecclesiastes 5:12 (KJV)

When I was thirteen, I got my first job working for a local contractor. During those long, hot days, hauling bricks, I gained a respect for craftsmen, an admiration for those who labor, and a realization that when I grew up I wanted to wear a suit and work in a climate-controlled office.

Years later, celebrating the long weekend of Labor Day at our family's cabin, my feet were bare, and shorts and a T-shirt replaced my usual jacket and tie. The kids were splashing in the lake, the sun was high, and a slight breeze was blowing through the pine trees. That's when the carefully laid concrete blocks that make up our cabin caught my eye. My grandfather had built this place fifty years earlier with his big hands and happy spirit. Knowing him, I was sure he labored with a dream of all the good times his family would have here.

Labor. We all have our own style of work, and it's pretty amazing how it all comes together. Bridges and roads, skyscrapers and modest houses, plumbing, electricity, the cars we drive, the foods we eat, health-care workers, service industries, the stores, the restaurants…the list is endless. We are all laborers, serving one another, building dreams.

Today, I pause to give thanks for this concrete-block cabin and the road that brought me here, for the food we'll enjoy tonight and all the other amenities of the good life, which the labor of others affords. And as I walk down to the shore, ready to dive into the lake, I smile at the good news of Jesus's words: "Come…all who labor…and I will give you rest" (Matthew 11:28, RSV).

Thank You, Father, for the satisfaction that hard work brings and for all of Your children who labor for one another. —Brock Kidd

Digging Deeper: Proverbs 14:23, 28:19; Luke 10:7

Tuesday, September 6

Everything that lives and moves will be your food.
—Genesis 9:3 (GW)

Harry Oppenheimer's stood on Broadway at Ninety-Eighth Street, and Harry the butcher presided behind the counter in a white apron, knife in hand, peering through his thick glasses, barking at his assistants, ripping out sheets of white paper for his scale.

I was all of twenty-four and figured that he would bark at me too. I had six dollars in my pocket and six friends coming for dinner that night. What was I going to feed them? Could I make some soup out of one of those bones he had? Was there something I could do with a ham hock? But what I really wanted to make was beef stew.

I waited in line, dreading Harry's fierce scowl. I could have gone to the supermarket and picked up ingredients for macaroni-and-cheese or made some spaghetti, but I felt drawn to Oppenheimer's—the white tile floor, the old sign, the butcher's sense of authority.

"Next," Harry said.

I took a deep breath and declared in rapid fire: "I have six dollars and six friends coming for dinner tonight. I've got some onions, garlic, and potatoes at home. Can I get enough meat to make a stew?"

He gazed over the top of his glasses, inspecting me, then heaped a huge pile of red meat for stewing on the scale. He scribbled some numbers on a piece of paper and declared, "Six dollars exactly. You're in luck. And let me give you some bacon to go with it."

What a feast we had! "Six dollars for all of this," I said. "The butcher said it was on sale." Funny thing, other times when I went into Oppenheimer's and had more money in my pocket, I never got a deal like that. But just when I needed it, when I was young and broke, a crusty old butcher took pity on me. Like the miracle of the loaves and fishes, generosity can be a miracle in itself.

Lord, let me see the ones whose lives I can ease with gifts of my own. —Rick Hamlin

Digging Deeper: Proverbs 11:25

Wednesday, September 7

WHAT THE SAINTS HAVE TAUGHT ME
Joan, Companion of the Falsely Accused

Blessed are you when men...utter all kinds of evil against you falsely.... —Matthew 5:11 (RSV)

A few years ago my husband and I took a car trip tracing the life of Joan of Arc. We started in the little country town of Domremy in northeast France, where Joan was born in 1412. The simple peasant house with its stone floor and tiny windows still stands. We walked through the meadows where this illiterate shepherd girl heard voices telling her to free France from the English aggressors.

There are only a couple of walls left of the chateau in Chinon, on the Loire, where the dauphin, son of the late King Charles VI, was cowering in defeat. It shows his desperation that he agreed to let this determined seventeen-year-old girl lead the troops trying to lift the English siege of Orleans.

Our next stop was the armor-clad statue of Joan in the coronation cathedral of Reims. She'd lifted the yearlong siege in nine days and had gone on to lead the string of victories that allowed her to stand there beside the dauphin as he was crowned Charles VII. Joan continued the struggle, attacking the enemy's remaining strongholds, until she was captured by allies of the English.

We drove last to Rouen, where Joan was imprisoned while a series of preposterous charges of witchcraft were brought against her by a court of churchmen in this city still under the control of the English. She was burned at the stake in the market square on May 30, 1431. She was nineteen.

Today a stunning modern church stands at the site. We sat in the light-filled space beneath the dramatic curved-wood ceiling and thought about the church council that, in 1455, twenty-four years too late, pronounced Joan innocent. And we thought how belatedly we, too, recognize the good that comes in unexpected forms.

Father, let me be slow to judge. —Elizabeth Sherrill

Digging Deeper: Proverbs 31:9, Matthew 7:2

Thursday, September 8

My God will fully satisfy every need of yours according to his riches in glory in Christ Jesus. —Philippians 4:19 (NRSV)

Last night my husband was on a business trip. As usual, when Kris is out of town, I had trouble getting to sleep. I played solitaire till nearly midnight. By that time it was too late for reading, my usual way of falling asleep, so I got in bed and turned out the light. After a few minutes, it occurred to me that I might not have locked the front door.

"Yes, you did," I told myself. (I talk to myself more when Kris is away.) "Remember? You moved that grading folder out of the doorway and into your book bag."

I sank back in the covers and started drowsing. Then I jerked myself up with the worry that I hadn't turned on the pump of our saltwater fish tank after feeding the fish.

This time I was less successful calming myself and finally trudged back downstairs to see, turning on all the lights as I went, thereby undoing any remaining sleepiness.

So I read after all, sinking into a long night of dream emergencies, waking the next morning with my reading glasses pressed into my cheeks and my book crumpled beneath me. At breakfast, after failing to make myself a cappuccino with our complicated machine and fixing a tea instead, I was uncharacteristically conscious of my husband's daily love and my dependence on him. *When did I become so helpless to provide for myself?* I wondered. The answer to my question steamed up from my tea. *Always. You were helpless from birth—even before birth. You're always helpless, always in need, and always fabulously provided for.*

Father God, thank You for Your magnificent and unmerited love. —Patty Kirk

Digging Deeper: Deuteronomy 8:7–18

Friday, September 9

The Lord is good to all, and His tender mercies are over all His works. —Psalm 145:9 (NKJV)

On our family cattle ranch, calves usually weigh seventy to ninety pounds when they are born. But Mini started life as a vigorous, full-term, twenty-pound calf. She was so petite, it was comical. She made people smile whenever they saw her. Her sunny, friendly disposition grew as she got older, but her body never did. As the time came to wean the calves from their mothers, Mini was more than two hundred pounds lighter than her age group.

A new worry developed: *What do we do with Mini?* We couldn't keep her, but we didn't have the heart to send her to some anonymous auction yard. We ran an ad online. Every day I prayed, "Please, Lord, help us find a home for Mini." Weeks passed, and I began to lose hope that anyone would want a runt calf who would never really grow up.

I don't know why I worried. God looks after even the least of us. A family living fifty miles away called. They had young children and a tiny farm. They wanted a small, friendly cow for their kids, but they didn't want to start a herd. It was a perfect fit. God saw to it that Mini would continue being showered with big smiles for the rest of her life.

Thank You, Lord, for giving Mini a forever home. You have shown me that the greatest charity happens when it is directed toward the least among us.
—Erika Bentsen

Digging Deeper: Proverbs 14:21–22, 1 John 4:16–19

Therefore encourage one another and build
each other up, just as in fact you are doing.
—1 Thessalonians 5:11 (NIV)

I have every *Daily Guideposts* I've ever contributed
to lined up on my bookshelf. The year 2006 was
my first one, and the devotions written then are
sweet, full of adventure and optimism, absent of
pain.

With each year's edition, my stories became
buried in sorrow. My hurt and brokenness splattered
on the pages for all to see. These devotions were
beyond work assignments; they were tearful prayers,
desperate attempts to make sense of my heartache
and my slow road to healing.

I remember people telling me that God was going
to use these experiences to make me stronger, to
be an encouragement to others. "I don't want to be
strong!" I argued back. "I just want to be happy!"

But then the letters came. *Daily Guideposts* readers
from different parts of the country sent me notes of
encouragement. They cried with me, shared their
own struggles, told me that my stories gave them
strength. They thanked me for my vulnerability and
my willingness to let God use me in my storytelling.

The process of becoming a strong person is not
easy. But comparing myself with the person I used to

be, I'm thankful and honored to be the woman God has allowed me to be today.

Thank You, Father, for seeing me through my pain and giving me the strength and the voice, and, oh yes, the optimism to encourage others. —Karen Valentin

Digging Deeper: Romans 5:3–5

Sunday, September 11

Worship the Lord with gladness.... —Psalm 100:2 (NIV)

My mind was far from worshipping God. I'd learned that a project I'd been working on needed major changes. I had no idea how to begin. I wasn't even sure I wanted to. I felt stupid, incapable, exhausted.

My husband, Rick, and I found our usual seats at church. When the praise music began, I was a million miles away, thinking, worrying, pouting, doubting. I mumbled the words to the song and faked my way through the second one. Before the final song, the worship leader said, "If you're comfortable doing this, let's try something new. Place your hand over your heart as we sing this next song."

Oh, great. I don't want to. Maybe no one else will either.

The worship leader's voice softened. "I want us to draw near to God. He is worthy of our worship. He

is holy. He longs to hear our praise in His sanctuary."
Then the pianist began playing. "Holy Spirit, Thou
art welcome in this place…"

The words filled the sanctuary, and the music
lifted high above our heads toward heaven. I could
see hundreds of people slipping their hands over their
hearts, even Rick. They weren't following directions
because they had to; they wanted to.

Forgive me, Lord, I prayed silently.

I raised my right hand and covered my heart.
The very instant I let go of my will and praised Him
in His sanctuary, my spirit connected with His. All
heaviness, fear, and doubt left me. With His help, I'd
face my fears head-on.

**"Holy Spirit, Thou art welcome in this place and
in my heart."** —Julie Garmon

Digging Deeper: John 4:23

Monday, September 12

…So that you may stand mature and fully assured in
everything that God wills. —Colossians 4:12 (NRSV)

It was Benjamin's first day at school. I wasn't sure
who was more nervous, him or me. But why was I
nervous? We knew this school well. Frances had gone
to preschool here and loved it. Benjamin would be in
her old classroom with a new teacher.

Maybe it was the sight of my son in his blue shorts and red shirt, the school uniform that all students wear, preschool through eighth grade. He looked so grown-up, a true boy, no trace of the baby he'd been just a few years ago. Or maybe I worried he'd have trouble distinguishing himself from his outspoken, hard-charging older sister.

Watching the emergence of my children's unique personhoods is by far my favorite part of being a parent. It feels like witnessing a holy mystery. But it's also nerve-racking. The whole process seems so tenuous, so beset by uncontrollable variables.

We got to the door. A few other children were clinging anxiously to their parents' legs. Not Benjamin. He remembered the room from the tour we'd taken a few days earlier. He made a beeline for the toys and began assembling a truck, trading pieces with a boy next to him.

"Give me a hug, buddy," I said, getting ready to go. Benjamin hugged me quickly, then turned back to play. A moment later he looked up and spotted me at the door. We waved. He grinned.

I watched him for a moment, savoring the intent look he always gets when playing by himself, something he does far more easily than his sister. I didn't need to worry about Benjamin's emergence. His personhood was already here, made and shaped by the Teacher Who made and shaped us all.

Each day I become a little more the person
You are calling me to be, Lord. —Jim Hinch

Digging Deeper: 1 Corinthians 13:11,
Ephesians 4:11–13

Tuesday, September 13

On the day the Lord gave the Amorites into the power
of Israel, Joshua spoke to the Lord…"Sun, stand still
at Gibeon! and Moon, at the Aijalon Valley!" The sun
stood still and the moon stood motionless until a nation
took revenge on its enemies. —Joshua 10:12–13 (CEB)

Our telescope is down from the loft in the barn, set up
on the lawn, and positioned at a perfect angle to the sky.
The boys want me to wake them if there's a good view.
My husband snores, and I am watching the clock, which
reads 3:05. Outside a rare lunar eclipse is happening.

I stare into the darkness, searching for the "blood
moon" that the news has hyped, but it's obscured
by a blanket of clouds. I look and look, waiting for
a break, a slight glimpse of the phenomenon, and I
think of Joshua's prayer for the sun to stand still—an
impossible prayer that was answered nonetheless.

I look into the early morning sky and think of the
many impossible prayers I've prayed staring out this
bedroom window during dark times in my life, when
fear and worries about health and family kept me awake.

Right now is different. I'm overcome by how peaceful it is, how grateful I am to be here, enjoying this sacred space, this darkness. And even though I'm missing the celestial event, I feel close, so very close, to God, as if anything is possible, as if a miracle is happening—and it is.

Heavenly Father, thank You for this beautiful unexpected moment of knowing Your incredible love in the deepest places of my heart. —Sabra Ciancanelli

Digging Deeper: Romans 8:37–39, 1 John 3:1

Wednesday, September 14

This is the message we have heard from him and declare to you: God is light; in him there is no darkness at all. —1 John 1:5 (NIV)

"We'd all be better off without religion."

I was sitting in a little doughnut shop, having a morning coffee. I glanced over at the man who had made the statement. He was looking at a newspaper and shaking his head over a story about yet another senseless terrorist act. "More bad things are done in the name of God than good things," he said to no one in particular. "History proves it. If there is a God, why does He put up with it?"

It was too early in the day to engage a stranger in a debate about religion. I've heard this argument more often these days, that religion is to blame for the world's ills. And, yes, for thousands of years virtually all of the world's religions have used faith as an excuse to wage war, to oppress and persecute. But is that God's fault or man's?

The God I believe in is not a God of terror but of love. I know people of many different faiths, and none of them believe their God is a God of terror. My friends practice their faith as a way of worshipping their creator and ordering their lives. Their devotion deepens their capacity for love, not hate. And when hateful things happen in the world, it is my faith that helps me understand that God is not to blame for evil. Christ brought peace into a violent world. His peace is still the greatest answer to man's worst deeds; His love is the antidote to our violence.

Maybe it was the coffee kicking in, but I suddenly felt tempted to start a conversation with the man. He was already gone, leaving his paper on the table. I said a little prayer that someone might change his mind.

Father, that man asked, "Why do You put up with us? With our brutality and prejudices? With our trespasses and misdeeds?" I believe the answer is that You are a God of love, not hate; of peace, not terror. Help me convince the next doubter I meet of Your goodness.
—Edward Grinnan

Digging Deeper: Deuteronomy 13:4

Thursday, September 15

As for God, his way is perfect: The Lord's word is flawless; he shields all who take refuge in him.
—Psalm 18:30 (NIV)

Chalk it up to crazy expectations, but I count on my eight-year-old son to put his belt in his dresser drawer every single day. You see, he has to wear the belt to school for his uniform and I'd rather not spend our entire budget on belts.

Mean mom, right? Even worse, because he has only one belt, if it gets stuffed under his bed or slides behind the closet doors, he's not able to find it when he's getting dressed for school.

It seems so simple, but we have "lost-belt drama" at our house two or three mornings every week. The kid doesn't seem to learn! We find the belt in the laundry room or in the back of the car or underneath the dog. Every time I remind him how easy it would be to find if he just put it away in the same spot, he says to me, "I know, Mom. From now on, I will."

How many times do I say the same thing to God? He's given me everything I need to live life abundantly, yet I get caught up in my own life and set Him aside. I push Him to the back of my closet and close the door. Then I start to panic and search frantically for Him when I need Him most, only to find Him right where I left Him, waiting.

I should know where to find You, Lord, if I just remember to put You where You belong—front and center. Amen. —Erin MacPherson

Digging Deeper: Proverbs 21:2, Isaiah 55:8

Friday, September 16

"You must love and help your neighbors just as much as you love and take care of yourself."
—James 2:8 (TLB)

If my dad's genes are any indication (he's ninety-six), I have many productive years ahead of me. I thought about helping seniors write their life stories or delivering meals-on-wheels or reading to patients in the local hospice center. But, sad to say, I never got my act together.

Then, one day, I was hiking around a lake near my home with my sister Catherine. "Look at that huge great blue heron!" I exclaimed. "It must be three feet tall." I snapped a few photos as did Catherine.

I turned to head back to the path and nearly jumped out of my skin. "Holy smoke! There's an alligator!"

Catherine jumped a foot. "Where?" she screamed.

"Right there," I pointed.

Ten feet from us was a nine-foot alligator, sunning itself in the grass. "How did we miss it? It's right under our noses!" We took some photos before it slid into the water and disappeared.

That night I thought about how close that alligator was to us. Then I began to think about all the neighbors around me, right under my nose, who could use my help. I decided that there were plenty of volunteer opportunities. I could sit with my friend Shirley's husband, who has Alzheimer's, so she can get out of the house once in a while. I could bring the mail upstairs for my neighbor who broke her leg. I could take Norma, who has moved into an assisted living residence, out to lunch more often. I could share more of my home cooking with Lou, a widower who lives in my building. The list is endless.

Father, help me keep my eyes open and reach out to help those who are right under my nose.
—Patricia Lorenz

Digging Deeper: Luke 11:25–37, Acts 20:35, 1 Corinthians 16:16

Saturday, September 17

For by him were all things created, that are in heaven, and that are in earth, visible and invisible, whether they be thrones, or dominions, or principalities, or powers: all things were created by him, and for him.
—Colossians 1:16 (KJV)

I took our nine-year-old son to the Maker Faire on the grounds of the New York Hall of Science in the borough of Queens. The exhibitors at the fair run the gamut from school kids to large corporations. The exhibits include the latest in 3D printers, circuits and kits for do-it-yourself projects, robots performing a multitude of tasks, Tesla coils, and Van de Graaff generators playing music along with lightninglike sparks.

Stephen has an engineer's delight in putting things together and taking them apart (more the latter than the former, alas). Snap-together electrical circuits, sun-powered LEDs, and Lego robots are high on his list of activities. His dad, however, is very different. I have neither the patience nor the fine-motor coordination to be a maker. But that doesn't stop me from spending six hours in the hot sun with Stephen, walking through the fair. My eyes glaze; his eyes glow. But to see that glow makes the whole day worthwhile.

Sometimes I like to imagine God looking at His world with an engineer's eye, captivated by the intricate mechanisms of a living cell or the amazing revolutions of the stars and planets. He is, after all, the Maker of makers. Every other maker is a maker only because He has made them and given them a little share of His own power to make something new. It's the reflection of His engineer's eye that I see glowing in Stephen's.

Lord, make me a maker so that I may share Your
goodness with others. —Andrew Attaway

Digging Deeper: Isaiah 44:24, Revelation 4:11

Sunday, September 18

Praise God in his sanctuary. . . .
—Psalm 150:1 (NIV)

I feel things deeply, but I'm not an exuberant
person. I sometimes wish I weren't so soft-spoken.
The man who sits behind my husband, Gene,
and me in church has a booming voice. I love the
way he praises God out loud during the sermon.
"Praise God!" or "Thank You, Jesus!" It seems like
I should be able to at least say an "Amen."

One Sunday in church, when Pastor Tom made an
excellent point, the man behind us voiced, "Thank
You, Jesus."

Why can't I do that?

Later on he expressed his praise in a totally
different way. He simply exhaled long and hard as
in, *"Wheeew!"* I translated this as, "Man, oh man,
that's good stuff."

Why did I stifle my own vocal praise and
welcome the ones from my neighbor? As we bowed
for the closing prayer, I asked God, "Please show me
how to praise You."

The next Sunday, an amazing thing happened. When Pastor Tom said something that stirred my heart, I surprised myself by singing in my heart, without making a sound, an old hymn by W. L. Thompson that I'd known since childhood. "Softly and tenderly Jesus is calling, calling for you and for me. . . ."

Behind me I heard, *"Wheeew!"*

"We praise Thee, O God, for the Son of Thy love, for Jesus Who died, and is now gone above. Hal-le-lu-jah! Thine the glory." (W. P. Mackay and J. J. Husband)
—Marion Bond West

Digging Deeper: Exodus 15:11, James 5:13

Monday, September 19

Anxiety weighs down the heart.
—Proverbs 12:25 (NIV)

Whose favorite room was this? What did she say about that doorway? I adjusted my earphone and tried to focus on the tour guide's description of the Byzantine architecture. Here I was, in the entertainment rooms of the Royal Palace of Dedinje in Belgrade, Bulgaria, yet I'd missed most of the commentary. I'd followed our group from room to room, but my thoughts were several thousand miles away.

An early morning e-mail from one of my daughters told me of an important decision she was facing. Since then, my mind went back and forth rehashing her options. I'd planned this amazing trip for months, wanting to savor every moment, yet I was so distracted with concern I barely noticed my surroundings.

I sighed, shaking my head. Then I remembered the horses.

My daily walk at home in Colorado takes me past our neighbors' horse farm; they breed Morgans. I enjoy watching these stately animals prance and kick up their heels in their pens. But I'd noticed something curious. Every time I see two of the horses in a pasture beyond the pens, they're walking back and forth along the fence. I keep waiting for them to enjoy the expanse of several acres, but they don't. I learned that horses often pace when they're anxious. Instead of running free, they wear a track in the ground from retracing the same spot so many times.

I was doing the same thing, letting anxiety carve a rut in my mind and missing the extraordinarily beautiful expanse looming all around me.

Lord, I turn this over to You. Lead and guide our daughter to do Your will. And thank You for this fantastic trip! —Kim Henry

Digging Deeper: Psalms 37:8, 68:19; Proverbs 14:31, 21:31

FINDING REST: Letting Time Pass

"But I say to you that if you are angry with a brother or sister, you will be liable to judgment; and if you insult a brother or sister, you will be liable to the council...." —Matthew 5:22 (NRSV)

I remember the first real fight my husband and I had almost twenty years ago. I have no idea what it was about, but I remember feeling angry and upset because we'd never argued much before.

My voice was raised; Charlie's wasn't. It hardly ever is. But he was giving back as good as he got, until at one point he abruptly left the room. I sat in the living room, caught between crying over the fact that we were fighting and steaming over what we were arguing about. I waited for him to return, becoming more distressed even as I marshalled my arguments for the next volley. The house was utterly quiet. Finally, I yelled into the silence, "So that's it? You think that just because you walk away, it's over?"

When Charlie didn't reply, I jumped up and charged down the hall. The bedroom door was closed. I barged in, drawing breath for my opening shot, and found him . . . fast asleep. It was about 7:00 PM and still light outside. The blinds were drawn, and he was in bed, under the blankets, gently snoring. I couldn't believe it! I spent the next hour pacing and fuming. Was this how every dispute was going to end? With his falling asleep?

More often than not, the answer's been yes. And over the years I've come to appreciate this, because when he got up the next morning, he was no longer angry and I'd had enough time to think about whether it was worth it to continue fighting. It wasn't. Usually it isn't.

**Father, thank You for reminding me that when
I rest in Your steadfast love, I rob anger of its power.**
—Marci Alborghetti

Digging Deeper: Lamentations 3:22, 24;
Luke 10:39–42

Wednesday, September 21

"Jesus . . . who went about doing good...."
—Acts 10:38 (NKJV)

A former student of mine is now a teacher herself, training teachers for Christian schools. Thilini has an uncanny ability to spot leadership qualities in her students.

She told me about the day when she was walking down the hallway of the college and four of her students were walking in front of her. There was a piece of trash lying in the middle of the hallway, but the first three young men just walked around it. The fourth one, however, picked up the trash and put it in the bin.

"He's my leader," Thilini said. "All four boys saw that trash, but this one did something about it. He could have argued that he didn't drop it there, so he didn't have to pick it up. Or that he is not the janitor, so that's not his job. Instead, he took ownership of the problem and solved it. He has a servant's heart. He will do well."

Thilini's wisdom inspired me because it reminded me that I can be a leader at any age and in any circumstances. I don't have to be forty years old, with a PhD, a political party, or a charismatic personality. I just need to notice needs and take care of them, like Jesus, Who "went about doing good." Or like my neighbor who helped me back my car out of the drive when my windows were frosted. And that driver downtown who got out and directed traffic around an accident.

It's not easy spotting those needs. It's even harder to take care of them. When I see my wife is overworked, I should grab a towel and help with the dishes. When I do take the time, I feel better about myself, as if I am doing what Jesus would have done.

It's nice to be needed, Lord. It brings me deep pleasure.
—Daniel Schantz

Digging Deeper: Isaiah 6:8, Matthew 25:40

Thursday, September 22

Even though I walk through the darkest valley, I fear no evil; for you are with me; your rod and your staff—they comfort me. —Psalm 23:4 (NRSV)

I have never really been in a fight. Throughout my school years, I gratefully avoided those scuffles—and worse—that boys seem to engage in between classes, after school, and on the playground. Even my brother and I would push each other around, but never hit.

Still, adrenaline really kicks in whenever I'm around heightened anger. For instance, at a stoplight the other day, I watched as two young men, probably intoxicated, got out of their car and pounded on the one next to theirs, angry about something that had just taken place on the road. After about sixty seconds, the light turned green and, thankfully, they left. No harm done. Except that perhaps harm *was* done, because I always feel at those moments that I'm not doing what I'm supposed to do.

I recall a line from the writings of Mohandas Gandhi, who wasn't a Christian but was profoundly influenced by the teachings of Jesus: "It is better to fight than to be afraid." I think what he meant was that to be a peacemaker requires more courage than fighting does. And I believe he was right. To be a real peacemaker is not to sit by and watch in fear and trembling, but to be present, to say something, to stand up.

I will try to stand up for what's right, Lord, no matter where I am. You alone are my strength. —Jon Sweeney

Digging Deeper: Psalm 25:2, 4

Friday, September 23

"Do not store up for yourselves treasures on earth, where moths and vermin consume, and where thieves break in and steal. But store up for yourselves treasures in heaven...." —Matthew 6:19–20 (NIV)

My mother-in-law passed away two years ago. Like so many, she fought cancer. Unlike so many, she got a chance to use the lessons she learned before dying. Marie first survived breast cancer in 1983. That scare in her forties changed everything. She and her husband, Ralph, decided that retirement begins *now*. They were not going to wait to do the things they wanted to experience in life. They reorganized their outlook and their savings plans. They began to invest in each other, not just their bank account.

They still put money away. However, buying tickets to see Neil Diamond in concert was no longer a luxury; it was part of the budget. Ralph took glasswork classes; Marie studied watercolor. Special trips weren't deferred for someday; they were for next month. They planned and enjoyed time with each other. They camped. They fished. They bought a cabin in the Rocky Mountains. They took a cruise through the Panama Canal. They went to Italy.

I watched my in-laws grab life; I saw the joy in their example. My husband and I try to do the same, no longer deferring big plans. Life happens now. Good stewardship of our resources does not mean that every extra penny goes to savings. Good stewardship means we invest in the people we love too. Spending our money as well as our time together enriches our lives.

Dear Father, You smile when Your children enjoy life. Help me to see every day as a blessing from You. Amen. —Lisa Bogart

Digging Deeper: Ecclesiastes 3:22, 2 Corinthians 4:18, James 4:13–16

Saturday, September 24

He satisfies the longing soul.... —Psalm 107:9 (NKJV)

I set off on a road trip, heading two hundred miles east toward the Cherokee National Forest and the little town of Tellico Plains, Tennessee—the birthplace of my father, Harrison Dunn. The next day found me following the twists and turns that lead through the pristine mountains where he had spent his childhood. I longed to find him there on paths leading down to the river, in the mist of Bald

Creek Falls, at the overlook where he served in the Civilian Conservation Corps.

Later, sitting in Tellico Grains Bakery, I looked out and saw the touchstones of my father's childhood: the old drugstore, the building that had housed his father's butcher shop, the train station where he had played kick the can. As I tried to connect to the boy he was, the words of Blaze Foley's song "Clay Pigeons" drifted through my mind: "I could build me a castle of memories, just to have somewhere to go." I suppose that's why my road trip brought me here: to find that place in memory where I could be with Daddy, because he was good and safe, and I was happy when he was near.

Later, I drove slowly through the mountains once more before heading home. I could smell the sweet green of the forests and feel the coolness from the running river. The ancient trees created patterns of light and shadow on the narrow road. I'd come looking for my earthly father. But I recognized a deeper longing, one I share with most of humankind; it wasn't for a person or a place or a time, but for a glimpse of God within...here...now.

Father, past our castles of memories, You fulfill our every longing and we are safe with You. —Pam Kidd

Digging Deeper: Psalms 42:1, 63:1, 84:2

Sunday, September 25

Then Jesus said unto them... Walk while ye have the light, lest darkness come upon you: for he that walketh in darkness knoweth not whither he goeth. —John 12:35 (KJV)

You know, everyone talks about praying to God, and appealing to God, and celebrating and praising and thanking God, but no one ever talks about arguing bitterly with God, so let's talk about that. I was arguing with the Mercy last night. I was saying that I am terrified for my oldest child, who has been lost in the darkness for years, and we are all exhausted dealing with her and her demons. While I love her beyond measure, she is driving me nuts, and I am furious and sad and down to my last drops of energy.

He says, *What, are you saying you want to quit? Because you begged Me for that kid, and I gave you that kid, and if you say you love her then you are going to have to prove it every day for the rest of your life.*

I say, "Can't You cut us a break here and lift her darkness? Is that so much to ask? Because we are all wiped out, and I worry that the fabric of the family is fraying, and I would give anything to see a happy, healthy, cheerful woman emerge like a phoenix from the mess of the present occupant, who seems like such a stranger sometimes that I wonder if I dreamed the first happy fifteen years of her life."

He says, *All you can do is love her. Trust that there is holy joy in her and maybe somehow she will find her way there. Trust that I abide in her and she in Me. Miracles are born in love and faith.*

Well, there's not much you can say when He is in this terse mood, and I knew He was right, so I piped down and went back to plodding on and praying. On we go, brothers and sisters. On we go.

Lord, I am quietly begging You here: heal my child. Bring her back to who she is and can be. Please?
—Brian Doyle

Digging Deeper: Isaiah 58:8

Monday, September 26

"For even the Son of Man came not to be served but to serve...." —Mark 10:45 (ESV)

I am in a clinic working to reform public-education funding in Connecticut. Throughout law school, I have been most proud of this assignment. The clinic is about serving others, and it is in doing this work that I feel closest to living a life consistent with Christ's teachings.

In 2013, our major lawsuit was barreling toward trial. I was asked to join the team. I wanted to say "yes," but going to trial is full-time work. I would be giving up two or three months of my third year in law school and a chance to play a major role on the *Law Journal.*

The journal is both an academic publication and a kind of sorting mechanism for law students. Membership and positions like editor-in-chief or executive editor are signs of prestige that follow lawyers for their whole careers. I was a member and wanted to try to secure one of the editorial spots, which could help land a clerkship for a federal appeals court judge. Going to trial meant giving up that chance.

I agonized over the choice, talking through every side of it with whoever would listen. Finally, in the middle of one more conversation with my wife, I thought, *Haven't I been chasing those proverbial gold stars long enough? Haven't I spent enough time going after whatever I believed would advance my career? Isn't it time to simply do what I know is the right thing?*

The choice was easy.

Thank You, God, for giving me chances to choose the right thing. —Sam Adriance

Digging Deeper: 2 Corinthians 9:7

Tuesday, September 27

For when I am weak, then I am strong.
—2 Corinthians 12:10 (NIV)

Why did I come here today? I wondered as I slipped into my seat at the round table of our weekly Bible study. I'd just been at the doctor's office, where he'd decided to put a heart monitor on me to keep track of my increasing problems with an irregular heartbeat. My shirt did not cover up the wires and suction cups or the bulky battery at my waist, and I could feel all eyes looking at me.

These women and I were just getting to know one another. I blinked hard to hold back the tears because I did not want to talk about the heart monitor or maybe because of my fears about tears in public. Yet they came, and someone plopped a box of tissues in front of me.

I felt totally revealed and had no choice. My words came tumbling out about feeling afraid and even a little ashamed because heart problems can come from not taking good care of yourself and not getting enough exercise or eating the wrong foods and that's not who I think I am and I don't want a heart problem and...

There were lots of sympathetic nods and good-listening faces and comforting words and someone praying for me. On the other side of all this compassion, I still felt a little embarrassed. But I also felt known and understood by this circle of women, my new small group. That's a good feeling.

Lord, today I learned that sharing fears—and even tears—in a safe place can be braver than trying to hide them. —Carol Kuykendall

Digging Deeper: Psalm 34:4–5, 1 Peter 3:8

Wednesday, September 28

It is written: " 'As surely as I live,' says the Lord, 'every knee will bow before me; every tongue will acknowledge God.' " —Romans 14:11 (NIV)

I'm fortunate to live in a house surrounded on all four corners by large oak trees. Just today I was walking around the yard, feeling grateful that my home is encircled by these strong, stately oaks. Yet the lesson that I've learned from these oak trees is not about their strength but about their weakness.

Years ago, the powerful winds from a hurricane uprooted a fifth oak tree in my backyard, the largest one of them all. When I returned home after evacuating, I stepped into my backyard, shocked and dumbfounded that the storm had uprooted this mighty tree. Its branches and massive trunk now covered the entire backyard. It wasn't until weeks later when I had it cut up and removed that I understood why.

"It's like this," the tree cutter said. "Oak trees are strong. They have sturdy trunks and branches. But that same quality renders them inflexible." He motioned over to the weeping willow growing by the backyard pond.

"See that?" he asked. "It didn't uproot because it has the ability to bend with the wind. It moved this way and that. Why, I've seen willows doubled over by the wind and the rain. Yet they always rise back up."

He shrugged his shoulders, leaned down, and cranked up his chain saw. Raising his voice over the loud motor, he stated, "As strong as the oaks are, they don't always have the flexibility they need to survive."

Lord, give me the strength of the oak with the flexibility of the willow. That way I can always be strong enough to bend to Your will. —Melody Bonnette Swang

Digging Deeper: Philippians 2:13, 4:13

Thursday, September 29

God said, "Let there be light".... —Genesis 1:3 (JPS)

I've been doing needlepoint for more than forty years. I learned how to stitch in a little shop in west Los Angeles. The owner, who taught the craft to her customers, was generous with her time and knowledge. One of the tips she gave me was to always start a canvas with the darkest yarn and work to the lightest, because the piece would stay cleaner if you didn't put the pale yarn on first.

When my husband got ill, I was his caregiver and there was no time for needlework. I put aside the canvas I'd just begun—a rendering of the first day of creation—and spent every minute with Keith. As he grew less able to do things, I made him the center and compass of my life and gave him all of my time.

Then he died. The first months after that were filled with paperwork and pain. Eventually, I began to emerge into a more normal routine. For the first weeks, I didn't want to be alone for long periods and my friends were very supportive. But I was at a loss to fill the hours at home since I couldn't concentrate on reading or writing or even watching TV. Then I remembered the needlepoint, fished out the canvas, and picked up where I'd left off.

As the weeks passed and the yarn colors changed from black toward pale yellows and white, it wasn't only the work that started with darkness and ended up in light; I began to emerge into the light too.

You communicate with me in so many ways, God, showing me Your light even in the threads of my needlework. —Rhoda Blecker

Digging Deeper: 2 Samuel 22:29

Friday, September 30

"I was a stranger and you welcomed me."
—Matthew 25:35 (NRSV)

For the umpteenth time, my suitcase falls against my seatmate in the cramped train rocking along the Ligurian coast. "I'm so sorry," I say.

She smiles over her novel and says in deliciously accented English, "Not a problem. Don't worry." Though we aren't facing the windows, I can easily view the turquoise Mediterranean Sea over my shoulder.

I've been paralleling it for nearly eight hours and have just crossed the border into Italy. Tonight I have a last-minute booking in Ventimiglia, just over the border. I'm anxious about the unknown hotel and navigating with a vocabulary limited to *ciao* (hello) and *grazie* (thank you).

Since Lorita has been gracious about my suitcase, I dare to ask her if she knows my hotel and show her the directions. She frowns, then announces, "We go together. We ask in the station." *Amid the rush-hour surge!* She speaks to a newsagent who gestures over, around, straight...*oh dear!*

Lorita returns. "It is complicated, so I will take you there. Come." I follow her out of the station, around a plaza, down an alley, past a church tolling the hour, and onto a thoroughfare. Two blocks later, she stops and points. "There is your hotel." I see the marquee, thank her, and we part with kisses, Italian style.

I am delightfully distracted by my fine accommodations, a two-block walk from the pounding surf, and remember a snatch of conversation. "Do you live here?" I had asked Lorita.

"No, I live in Acquadolce. It has a beautiful bridge."

I check my map; Lorita's hometown is twenty minutes farther south!

Grazie, Lorita. Grazie, Lord, for the kindness of strangers. —Gail Thorell Schilling

Digging Deeper: Proverbs 21:21

GOD'S ABIDING LOVE

1 _____

2 _____

3 _____

4 _____

5 _____

6 _____

7 _____

8 _____

9 _____

10 _____

11 _____

12 _____

13 _____

14 _____

15 _____

16 _____

17 _____

18 _____

19 _____

20 _____

21 _____

22 _____

23 _____

24 _____

25 _____

26 _____

27 _____

28 _____

29 _____

30 _____

OCTOBER

Oh give thanks to the Lord, for he is good,
for his steadfast love endures forever!

—Psalm 107:1 (ESV)

WHAT THE SAINTS HAVE TAUGHT ME
Thérèse, Companion in Daily Life

I am small and despised, yet I do not forget thy precepts. —Psalm 119:141 (RSV)

Reading the lives of saints, I often feel overwhelmed. The giants of our faith, the heroes and martyrs, can be daunting company! So I was delighted to meet Thérèse of Lisieux.

You can't be in France long without seeing a photograph of her round young face in its sober nun's wimple and hearing her quiet, undramatic life story. Born in 1873, the youngest of five daughters of a prosperous middle-class family, she lost her mother at age four but was raised by a doting father and sisters. At fifteen she entered the Carmelite convent in her hometown and died there of tuberculosis at twenty-four.

Puzzled as to how this made her "the greatest saint of modern times," I went to visit her childhood home. It's a handsome three-story redbrick mansion set in a large garden, with nothing in the bric-a-brac and massive Victorian-era furniture to suggest sainthood. Silver-framed photos of Thérèse show a sweet-faced child with a mass of wavy blonde hair, dressed in the frilly tucking and bows of the period.

What made Thérèse a saint? Her diary. At her superior's direction, she kept a daily record of the progress of "a very little soul, who can offer only very little things to our Lord." Performing each everyday action, suffering each trivial hardship or unkindness, for love of God, Thérèse found what she called "the Little Way" of spirituality. When the diary was published after her death, the publisher could not keep it in stock. Today millions of ordinary readers, who like me, will never perform great world-shaking deeds, turn to it for guidance in their daily lives.

Help me, Father, to make the routines of this day an offering of praise to You. —Elizabeth Sherrill

Digging Deeper: Hebrews 13:15

Sunday, October 2

Exercise yourself spiritually, and practice being a better Christian because that will help you not only now in this life, but in the next life too. —1 Timothy 4:8 (TLB)

I came across a blank book I'd given to my mother just fifteen months before she died. I had wanted her to record her thoughts and observations as she navigated her way through ALS, the disease that took her life. She made only six entries before she was unable to write. Tucked inside one of the blank pages was a handwritten poem (author unknown) on a slip of paper.

We squander health in search of wealth.
We scheme and toil and save,
then squander wealth in search of health
and all we get is a grave.
We live and boast of what we own,
We die and only get a stone.

Mom must have been having a bad day when she tucked that poem in her journal because the most important gift she left me was her amazing faith. And yet it made me sad when I read those words because even though my mother never squandered her health, she knew she was coming to the end of her life. The more I read that poem, the more I felt I had to write something different and add it to her book:

Life's about morning walks and lengthy talks.
Smelling flowers, enjoying showers.
For writing books, exploring nooks.
I'll squander not my health for wealth.
For when I die, I'll call your bluff.
I'll leave my thoughts, instead of stuff.

As I tucked that little poem into her blank book, I knew that I would try even harder to have a life of beautiful faith in God as Mother did, knowing life in heaven is by far the ultimate gift of our Creator.

Father, thank You for my mother's incredible gift of faith that she handed down to me. —Patricia Lorenz

Digging Deeper: Psalm 42:9–11, Proverbs 17:22, 1 Timothy 4:7–10

Monday, October 3

The patient in spirit is better than the proud in spirit. —Ecclesiastes 7:8 (RSV)

I wasn't in my best form last week when I went to the neighborhood branch bank. Though a few chairs were available, I didn't settle in, content to read a book or pray. I flinch to admit it, but I paced back and forth across the lobby, intentionally trying to make a statement.

Someone eventually called my name, but when I described my request, he didn't know how to expedite it. He offered me coffee, but I'd have to wait for a specific individual and she was still assisting another customer. I returned to my worries and pacing. Finally, a second bank representative stepped out of an enclosed office and asked if he could help. And, yes, he did so, politely and efficiently. "Thank you for your patience," he said with some irony.

"Right," I muttered.

I can't say that I regretted my attitude and silent protest until I returned to the bank yesterday and saw those harried employees. They didn't need or deserve my public display of irritation. They needed my prayers. At least during the workday, they are part of my neighborhood. If I had taken a seat and settled myself, I'd have seen that they are the neighbors I might have spiritually embraced, asking

God that they would thrive in their careers, cope with their demanding workload, and quickly attend to the needs of the waiting queue.

Lord, help me to mind my attitude and mend my restless impatience. —Evelyn Bence

Digging Deeper: Psalm 40, James 5:7–8

Tuesday, October 4

Taste and see that the Lord is good; blessed is the one who takes refuge in him. —Psalm 34:8 (NIV)

The most wonderful thing happened to me recently involving honey. I needed it for a new recipe, and after searching my cupboard I realized I didn't have any. I wrote it down on my shopping list, and when I was at the big-box store I wasn't sure I could use an entire half-gallon. But the price was reasonable, so I made the purchase. As I set it in my cupboard, lo and behold, I found the small jar I'd been looking for earlier.

Two days later I had lunch with an acquaintance who, unbeknownst to me, kept bees. Thanking me for some advice I'd given him, he brought me two quart-size jars of honey.

Then I spoke at a breast cancer awareness luncheon. One of the sponsors distributed honey, and as a special thank-you, the chapter president set aside a large bag full of honey-bear bottles for me to take home. By this time I found the entire honey episode rather amusing.

The next morning, during my devotions, I read that honey is a symbol of God's blessing and abundance. After months of grieving the death of my son, it was as if God had placed His loving arms around me and promised me blessings beyond measure.

Lord, the reminders of Your love are all around me. May I remember to share them with others so they, too, can taste and see that You are good.
—Debbie Macomber

Digging Deeper: Psalm 19:9–10

Wednesday, October 5

Give generously to them and do so without a grudging heart.... —Deuteronomy 15:10 (NIV)

I ran into my neighbor Jessica on the street this morning. She's had a rough year: her teen was in constant rebellion and her junior high kid badly bullied. When we met, she was despairing over how her older child seemed ungrateful and rude all the time.

I hugged her and sighed. "It took me a while to figure out that some kids will learn thoughtfulness from your example and others will simply let you do all the work," I admitted wryly.

Jess nodded grimly. "But what do you do then?" she asked. "I mean, so you don't get utterly depleted?"

"This sounds kind of lame," I offered, "but I've had to learn to figure out *why* I do things. When I'm kind or generous for my kids' sake, I get angry if they react with selfishness. But if I do something thoughtful because that's the kind of person I want to be, I have serenity."

Jess thought about that for a moment and then said, "Yes, but that's hard."

I gave her another hug. "Yeah, but it's not as hard as being angry all the time."

Lord Jesus, teach me to be generous like You: without resentment. —Julia Attaway

Digging Deeper: Romans 12:8–9

Thursday, October 6

Every perfect gift is from above, and comes down from the Father of lights.... —James 1:17 (NKJV)

There's no better way to meet God face-to-face than to say *yes* when He offers you a job. My offer came in 1999, standing on a dirty Zimbabwe city street in the early morning, watching children emerge from back alleys and storm drains. I silently screamed every bad word I knew straight into God's ear. "Why don't You send someone to help these children?"

Silence. Then, as clear as a bell, God answered: *I did. I sent you.*

I had no contacts, few resources, and no clue as to how I could help. That's how I learned that saying yes to the impossible is God's delight.

At first, our goal was to save a few children from starvation, then to support a woman serving them. Next, it was a rural farm where a couple takes in AIDS orphans, raises them in a safe family, and teaches them to reach out to rural people in need. I wrote about our project in *Guideposts* magazine, and a man named Larry sent us a check. That was the first of many. Today, we have a loving network of people still sending money, though we have never asked a single person for any.

God already knew the woman in Hawaii, the banker in New York, the cranberry grower in Wisconsin, the rancher in Texas, the kind lady in Arizona.... He just needed a go-between who would make sure every gift, from milk money to a greenhouse, would go where the giver wanted it to go.

I am where I wanted to be from the beginning: face-to-face with God, seeing Him in the joy of each person who gives.

Father, can I ever adequately thank You for showing Yourself to me through those who give so freely to Your children in need? —Pam Kidd

Digging Deeper: Psalm 13:6, John 16:24

No matter what happens, always be thankful, for this is God's will for you who belong to Christ Jesus.
—1 Thessalonians 5:18 (TLB)

On a recent visit to Colorado, I drilled my youngest grandson, Caden, on words for his Friday spelling test. Spelling is not his favorite subject, but he managed to get all twenty words right before he headed off to school.

When Caden returned that afternoon, he showed me his weekly school report. It wasn't from the teacher, as I expected, but was his own listing of "highs" and "lows." Some of the high points were predictable: "I got to miss school to play in a hockey tournament"; "I liked learning about medieval England." To my surprise he also listed "spelling test" as a high. "I only missed one word and it's a whole week before another test," he explained. "So my week was all highs, no lows."

I wish my week was like that! I thought. Lately I seemed to have all lows, no highs. My granddaughter was struggling with health issues. I had developed some back and hip joint problems. Continued drought meant lower yields for our corn crop.

I looked at Caden's report again. Could it be that my viewpoint was faulty? After all, we'd had the pleasure of watching him play hockey, plus a good visit with a son and daughter-in-law. Our grandsons were all well. Our granddaughter was receiving helpful therapy. My health issues were annoying and sometimes painful, but not serious. Our corn would yield enough to pay expenses plus some.

My week had lots of highs. I just needed help from a ten-year-old and a spelling test to see them.

Lord Jesus, there will always be highs and lows in life. Thank You for helping me understand that the difference between them is often my attitude.
—Penney Schwab

Digging Deeper: John 16:33, Philippians 4:8

Saturday, October 8

But the Comforter, which is the Holy Ghost, whom the Father will send in my name, he shall...bring all things to your remembrance.... —John 14:26 (KJV)

I was visiting a class the other day, and a boy asked me about memory and writing, and I have been pondering that odd lovely marriage ever since. I tried to tell him this: I believe that everything that ever happened to me is inside me somehow, and if I can only find the key, then I can unlock a moment, a remark, a joke, a terror, a tumult, an epiphany. A snippet of song is a key, a sidelong scent, a certain angle of light—anything. And always it's unexpected, and you cannot seek it out but just be open to it when it arrives, startled.

I see a little girl, age four, hopscotching in the playground, and instantly it's fifteen years ago and she is my daughter, leaping from Oregon all the way to Maine, Dad! And she still holds my pinkie when we walk, and she is not yet a teenager sometimes so surly that I have to go fold laundry to calm down. An old man on the train unfolds his eyeglasses and I am six and he is my grandfather and we are going to the city to see the Knicks. I smell bleach in a school hallway and my son, now twenty, is suddenly two again and I am desperate in a hospital hallway, watching him be carried to surgery.

It all abides in you, brothers and sisters. There is no passage of time, only a wholly inefficient storage system. The dead are not dead when you see and hear and speak of them. We mourn lost time and love, but the only duty is to remember and sing the glory of what was, so as to save it from the thirsty void. What else can we do but sing? What else can we do?

Lord, I assume that someday I will lose what there is of my muddled intellect and weirdly excellent memory, and when that happens I will be sad. But meanwhile thanks for letting me remember pretty much every sweet moment I ever had. —Brian Doyle

Digging Deeper: Psalm 96

Sunday, October 9

"Abigail...was a woman of good understanding and beautiful appearance...." —1 Samuel 25:3 (NKJV)

It's Sunday morning. I am standing in the church foyer, admiring my wife through the big window of the church library, where she sits at the librarian's desk. She is smartly dressed in navy blue, with a red pearl necklace and matching earrings. She is animated, laughing, charming the patrons who have come to chat and sample her homemade chocolate chip cookies. "Librarian" can be a tedious job, but Sharon has made it festive.

She has done many things in her life: full-time mother, literature professor, teacher's aide, public speaker. But this volunteer job seems to bring all of her best gifts into focus: her knowledge of literature and people, her understanding, her hospitality.

Church members are looking for more than books at her library; they are looking for wisdom. "What would be good for an eight-year-old boy who has picked up some swear words?" a desperate mother asks.

"*Hmm,* it sounds to me like he has a problem with anger. Here's a book on helping people with anger issues," Sharon says. "If you can get his temper under control, the words should fade away, I think."

As I watch church members come under her spell, I am convinced that what we do instead of our real job *is* our real job.

Maybe there's not much I can do about my regular job. It is what it is. But somewhere there is a volunteer job that will bring out all of my best instincts. A job that will use all of me, body and soul. No, there won't be a paycheck and gold watch when I retire, but there will be a sense of satisfaction, knowing that I am doing this for God alone and not for my glory.

Somewhere, Lord, there is a volunteer job with my name on it. Something I was born to do. Help me to find it. —Daniel Schantz

Digging Deeper: Nehemiah 4:6, Isaiah 6:8

Monday, October 10

He will cover you with his feathers, and under his wings you will find refuge.... —Psalm 91:4 (NIV)

I headed into the local Caribbean restaurant to have lunch. Normally I eat a sandwich at my desk, but this particularly stressful day I felt like treating myself to a Spanish meal. The smells alone took me back to my *abuela's* (grandmother's) kitchen.

I sat at the table, just like when I was a little girl waiting to be served. Even the setting was similar, with a layer of plastic over the floral print tablecloth. An older woman with a warm smile placed the familiar platter of white rice and black beans with roasted chicken in front of me, with a salad with avocados on the side. Other women from the family-owned business sat at a nearby table, peeling a large white hill of garlic as they chatted in Spanish. The television above them showed an overly dramatic *tele-novela* (soap opera) like the ones I used to watch with my abuela.

For a moment, I wasn't the busy children's director at work or the overtaxed mother of two boys. I was a child in my abuela's kitchen, eating her wonderful food, listening to her beautiful language, and feeling the warmth and safety of her home.

I no longer felt the stress I walked in with. Though my abuela is gone and I'm a grown woman with much responsibility, I'm still God's little girl.

Gracias, Dios, for showing me that no matter what, I will always be Your precious child. —Karen Valentin

Digging Deeper: John 1:12

Tuesday, October 11

"You are a good and faithful servant! You've been faithful over a little. I'll put you in charge of much. Come, celebrate with me." —Matthew 25:21 (CEB)

Football is all about numbers: yards gained, penalties assessed, time remaining on the clock. But in the end there's only one set that really counts: who won and who lost. Or so I thought, until I watched an interview with Nick Saban, the University of Alabama football coach, considered by many to be at the very top of his profession. What, the interviewer asked him, was the key to his sustained success, to all those wins? "Don't worry about winning," Saban said. "Just focus on doing your job at the highest level, every single play, and the wins will follow."

Easy for him to say, I remember thinking. Until I related that quote to a friend of mine the following day.

"He's exactly right," Susan said. "Last year, I set a goal of writing two books in a year. It was such a big goal, it paralyzed me. I couldn't do it. But guess what? This year, writing just twice a week for my blog, I've done over 115,000 words. The average book is about sixty thousand words, so I've written two books after all."

What does all that mean for you and me right now? I think it means setting aside those big goals—a promotion, losing seventy pounds, winning a bake-off—that can seem unreachable. I'll try to keep things simple: writing one supportive e-mail each day, taking one volunteer opportunity each week, making prayer a twice-daily pattern, "doing my job every single play."

Thanks, Coach Saban. And good luck this season... though I suspect you'll do just fine.

Whatever I do today, God, help me to give it my best effort, trusting that You will use it for Your ultimate ends. —Jeff Japinga

Digging Deeper: Matthew 25:14–30, Galatians 5:16–26

Wednesday, October 12

You know when I sit down and when I rise up; you discern my thoughts from far away. You search out my path and my lying down, and are acquainted with all my ways. —Psalm 139:2–3 (NRSV)

It was bedtime prayers with Frances. The evening was warm, so my seven-year-old lay outstretched on the sheets. Her feet, I noticed, reached close to the bottom of the bed. I couldn't help myself. "You're so tall, sweetheart!" I exclaimed, forgetting that kids find such obvious statements ridiculous.

Frances said nothing and I went on, caught up in memories. "I remember the day you were born. I could hold you with one arm, just like this." I made a cradling motion. "I used to hold you right up to my face and talk to you all day long. And I could make you fall asleep just by wrapping you in a swaddling blanket and sitting in the rocking chair, patting your back. *Zonk*, you were out. And now you're so big, becoming such a grown-up girl, with your gymnastics and your schoolwork. I just love what a strong, clever, interesting person you're becoming."

I stopped myself. Frances must have been quite embarrassed by now, so it was back to the prayers.

But Frances wasn't embarrassed. Grinning, she sat up, threw her arms around my neck, and squeezed tight. "I love you, Daddy," she said, giving me a rare kiss on the cheek. Then she lay back down.

I thought of Psalm 139:1 (NRSV): "O Lord, you have searched me and known me." Maybe, I thought, my memories weren't just nostalgia. Maybe they gave Frances a glimpse of the immensity of my love for her—a glimpse of even greater Love searching and knowing us both.

Today, Lord, I will rest secure in Your love for me and I will share that love with others. —Jim Hinch

Digging Deeper: Jeremiah 1:4–5, Matthew 10:29–31

Thursday, October 13

He explores the mountains for his pasture and searches after every green thing. —Job 39:8 (NAS)

How do I tell the story of a mountain beagle named Lucy? A low-to-the-ground patchwork wonder who roamed woods and fields fearlessly. Who wasn't afraid to chase off a bear. Who thought all deer were hers to annoy. Who didn't let what *could* be there—wolves, cougars, moose—stop her.

I met Lucy only a year ago, on trips to north Idaho's Gold Cup Mountain prior to our move here three months ago. She was the mountain icon poking her free spirit everywhere. She belonged to everyone, although she lived with Leroy down the road. I felt braver traversing the mountain with Lucy along.

An outdoor animal of at least twelve, she was an independent thinker who knew how to take care of herself without complaint. Yet, she accompanied residents and visitors alike for most any reason... and if you were inclined, she'd sit and be petted, look at the view, and share your muse. When I saw her withdrawn in a nest of pine needles the other evening, something didn't seem right. Two days later Leroy was transporting her to the vet. Her kidneys were failing.

We lost her today. Leroy buried her in her favorite spot beneath the pie cherry tree. She's back on the mountain where she belongs, only not in the way I had hoped. I wanted the pleasure of her presence... I wanted more time.

In the months we had, Lucy inspired me to stretch beyond discomfort and fear, to walk my path confidently, to welcome detours. A small ball of fur on a big mountain, she never considered the odds. Lucy only measured in opportunities, and they were all her size.

Dear Lord, Lucy was such a servant from Your animal kingdom. I can see her brown eyes now bidding me on to the next opportunity. —Carol Knapp

Digging Deeper: Genesis 9:8–17, Isaiah 32:15–18, Hebrews 11:1

Friday, October 14

Where can I go from your Spirit? Where can I flee from your presence? If I go up to the heavens, you are there; if I make my bed in the depths, you are there. —Psalm 139:7–8 (NIV)

The news came unexpectedly in the form of a tiny report: the adoption agency my brother and sister-in-law were working with was being shut down for fraud. Overnight, every family, child, and employee associated with the company was cut off from information, from much-loved and much-wanted kids, from hope.

My nephew "E"—the baby we had prayed for, saved for, treasured through photos, and dreamed of holding—was still waiting for an official exit visa from his country of origin. While he legally belonged in my brother's family, it would now take miles of paperwork and thousands of dollars to get him home. It was one of those moments when the entire world tilted and God's voice seemed to go silent.

But God was there—working miracles, answering prayers, standing firm when all else crumbled. He was there when we started to doubt if He had really led my brother's family to this adoption to begin with. He was there when officials met to decide the fate of these lost children. He was even there when we found out the agency not only stripped away the hope of hundreds, but also stole the hard-earned dollars of families whose hearts were with these precious kids.

And now in our darkest moments, God, in His all-knowing and all-powerful glory, is carefully orchestrating a plan. Because of that, I know He will be there when dear "E" is finally carried off that plane and into our waiting arms.

Lord, in my darkest moments, fill me with the Your presence. Just knowing that You are there is all the comfort I need. Amen. —Erin MacPherson

Digging Deeper: Joshua 1:9, Romans 8:38

Saturday, October 15

Even to your old age I am he, and to gray hairs I will carry you. I have made, and I will bear; I will carry and will save. —Isaiah 46:4 (ESV)

Huffing and puffing, my golden retriever, Millie, and I reached our usual trail juncture on this particular mountain hike in western Massachusetts. We sat on our respective rocks and had our usual water break. The day could not have been more to my liking. We were a week or so beyond "fall peak." I love this stage of autumn when most of the leaves have dropped, but a few spectacular ones still rage against the dying light (to borrow from poet Dylan Thomas). I like the air getting crisper and the smell of cold dirt. It seems that everything important in my life has happened in the fall. Each time it feels like I am returning to a place of glory.

Millie's booming bark informs me that I have done sufficient reflecting. She is standing expectantly at the head of Indian Monument Trail. I'm surprised. Usually my big, strong, one-hundred-pound retriever insists on Squaw Peak Trail to the top. Steep and rugged, it has glorious views along its jagged cliffs. I've had arguments with Millie over which route we'll take when I thought we'd done enough steep climbing for the day. Now here she was urging us to take what we'd always called "the old lady's trail."

Millie is almost pure white from tail to nose, yet somehow I know the white on her muzzle has grown a touch whiter of late. Her flanks expand like bellows as she stands there panting. Secretly I'm glad about not going up Squaw Peak. I wasn't sure I had that gear today and I knew I'd feel it that night.

As a baby boomer, I was conditioned to never give in to age. Now I hear myself say, "I guess we're getting old, aren't we, Mil?"

Another bark. She doesn't seem bothered by it. Really, neither should I.

God, You are with me through all the seasons of my life, especially the one I am entering now, my favorite. —Edward Grinnan

Digging Deeper: Proverbs 16:31

Sunday, October 16

"See, I am sending an angel ahead of you to guard you along the way and to bring you to the place I have prepared." —Exodus 23:20 (NIV)

I'm in bed in beautiful twilight sleep, where I'm just about to drift off when I hear it: *You have to check that date. The big meeting is tomorrow.*

Tomorrow? I think to myself, opening my eyes. *I'm pretty sure it's the day after. I checked it yesterday.*

You'd better check again. The nudge is persistent and now my eyes are open, looking at the clock. I groan, flipping back the covers and getting up. There's no point in trying to go back to sleep now without making sure. Otherwise, I'll just lie here and worry.

Grudgingly, I walk to my office in the dark. It's bad enough I'm awake; I don't want to bother the rest of the house. I open my laptop. "This is pointless. I know it's not tomorrow," I mutter.

I log in to my e-mail and look at my schedule. I scroll to tomorrow and see the bright-red, high-priority, exclamation-marked meeting. How on earth had I been wrong? I do have a meeting. Tomorrow morning, first thing. If I hadn't checked, I'd have been too late to make it. Now I can shift a few things and everything will be fine.

Back in bed, I reach over to the clock and change the alarm for an hour earlier. Closing my eyes, I say thank You to God and to the heavenly angel who nudged me awake and saved the day.

Dear Lord, thank You for caring about the details in my life and for sending an angel to help keep my appointments. —Sabra Ciancanelli

Digging Deeper: Psalms 91:11, 103:20

Monday, October 17

But if a woman has long hair, it is her glory?...
—1 Corinthians 11:15 (NRSV)

I rarely have a bad hair day. Aside from two frizzy perms and one unfortunate hair-coloring episode years ago, I'm happy with my blow-and-go do. I should have left well enough alone, but two days before leaving for Turkey and my son and daughter-in-law's wedding reception, I chanced a trim with a new stylist.

Big mistake. She lopped off at least an inch too much, so instead of graceful shoulder-length hair, my neck stood out like a stalk. I looked ridiculous.

No sooner had I begun to mourn the damage than I thought of an e-mail from Cathy. She had posted a new photo, her head covered in a brilliant scarf of fiery colors so suited to her dark eyes—a scarf to cover her baldness from chemotherapy. Her upbeat letter shamed me instantly.

I wish I could report that I never again thought of my hair, but I'd be fibbing. Whenever I pass a mirror or even just recall my gawky hairstyle, I still wince. Then I remember Cathy with no hair at all and pray for her continued healing. Thanks to my botched haircut, I now pray for her a dozen times a day instead of just in the morning. I trust that soon her cancer—and my vanity—will both disappear.

Compassionate Father, please heal my friend Cathy and forgive me when I fuss over trivial things.
—Gail Thorell Schilling

Digging Deeper: Ecclesiastes 1:2, Romans 8:28

FINDING REST: From Death to Life

He said, "Go away; for the girl is not dead but
sleeping." And they laughed at him.... He went
in and took her by the hand, and the girl got up.
—Matthew 9:24–25 (NRSV)

This story of Jesus raising the little girl is one of the
first Gospels I remember from childhood. It could
be because of the fascinating events leading up to
Jesus coming to the house, or how He reprimands
the mourners and is derided, or His astonishing
statement that the girl is sleeping, not dead.

Most likely it is because when I was eight, my best
friend was dying of cancer. I knew she would die. I went
to the hospital with my parents. I watched her regress
from a little girl's bed to a large crib, so she wouldn't fall
out as she became smaller and frailer. I saw her mother
and my mother, also best friends, cry together. When
she died, I wanted Jesus to come and say, "Don't cry.
Don't worry. She's just asleep. Watch this!"

A few years later, when both of my grandfathers
died, I wanted the same thing. *Come, Jesus. Say they
are just asleep and You will wake them.*

At every funeral, a minister would say something
about meeting again in the future when we would
be at rest and at peace together. As a child, that time
seemed like a long way off; I couldn't wait! As an

adult, I've come to see how all those that I've "lost" aren't lost to me at all. They are part of me, shaping who I am, firing my faith, making me love Scripture passages about God's power over death. And when I rest with them in Jesus, Who can waken us from death to life, there are others who will remain here and I will become part of them.

Jesus, as I come closer to the end of this life, help me to trustfully and joyfully anticipate resting in You with all of those who have gone before me. Amen. —Marci Alborghetti

Digging Deeper: Matthew 10:29–31, Luke 7:28

Wednesday, October 19

But God has surely listened and has heard my prayer. —Psalm 66:19 (NIV)

I scanned my bookshelves and pulled out a hodgepodge of old prayer journals. I made myself comfortable on the couch and began my search. Guideposts had recently sent out a request for prayers to include in the *Daily Guideposts Prayer Companion*. I wanted to see if there were any that I might be able to submit.

As I sat there, flipping through the journals, a sense of awe overwhelmed me—so much so that I had to stop and blink back tears. Every single journal was filled with prayers—ones that didn't come to fruition and those that did. There were prayers I remembered and prayers I'd forgotten all about. There were big prayers about infertility, adoption, my dreams for my family and my career. There were small, everyday prayers that seemed silly and insignificant all these years later.

However, it wasn't the prayers that left me in awe. It was the fact that God heard every single one. None of them fell on deaf ears or got lost in the cacophony of human pleas. How amazing that we worship a God Who bottles our tears and hears our cries!

What an awesome God You are, to hear every last one of my prayers! Thank You that I can trust my prayers to You, knowing You will answer according to what is best. —Katie Ganshert

Digging Deeper: Psalm 18:6, Hebrews 4:16

Thursday, October 20

"Blessed is she who has believed that the Lord would fulfill his promises to her!" —Luke 1:45 (NIV)

A few days ago I learned that my friend Jaynie's stage-four cancer had recurred. Tests showed the growth of new tumors.

I'm a stage-four ovarian cancer survivor, almost ten years beyond a diagnosis that gave me a two-year life expectancy. When I hear about someone who's just been diagnosed or who's had a recurrence, the news opens a place deep inside me where I've stored the memories that still feel fresh. I long to connect with that person but recognize that each one's journey is uniquely individual. Some welcome connection; others need privacy.

When I got up early this morning, I prayed for Jaynie in the still darkness and then wrote her an e-mail ending with: "Today I'm claiming this Bible verse for you. It's what Elizabeth told Mary when she faced the preposterous news of her pregnancy as a not-yet-married woman. What an enormous challenge to trust God's faithfulness in her unknown future. Elizabeth said, *'Blessed is she who has believed that what the Lord has said to her will be accomplished!'* I pray that as you continue your journey, you will be blessed by believing what God has told you. Day by day. Trusting that He will light your way and accomplish what He promises."

For a moment, I wondered whether to send the message. Would I be intruding? Or sound self-serving? I paused, then hit the Send button.

Lord, You redeem our pain and suffering when we share prayers with others going through experiences similar to our own. Please surround my friend with light-bringers on her journey. —Carol Kuykendall

Digging Deeper: Psalm 119:105, Proverbs 3:26

"Sing to the Lord a new song...." —Psalm 149:1 (NIV)

Some time ago I made a commitment to pray daily for my friend Gloria, who has metastasized breast cancer. Gloria is a musician, both at church and in my favorite anecdote about her, in which, as a teenager, she was always getting in trouble for being cranky at breakfast. She prayed about the problem, she says, and soon found herself waking up each morning with a beloved hymn in her mind.

Inspired by her story, I decided to pray whatever song entered my mind in a given day for Gloria—with some surprising results. I discovered that I'm regularly visited by almost forgotten hymns from my childhood. And lines that once bothered me, like "The Father turned His face away" from Jesus on the cross, acquired new significance: God can't bear to see His children suffer.

Although I was praying these songs for Gloria, certain lines like "I nothing lack if I am His!" lodged in my own consciousness and comforted me for weeks.

Not every day's song was a hymn, of course. I prayed "King of the Bongo" to God for Gloria and "Hello my baby, hello my honey, hello my ragtime gal!" and James Taylor's "Something in the Way She Moves." I often heard such songs in my mind as God singing to Gloria—His baby, His ragtime gal, His beloved, who'd been with Him now such "a long, long time."

Every day's song, even the quirkiest, broadened my knowledge of God's love, not only for Gloria but for me.

How delightful songs are, Lord! Surely we inherited the urge to sing from You. —Patty Kirk

Digging Deeper: Psalm 40

Saturday, October 22

Contribute to the needs of God's people, and welcome strangers into your home. —Romans 12:13 (CEB)

For the men's dinner at church, my pal C.J. was cooking up a storm in the parish house kitchen—a true Oktoberfest. More than twenty guys had signed up, and C.J. looked like he was well prepared. We'd have plenty.

I was setting the tables when the doorbell rang. I opened the door to a nice-looking young couple pushing a child in a stroller. "Could we talk to a minister?" the man asked.

I found our pastor and went back to setting the table, but I couldn't help overhearing the conversation that ensued. The couple said they were looking for a meal. They'd heard we have a soup kitchen on

Saturdays. But as was explained, the soup kitchen was finished by noon, with over two hundred people served, and nothing remained. "We're having a men's dinner tonight," our pastor said. "They might have a little extra food."

The next thing I knew, C.J. was spooning out two deep dishes of sauerkraut, sausages, potatoes, salad, ham, and apple strudel. They went to that young couple, our first guests—not the ones who'd been invited, but the ones who had appeared and were in need.

I was reminded of the parable Jesus told of a man who hosted a feast and invited many, but all of them made excuses about why they couldn't come. Finally he said to his servant, "Go quickly to the city's streets, the busy ones and the side streets, and bring the poor, crippled, blind, and lame.... Go to the highways and back alleys and urge people to come in so that my house will be filled" (Luke 14:21, 23, CEB).

Our parish house was full indeed that night for a fine evening of faith, fellowship, and hearty food. Nearly thirty guys showed up—more than expected—but our best guests were the first ones served, a pair from the streets of a busy city.

In Your world, there is always plenty, Lord. Help me to share. —Rick Hamlin

Digging Deeper: Psalm 23:5, Luke 14:13

Sunday, October 23

If any of you lacks wisdom, you should ask God…and it will be given to you. —James 1:5–6 (NIV)

The television spewed a hissing noise and white fuzz covered the screen. I glanced at my watch. The show with the wild horses, which a friend at work had told me about, was starting. Knowing that I don't watch TV, he even gave me the channel. But try as I might, I couldn't get reception. It was as frustrating as the last few days of my prayer life. I'd been asking for advice, but I couldn't find God's channel either.

The next day I was greeted with, "Wasn't that show incredible?"

"I couldn't get reception," I replied, shrugging my shoulders.

"Did you ever hook up the box that switches the signal from analog to digital?" he asked.

I nearly melted under my desk, embarrassed. What seemed like forever ago I'd purchased the box. But since I don't watch TV, I hadn't hooked it up and completely forgot about it. All I needed was the black box. How simple was that? Then a thought pricked my mind: *And my answers are in the black book. All I need to do is still my thoughts and meditate on God's.*

In my prayer time the next morning, I switched my analog thoughts for God's digital ones. I had the solution.

Lord, when I'm looking for answers, please remind me to rest in Your Word. Amen. —Rebecca Ondov

Digging Deeper: James 1:6–8

Monday, October 24

The wilderness and the wasteland shall be glad for them, and the desert shall rejoice and blossom as the rose.... —Isaiah 35:1 (NKJV)

So I'm standing at the edge of the Kubuqi Desert in Inner Mongolia, holding a shovel. I'm part of the University of Pittsburgh's contingent to Future Forests, a Chinese/Korean/American student project aimed at combating the spreading desert by planting hundreds of thousands of trees—an undertaking that will go on for years, maybe decades. We're here at the invitation of former South Korean Ambassador Kwon Byong Hyon, the founder of Future Forest and a loyal Pitt grad.

This is hard work. To secure the newly planted trees against the relentless wind, you first affix a square wooden framework in the sand. Each frame is homemade—a cluster of sticks tied together with twine and embedded into the plot. Before me are scores of students kneeling, hats tied under their chins and bandannas around their mouths to shield against the blowing sand, deftly tying twigs together, digging holes, planting, watering, starting again.

Standing back, taking in the larger, breathtaking picture, makes this venture seem fruitless. Could hundreds (thousands, millions) of trees really stop a relentless desert, whose ever-shifting, ever-expanding sand blows thousands of miles, adding to the pollution woes of cities like Beijing, sometimes all the way to Seoul?

But that's not what I see. I see commitment against the wind, the odds. With their bandannas pulled high and hats pulled low, it's impossible to tell who's Chinese or Korean or American. And Whoever is looking down upon us as we hurtle through space, third rock from the sun, sees the same thing: a bevy of young people laboring together to make a desert blossom. It's work that's good for Seoul. It's good for any soul.

Lord, lift the veil from our eyes and let us see what You see: people as people, in unity and peace.
—Mark Collins

Digging Deeper: Deuteronomy 32:10, Job 24:5

Tuesday, October 25

The heavens declare the glory of God; and the firmament shows His handiwork. —Psalm 19:1 (NKJV)

"What a rotten day," I growled at the darkness, lit only by my headlights on the narrow, windy mountain road. I was driving back to the family ranch, thirty-five miles from town, after an extremely stressful meeting. I slouched in the seat, letting my worries hang around my shoulders like an anchor. "This is horrible, Lord," I prayed or, rather, complained. "What a terrible world this is."

I rounded a corner and, lo, before me was the moon, so full and large it seemed to pervade the whole sky. Moonlight reflected in a nearby stream, turning it into glowing silver as it zigzagged in a shimmering path across an open field.

It took my breath away. I was in the middle of God's majestic handiwork. The seemingly monumental weight of my burdens vanished in the awesome splendor of the painted landscape. *What can mere man do that is more powerful or can last longer than this?* I thought. Even though my problems had felt enormous, God was bigger and far more powerful.

My worries evaporated. Just as the moonlight filled the quiet stream with an overflowing glow, God's peaceful beauty replenished my troubled heart with overflowing joy. I needed only to look around to remember He was everlasting and only a prayer away.

Lord, "I will lift up mine eyes unto the hills, from whence cometh my help" (Psalm 121:1 KJV).
—Erika Bentsen

Digging Deeper: Psalms 24:7, 150:2; Luke 9:43

Wednesday, October 26

So we have known and believe the love that God has for us. God is love, and those who abide in love abide in God, and God abides in them.
—1 John 4:16 (NRSV)

You know how you listen to an old song later on in your life and it has a completely different meaning? That happened to me just the other day. I was in the grocery store, and "I Love You Just the Way You Are" by Billy Joel came across the speakers. As I absently hummed along to this "oldie but goodie," a strange notion came to mind: *Billy Joel is a theologian.* As I paid closer attention to the lyrics, the song suddenly transformed from one that some guy wrote for his wife to an exchange of love between God and me. I stopped looking for my favorite brand of strained tomatoes and listened.

I listened as the lyrics talked about seeing me and accepting me just as I am. I listened to lyrics that told me I would never be left alone, even in times of trouble. I listened as the lyrics spoke of a love beyond comprehension.

Sometimes God shows up in the grocery store to tell you that you are loved, even in your sweats and ponytail, standing in the middle of the aisle, listening to Muzak! I'm sure that's not what was intended when that song was added to the store's playlist. I'm sure its objective probably had more to do with sensory shopping. Still, I'm glad for that unexpected moment of connection with the Divine and the reminder that I am known and loved.

Hey, God, I love You too. Amen. —Natalie Perkins

Digging Deeper: Psalm 139:13–16,
1 Corinthians 13

Thursday, October 27

...Shew I unto you a more excellent way.
—1 Corinthians 12:31 (KJV)

I have a stubborn nature and tend to resent instruction. Not because I don't need it. I do.

My husband's daughter Shelly came to see us when Gene broke his hip. She's a speech therapist and a sharp cookie. Shelly delights in helping people. When we went to visit him at the Oaks Rehab, she quickly told me that taking the loop around the city was faster than the familiar way I traveled.

"I like my way," I told her. The next day I complained that the padded little rug at our kitchen sink was hard to clean.

"Just throw it in the washing machine," Shelley said. I ignored the comment. As we got into my car one day, she observed that our garage door opener wasn't functioning properly.

"See that chain. It's a bit loose. Better call someone before the motor blows up."

"It's working fine." I opened and shut the door several times to prove my point.

"You really need to call a garage door company. Now."

Shelly had to get back to her school in California, and I took her to a bus that would get her to the airport. We hugged, and I promised to keep her updated about Gene's progress. Then I went home and washed the green rug in the washing machine. It came out looking brand-new. When I opened the garage door to back out my car, it wouldn't move an inch. The man who came to repair it said, "Sorry. You'll have to have a new motor. You blew the old one by continuing to use it when the chain became loose."

Driving to see Gene that day, I took Shelly's route. Only fifteen minutes to get to the Oaks instead of my twenty-five.

Father, show me how to gratefully receive instructions.
—Marion Bond West

Digging Deeper: Isaiah 6:5–6, Luke 7:18

Friday, October 28

"My stronghold and my refuge, my savior; you save me from violence." —2 Samuel 22:3 (ESV)

I wasn't sure I'd be much help on a mission trip to Appalachian Kentucky. I volunteered to teach a Bible study; our main purpose was construction work. But I'll never forget a certain downtrodden woman. Spotting her, I thought, *She's why I'm here.*

Keeping her gaze on the ground, she held her children's hands and entered the shelter where we served meals. I smiled and motioned for her to sit with me.

"I had to get away from my husband," she whispered. "I was afraid to leave him, but I had to protect the children." Her deep blue eyes searched mine. She wanted to know on some level that I understood, that I cared.

Oh, how I cared! I'd never been in her position, but months earlier one of our daughters phoned around midnight. Her dad answered. I heard him say: "Get in the car and come home. Don't look back. Leave. Now."

Sitting beside this woman, I said, "I understand." Tears caught in my throat. "You've done a brave thing. I'm proud of you."

I noticed a crochet needle and a ball of red yarn in her tattered purse. "Are you coming by for breakfast tomorrow? I'd like to tell you good-bye."

"I'll be here."

Early the next morning, I bought a dozen skeins of red yarn. "For you." I handed my new friend the yarn. "Anytime you consider going back, get busy making a blanket. You wrap yourself and your children in it, the same way God wraps us in His love. You'll be safe."

Her eyes filled with grateful tears. "Thank you. I will."

"You promise?"

"I promise."

> **Lord, that precious woman and my own daughter . . . thank You. You rescued them.**
> —Julie Garmon

Digging Deeper: 2 Thessalonians 3:3, 1 Peter 2:9

Saturday, October 29

Lo, I am with you always, even unto the end of the world. Amen. —Matthew 28:20 (KJV)

I turned sixty-five. Somehow, I never really expected to turn sixty-five. At eighteen, sixty-five seemed farther away than Halley's Comet; in my misspent youth, I doubted I'd live long enough to get there. The truth is I don't feel sixty-five, or at least it doesn't feel like I'd imagined it would. Oh sure, I've got an ache here and a pain there, but nothing serious. I always get a shock of surprise when I look in the mirror and see this guy with neck bands (yes, that's what they're called) and a white beard looking back at me.

But there was one thing about turning sixty-five I'd been looking forward to. On my birthday morning, I put on a jacket and walked briskly to the subway. I got off in the Financial District, spent twenty minutes getting lost within its winding streets, and finally found the building I was looking for. The ground-floor office was full of people my age and older, all with the look people get when they have to sit around in government offices. I got in line and then handed in my paperwork. The clerk told me to take a seat until my name was called. When it was, I had my picture taken. Fifteen minutes later, there was my photo, neck bands and all, looking back at me from its shiny surface: my half-fare Metrocard!

I found my way back to the subway, swiped my card, and heard the satisfying *ching* permitting me to go through. As an official senior citizen, I took my seat on the train, and my thoughts took a more serious turn. There are more wonderful things than a discount awaiting me at the end of my journey, and I won't need a Metrocard to get there.

Lord, it's Your grace that's brought me safe
thus far; may that same grace lead me home.
—Andrew Attaway

Digging Deeper: Genesis 28:15, Exodus 40:38

Sunday, October 30

But when you pray, go into your room, close the door and pray to your Father, who is unseen. Then your Father, who sees what is done in secret, will reward you. —Matthew 6:6 (NIV)

At lunch one afternoon, my mother-in-law mentioned her prayer closet. "Prayer closet?" I asked. Peggy explained that she'd designated a special place in her home, free from distractions, to meet God.

That's what I need, I thought. When I sit down to have my Bible study at the dining table, my mind wanders. Chores, bills, errands, and e-mails volley for my attention. *I bet I could focus on God better if I had a nice, comfortable spot.*

Peggy has exquisite taste. I imagined her stylish nook with lavish decorations—maybe she used an animal-print fabric with turquoise or bold-red accents. Had she fashioned an altar with faith icons and other symbols? Maybe she put a comfy chair in the corner of her immaculate walk-in closet.

Days later, I stopped by her house. Peggy led me through the laundry room to a door. She flipped on the light. I followed her inside the storage area underneath the staircase. We walked about ten paces past cleaning supplies and shelves stocked with canned goods. We turned the corner. "Watch your head," she said, crouching low into a hidey-hole spot about four feet high by three feet wide. There were large throw pillows on the floor and shelves bare except for a metal cross and candle. It wasn't at all what I'd envisioned!

Peggy must have sensed my disappointment. "My first instinct was to decorate, but once I came in here I discovered the emptiness was liberating. Instead of filling this space with stuff, I want to fill myself with God."

God, show me my unlikely, humble prayer closet where I can focus solely on You.
—Stephanie Thompson

Digging Deeper: 2 Chronicles 7:14, Luke 18:10–14

Monday, October 31

"For my thoughts are not your thoughts, neither are your ways my ways," declares the Lord.
—Isaiah 55:8 (NIV)

On a family trip to New York City, the last place I expected to see something interesting was on the hotel room's bathroom wall. But there it was, a sampling of incomplete sentences written in script, some of the phrases covered by a smoke detector.

Part of one line was clear: "...the world our way not his way."

At the bottom were the author's name and the title "Manifesto." I made a note to look it up later, but sightseeing doesn't allow much time for research and I reminded myself, *It's just words on a bathroom wall.*

Yet during those many subway rides around the city, I found myself coming back to that haunting line: "...the world our way not his way." I struggled to put the words into context. The more I thought of it, the answer seemed obvious: the line was speaking to human beings' insistence on seeing the world our way instead of God's way. Over the course of the vacation, I prayed about my tendency to see things from an earthly perspective and asked God if I might see the world through His eyes.

Several days after we were back home in Alabama, I looked up the full text. It was about art, not God: "It is our function as artists to make the spectator see the world our way not his way."

Perhaps people are right when they say art is subjective. If we look for spiritual guidance, we can find it anywhere...even on a bathroom wall.

Help me to see the world through Your eyes, Lord.
—Ginger Rue

Digging Deeper: 1 Samuel 16:7, Luke 16:15

GOD'S ABIDING LOVE

1 _____

2 _____

3 _____

4 _____

5 _____

6 _____

7 _____

8 _____

9 _____

10 _____

11 _____

12 _____

13 _____

14 _____

15 _____

16 _____

17 _____

18 _____

19 _____

20 _____

21 _____

22 _____

23 _____

24 _____

25 _____

26 _____

27 _____

28 _____

29 _____

30 _____

31 _____

NOVEMBER

*And let us not grow weary of doing good,
for in due season we will reap, if we do not give up.*

—Galatians 6:9 (ESV)

Tuesday, November 1

Bear with each other and forgive one another if any of you has a grievance against someone. Forgive as the Lord forgave you. —Colossians 3:13 (NIV)

As I was cleaning my home with my playlist on shuffle, the song I had danced to with my father on my wedding day came up. After my divorce and for a number of years, I might have turned it off or changed the song. But as I listened to it now, it made my heart happy.

I remembered that dance, cheek resting on my father's shoulder and feeling all of his love for me, his little girl. I felt grateful for my wedding day. Despite a failed marriage, I got to experience my father walking me down the aisle. I was able to see and feel the love and support of so many who still love and support me today. It was a fun-filled occasion and a celebration of love in so many ways.

And as justified as I can feel at times to despise my ex-husband, that will never happen. There were great times, he was part of my life, and we have two beautiful boys. He has to live with his choices and I with mine. For now, I'm basking in the glow of love given to me every day by my children, my family, and my friends. There's no room for hate here.

Father, thank You for teaching me how to forgive and for lifting the heavy burden of resentment from my heart. —Karen Valentin

Digging Deeper: 1 Corinthians 13:4–6

Wednesday, November 2

A good name is rather to be chosen than great riches.... —Proverbs 22:1 (KJV)

Corinne and I were tickled pink when we learned that we were having a second daughter. From the beginning, my son, Harrison, had bonded us into a family, and our daughter Mary Katherine made us happier still. This new baby would surely make our lives complete, and we wanted her to feel important.

"What about a special name?" Harrison suggested.

I loved his idea! Our family has always given great importance to names. While nothing material is bound to last, a name is yours forever.

So the debate began. "How about Susan as in Susan B. Anthony or Florence as in Nightingale?" Harrison suggested.

"How about Ruth?" Corinne added. "Her story is beautiful."

But my mind drifted to the past. "I was so young when my mother died that I hardly remember her,"

I recalled my grandfather, Pa, saying. "Except for this one day," he went on, "when we were in my daddy's butcher shop in Tellico Plains, Tennessee. The Depression was in full swing, and Daddy could extend no more credit. My mother, Ella, was at the counter when a man came in, pleading for food for his family. Daddy sadly shook his head. Mama didn't say a word. Tears fell from her eyes as she looked at Daddy. 'What good is money,' she seemed to ask, 'if your neighbor's hungry?' Within minutes, Daddy called the man back and filled his arms with food." Pa added, "If you can have only one memory of your mother, could there be a better one?"

After sharing the story with my wife and kids, I asked, "How does Ella sound to you?"

"It's perfect," Corinne answered, a little teary. "And let's add Grace. God's grace."

Lord, help us to live up to Your gifts and to remember always the grace You bestow upon us.
—Brock Kidd

Digging Deeper: Ecclesiastes 7:1, Isaiah 43:1

Thursday, November 3

And let us consider how we may spur one another on toward love and good deeds.
—Hebrews 10:24 (NIV)

We did a series in *Guideposts* magazine on the challenges faced by our returning troops. It was my honor to interview US Army S.Sgt. Bobby Henline, who had been horribly injured in a roadside bombing in Iraq. I had my list of questions ready, but when I sat across from Bobby, I must have paused a bit longer than I thought. He was missing one ear completely and half of the other one. His scalp and face were a gruesome patchwork of scars and skin grafts. The lower half of his left arm was gone. Finally, he leaned in and whispered, "You should have seen the other guy."

Was I supposed to laugh? Bobby smiled. "Chill out. It's a joke."

A joke? How could this man think anything was funny? He'd been in the hospital for six months and had endured forty-five surgeries and counting. I started by asking about the accident.

"Oh, it was no accident, Edward. They were definitely trying to get me."

Now I did laugh. How could I not? Bobby went on to say that the injury occurred on his fourth tour of duty in Iraq. "That's when I realized my lucky number was three."

Then Bobby got serious. He told me about lying in a bed, night after night, begging God, Whom he never believed in, to take his life. Finally, with the help of his wife, he decided to give his life to Christ instead. That's when everything changed. Which didn't mean

Bobby still wouldn't be a wisecracker. He'd always been the cutup in his unit (another Bobby joke). His physical therapist had a connection with the manager of a comedy club, and when Bobby was well enough, he auditioned.

Today he is a stand-up comedian and an inspirational speaker.

Lord, help us remember every day that our sacred obligation to our servicemen and service-women doesn't end when the fighting does. For so many, the fight has just begun and they need our help more than ever. —Edward Grinnan

Digging Deeper: Psalm 126:2

Friday, November 4

WHAT THE SAINTS HAVE TAUGHT ME
Francis, Companion of the Poor
"Go, sell everything you have and give to the poor…." —Mark 10:21 (NIV)

When I visited Assisi, only the lower part of the huge Basilica of Saint Francesco had reopened following a massive earthquake. I knew Saint Francis only as a peaceful carved figure decorating gardens. But in his impact on his world, Francis was actually like an earthquake unto himself.

Born in 1182 to a wealthy cloth merchant, Francis was a rich young playboy repulsed at the very sight of sickness or poverty. Until one day, passing a hideously deformed leper, he abruptly leaped off his horse and handed the man his cloak. About to remount, he turned around instead and kissed the man on his lipless mouth.

Now Francis spent his time praying. He was kneeling one day in the dilapidated chapel of Saint Damiano when he heard a voice say, *Francis, restore My church.* Needing money to buy building materials, he helped himself to a bale of cloth from his father's warehouse. His father had no such instant conversion. He hauled Francis before the bishop for a public trial. Francis not only gave back the money, but he also stripped off every stitch of his clothing while the embarrassed bishop hastily wrapped a cloak around him.

Slowly it dawned upon Francis that the voice hadn't meant "repair a building." His monumental calling was the reformation of the rich, corrupt church of his time. Embracing a life of poverty, Francis was astonished when other privileged young men flocked to him. His radical movement fanned out across Europe with the message that Jesus wanted not ostentatious buildings but service to the poor. For Francis, all creation was sacred—birds, water, rocks. He sang of Brother Sun, Sister Moon, and Mother Earth until in 1226 Kind Sister Death called him home.

Father, show me Yourself in all I see today.
—Elizabeth Sherrill

Digging Deeper: Proverbs 14:31

Saturday, November 5

It is clear that the righteous one will live on the basis of faith. —Galatians 3:11 (CEB)

Do you remember the old game show *Name That Tune*? Contestants would try to predict how few notes they would need to hear in order to correctly identify the song being played: "I can name that tune in four notes!"

Well, I hardly ever do things briefly. I have lots to say, and it's all important! Until I was challenged by a project one of my students was doing in her church: summarize your faith in six words.

Impossible! I thought, until I started wrestling with what I might actually say in six words. What, amid all I knew and talked about, really mattered to me?

I'll tell you in a minute what I finally came up with after literally hours of struggle and false starts. But perhaps more important than the six words has been the impact of them on my life. They have served as a touchstone against which I now measure the thousands of words I say and hear every day. Not because those six words are so right or are the full essence of my faith, but because they have helped me more consistently live what I say I believe.

My six words? *God's grace invites me to serve.*

What might your six words be? What impact might they have?

Sometimes we make faith so complicated, God. Might You help me find a few words that will focus my witness for You today and every day? —Jeff Japinga

Digging Deeper: Joshua 24:14–24, Ephesians 4:1–16

Sunday, November 6

"Oh, there is so much more I want to tell you, but you can't understand it now." —John 16:12 (TLB)

My wife's car died in the church parking lot, so I came with my car to tow it home. I hooked up a rope between my car and hers, then instructed her: "You drive the lead car and I'll drive your car, because without power steering it will be very hard to steer. Just start out slowly until the rope tightens and then drive moderately."

Sharon climbed into the lead car, and I walked back to her car and got ready. She did indeed start out slowly, but then she suddenly took off like a jackrabbit. I watched in shock as the rope tightened up with a loud *twaaannnggg* and the front end of my car leaped into the air like a hooked fish.

There were four stops on the way home, and at each start-up I prayed, "Lord, please let the rope break before the front end of this car falls out." Somehow we managed to get home without killing anyone.

"That was kinda jerky" was all she said.

I said nothing because it was 100 percent my fault. I broke the very first law of communication, which is to find out what someone knows. I should have asked her: "Have you ever towed a car before?" "Do you know how to do this?" "Would you rather I call a tow truck?"

The next time I ask someone to do something tricky, like towing a car or learning a new computer program, I'll first have a conversation to find out where they are, like Jesus often did with His disciples. It may be that they don't know enough even to begin, and I will need to make other arrangements to get the job done.

Father, forgive me when I ask too much of others. Help me to be more realistic in my expectations.
—Daniel Schantz

Digging Deeper: Psalm 116:6, Ecclesiastes 7:8

"Blessed are those who mourn, for they will be comforted." —Matthew 5:4 (NIV)

It wasn't until after our son Dale died that Bogie, our dog, started sleeping with my husband and me. Even now, I'm not sure how it started. Until that point, Bogie slept in our bedroom in a small crate. I know that both Wayne and I receive comfort having Bogie there between us. Many a morning I wake with his small chin resting on my shoulder and his dark brown eyes looking into mine as if he understands the agony I suffer.

Just recently a good friend told us about her grandson who was injured in Afghanistan. His physical injuries, while serious, pale in comparison to his mental ones. In an effort to help her grandson deal with the aftermath of war, the army provided him with a service dog. The dog was a tremendous help to him. As a constant companion, the dog made it necessary for her grandson to engage in life outside the confines of his home. He was responsible for feeding and walking the dog. My friend called him a "comfort dog."

In that moment, I realized that just a year before our son died, God knew what the future held and sent us a comfort dog of our own.

Lord, Your presence in my pain is visible in so many unique ways. How amazingly loved I know I am that You would provide comfort to my broken heart and peace to my wounded spirit. May others experience this overwhelming love that could come only from You. —Debbie Macomber

Digging Deeper: 2 Corinthians 1:3

Tuesday, November 8

There is neither Jew nor Gentile, neither slave nor free, nor is there male and female, for you are all one in Christ Jesus. —Galatians 3:28 (NIV)

For two years, my sister's spunky four-year-old foster daughter has brought much joy to our family. Recently, my youngest daughter, Jada, had a few questions about Britney that she needed answered.

"Mommy, is Britney really my cousin?" she asked, her bright eyes thoughtful.

"Well," I answered, wondering how much detailed information a kindergartner could understand about foster care, "she's like your cousin. But unless Uncle Ralph and Aunt Lori adopt her, not really."

"Oh, because she looks different from the rest of the family."

"Really? How?" I braced myself for her description of Britney's Asian features, quite different from our family's African American features.

"She has fat cheeks!" Jada declared.

I erupted in laughter, amazed at the purity of my daughter's heart. I don't know if she realizes Britney's eyes and skin tone don't resemble her own. Yet for whatever reason, those cherublike cheeks were the only features that stood out to her.

I wonder how often I look past other people's eye color or skin tone to see the precious soul within. Do I ever miss their beauty because they come from a different culture or race or class?

I am so grateful that God never judges us by our appearance, family backgrounds, or social standing. He loves the great big melting pot of us and celebrates the beautiful diversity we bring to the world. His love runs deep.

**Lord, give me the eyes of a child
to see others' beauty.** —Carla Hendricks

Digging Deeper: Revelation 5:8–10, 7:9–10

Wednesday, November 9

Remember your word to your servant, for you have given me hope. —Psalm 119:49 (NIV)

It had been a trying year at my century-old log cabin. I had furnace problems, wiring problems, water problems. Not to mention the trees I had to have cut down that bordered a neighbor's property. It had all amounted to a small fortune.

I adore giving gifts, but I had little money to spend. I decided to purchase the loveliest cards I could find and pen some old-fashioned handwritten notes to people who had touched my life or needed a bit of encouragement themselves.

Yet when I didn't hear from any of the recipients, I interpreted the lack of response as my being out of touch with the times. *I need to tune in to technology,* I thought. *I should have sent e-mails.*

Then I heard from a harried young mother who'd received one of my missives. "You wrote me a note," she said, "and I want you to know how that encouraged me. It's still in my handbag, in the secret middle compartment where no one roots around for tissues or gum. Your words came just when I needed them. I'm so grateful for I often feel like a dry well."

Oh, Lord, all too often I misinterpret the lack of feedback from others. Teach me to take action and trust You with the results. Amen.
—Roberta Messner

Digging Deeper: Psalms 18:2, 91:2; Nahum 1:7

Thursday, November 10

"Oh, that I could write my plea with an iron pen in the rock forever." —Job 19:23–24 (TLB)

I was thrilled when my daughter Jeanne gave me a journal for Christmas in 1990. I immediately glued small decorative pieces of paper on the first seven pages with the idea that I would write something fabulous on each page every day of that week. I didn't write a word.

In 1991, I glued newspaper headlines about the Gulf War to fourteen pages. Things like "Zero Hour," "Anxiety Everywhere," "Congress Okays Going to War." It was the first war of my adult life and it made quite an impact on me.

In 1993, I added two pages of notes about dating a widower named Wayne. Short sentences in extra-large handwriting: "New feelings. New friends. New opportunities. New man in my life."

I had only three sentences in 1994: "Wayne's been gone since last October. Now that we have a crash pad for pilots in our home, there are men all over the place…all married! But for some reason I am very happy."

Then nothing until 2004: "The crash pad lasted ten years, and now I've moved to Florida! I have never been this happy in my life. Just turned fifty-nine, and today Jack, my new main squeeze, and I voted for president."

Ten more years passed without a word, but in 2014 I added colorful hand-painted designs and pasted a postcard of Pope Francis that I got when I went to Rome that year. I also glued in one of the wedding invitations to Jack's and my wedding.

Truth be told, I am a pathetic journal writer. But even though my entries are scattered, I know it's good for me to keep track of my life, especially the answers to prayers. Each time I look at my journal, it can turn a blah day into a happy one when I see how wonderfully God has orchestrated these many years.

Father, this life You gave me is such an interesting journey. Keep me mindful of how You have blessed every single day. —Patricia Lorenz

Digging Deeper: Psalm 102:18, Romans 1:10–12, 2 Corinthians 3:2–3

Friday, November 11

For, "Everyone who calls on the name of the Lord shall be saved." —Romans 10:13 (NRSV)

I think a lot about language, and the most important question I've learned to ask is "What are its limitations?"

This question has become profound for me lately as I've meditated on the names of God in Scripture. Sometimes we unwittingly reduce God to one or two names. We like *Abba*, the Father God

Who appears more than two hundred times in the New Testament, evoking loving, parental care. Or *Emmanuel,* God with us. *Jehovah Shalom,* the Lord Is Peace, and *Jehovah Rapha,* the Lord That Heals, reflect reassuring aspects of God too.

Nowadays we tend to overlook *Jehovah Sabaoth,* the Lord of Hosts, the Commander of spiritual troops. Until I started doing some research, I confess, I didn't even know *El Olam,* the Everlasting God of Genesis 16, or *Qanna,* Jealous, a name that appears in Exodus and Deuteronomy.

Here's the thing: I don't like being reduced to one aspect of my being. I am Chinese, I am American, I am a journalist, and I am an introvert, but I am never only one of these things. I am *all* of them and more. If this is true for me, how much truer must it be for the One Who made us in God's own diverse, multifaceted image?

Our language is human, but God is divine. In all His majesty (*Adonai*) and might (*Elohim*), He's beyond words. To know Him is to try to grasp His complexity and to acknowledge our limitations. To strive for Him is to study His many names, calling on not just one or two. In all, the Lord Is There (*Jehovah Shammah*).

God, help us to know You better each day in all Your richness and diversity. —Jeff Chu

Digging Deeper: Psalm 148, Isaiah 9

Saturday, November 12

They are to be given daily, without fail, whatever they need.... —Ezra 6:9 (JPS)

I always knew there would be a lot of paperwork after my husband died, but I thought we had prepared for it as best we could. So when Social Security asked me to send proof of our marriage, I did at once, providing the date, location, and name of the rabbi who married us.

While I was waiting to hear from them, our bank informed me that, while they could find the power of attorney I'd signed, they had no record of the one Keith had signed. And the Department of Motor Vehicles told me and the couple who wanted to buy his truck that the State of Washington had not sent the required ownership documents.

On top of all of this, a letter arrived from Los Angeles County telling me that there was no record of our marriage. I began feeling like I'd spent the last thirty-six years in some kind of void. "Why is everything disappearing?" I asked God.

I hadn't received an answer by the time the cemetery admitted it had messed up the paperwork and buried my husband in someone else's grave. While we worked it out, I became even more convinced that God was trying to tell me something. *But what?*

Then one day, I suddenly understood. Even though the paperwork had vanished and Keith was no longer here, the only really vital record of everything we had had with each other was written where it mattered most.

I've lost so much that is valuable to me, God, but as long as You keep finding ways to make me aware of Your blessings, then I have what I need.
—Rhoda Blecker

Digging Deeper: Isaiah 51:12

Sunday, November 13

Jesus went down to Nazareth with them and was obedient to them. His mother cherished every word in her heart. —Luke 2:51 (CEB)

Oh, what hopes we have for our children, what dreams! Both of our sons were born in winter, and I can remember during Advent, when Carol was "great with child," how Mary's hopes for her son resonated with me. She heard the angel say that He would be God's Son and exclaimed in praise, "With all my heart I glorify the Lord!" She knew He was destined for great things.

And yet it is easy to lose track of those dreams, to forget the thrill of expectation. My sons have done marvelous things, far greater than I could ever have imagined. But there were moments when I wondered if they'd even get through algebra or

French or middle school or soccer or sleepaway camp. Fear can rob us of hopes and dreams.

The same thing happened to parents in the Bible. I was thumbing through the Good Book and noticed how, in the Gospel of Luke, only a few dozen verses after Mary gave birth to her firstborn, the angels' song ringing in her head, worries got the best of her.

Jesus was twelve years old and had gone with His parents to Jerusalem for Passover. Mary and Joseph were heading home when they realized He wasn't with them. They hurried back and combed Jerusalem for three days, only discovering Him, at last, sitting among the teachers at the temple. "Why have you treated us like this?" Mary asked. "Your father and I have been worried."

"Didn't you know it was necessary for me to be in my Father's house?" Jesus asked. Indeed, didn't she know? Hadn't she remembered?

Go ahead, dream great dreams for your children, commit them to prayer, give them all the love you have, and then let go. Let the Lord take our children far, leading us to places we'd never expect to go.

I turn my worries over to You, Lord, so I can be filled again with hope, not fear. —Rick Hamlin

Digging Deeper: Luke 1:45, 2:14

My son, do not forget my teaching, but let your heart keep my commandments, for lengths of days and years of life and peace they will add to you.
—Proverbs 3:1–2 (ESV)

I silenced my alarm again, ignoring the little voice reminding me that this would be the day I would make a change. That my time with God and my time bettering myself would start now. Instead, I rolled over for seven extra minutes of fitful sleep and then seven more.

I had legitimate reasons why I couldn't get started on my goals: working full time, raising my toddler, and being pregnant. Olivia disliked the stroller, so I couldn't sneak in a walking workout after work. By the time she was in bed, I was exhausted, staring at the mountain of laundry that needed folding. Even though I could have used my chore time to pray, I preferred to watch reruns on TV. I'd go to bed late and repeat the cycle the next day.

I was berating myself again when suddenly I heard: *Ashley, you're so focused on accomplishing that you aren't paying any attention to doing.* God didn't need me to have the perfect spiritual life at that exact moment; He simply needed me to turn toward Him.

The next morning my phone buzzed. I rolled out of bed to find an e-mail from a close friend. "Is anyone interested in doing an online Bible study with me?"

She'd e-mailed our group of six decade-long friends. Within an hour, everyone replied with a resounding "yes." We're a few months down the road now and have already covered Luke and Ephesians.

Instead of getting bombarded with spam, sales, and work e-mails, my in-box now overflows with commentary and insights from my best friends as we work to build ourselves into better servants of God.

God, thank You for giving me the answers I need, beyond what I could even dream of. —Ashley Kappel

Digging Deeper: Deuteronomy 11:18–23, Ephesians 6:11–17

Tuesday, November 15

"When you pass through the waters, I will be with you; and when you pass through the rivers, they will not sweep over you. When you walk through the fire, you will not be burned; the flames will not set you ablaze." —Isaiah 43:2 (NIV)

"I'm sorry for whining and demanding breakfast and making it so you couldn't think straight while you made your coffee," my daughter, Kate, had written in a lovely apology letter.

Next came my son Joey's carefully scrawled note: "I'm sorry for screaming 'food fight' and jumping onto the counter like a ninja."

I took a deep breath and tried to keep a straight face. Because what had been enough to cause a meltdown just a few minutes earlier now seemed petty in comparison to the bright-eyed children standing in front of me.

So often things like spilled milk and the occasional food fight cause my days to degenerate into craziness. I let the river sweep me away into frustration and anger, and I fail to see the beauty that stands just on the horizon: healthy kids with toothless smiles and independent personalities, quiet mornings with nowhere to go, laughter and togetherness in this messy thing we call life.

So I set the sweet notes from my kids on the counter and found them in the living room, where I pulled them onto the couch. We snuggled and laughed and talked about an imaginary world where food fights are common at mealtime and tiny robots scoop up soggy cereal and mashed strawberries so as not to leave a mess. Because it's not those frustrating moments that are going to define me but the ones when I allow God to refine me through the fire.

Lord, help me not to lose my purpose when life is frustrating or difficult. Amen. —Erin MacPherson

Digging Deeper: Matthew 11:28, 2 Corinthians 4:16–18

Wednesday, November 16

Love is patient; love is kind. . . .
—1 Corinthians 13:4 (NRSV)

The prayer service was over, and we all filed out to
the lawn to wait for dinner. We were at a fund-raiser
for an outreach ministry where several members of
our church volunteer.

I hadn't looked forward to this evening. Church
events are always the same for me. Kate, an Episcopal
priest, works or talks with other clergy while I look
after the kids. I feel like a bystander, a babysitter.

I looked around for Frances and Benjamin. They
were playing with another priest's kids in a garden
adjacent to the church lawn. The priest's husband
was there. I introduced myself, and we commiserated
about clergy spouse/babysitting duty. "Though, right
now it's not too bad," Dennis said, gesturing at the
setting sun and the kids happily absorbed in a game
of cartwheels.

I looked around. The church hosting the fund-
raiser was lovely, especially in the mellow evening
light. The kids, I realized, were old enough so
that looking after them really wasn't a big deal.
Here I was in a beautiful place, having a grown-up
conversation.

Suddenly, a mariachi band struck up behind us.
We turned to see colorfully dressed musicians and

folkloric dancers. Awash in sound and movement, I laughed at myself. My resentment was out of date. That old part of life—intensely watching over babies and toddlers—was gone. Life was freer now. Really, the only problem had been my impatience.

"This music is great!" Kate exclaimed, appearing beside me and taking my hand. "Are you having more fun than you thought you would?" I spotted the kids across the plaza, shyly imitating the dancers' moves. I grinned. Yes, more fun than I'd expected, more than my impatience deserved.

Lord, teach me to live on Your time, not mine.
—Jim Hinch

Digging Deeper: Habakkuk 2:3, 2 Peter 3:9

Thursday, November 17

So the Lord said to Joshua: "Get up! Why do you lie thus on your face?" —Joshua 7:10 (NKJV)

Years ago, children's author Maggie Kimmel asked me to coedit a book about *Mister Rogers' Neighborhood.* One day, we were sitting in Fred Rogers's office discussing Marian Wright Edelman, founder of the Children's Defense Fund and one of Maggie's heroes. "When I grow up," Maggie said, "I want to be Marian Wright Edelman."

We laughed—Maggie was quite grown-up by then. Well, everyone laughed except Fred. "I don't understand," Fred said in that entirely Mr. Rogers way. "Why would you want to be someone else? You're wonderful just the way you are."

I was thinking about this at her funeral last week: Fred was right.

Maggie had polio as a child and spent her life in braces and eventually a wheelchair. When she first came back from the hospital as a young girl, she took one faltering step inside her house and then fell over. Her mother reached to help, but her father stepped in. "Are you hurt?" he asked.

"No," Maggie said through her tears.

"Then, my child," he said, "get up."

Maggie did get up, a thousand-thousand times more. Maybe that's how heroes are made: it's the way you get up and do it again and again, every day, now and forever.

"When an old woman dies," begins Maggie's favorite African proverb, "a library burns to the ground."

Not to disagree with the recently deceased, but Maggie survives. Her words, her work, her life are wonderful just the way they are.

Lord, let Maggie's life remind us to see past the barriers to who we really are. —Mark Collins

Digging Deeper: Jeremiah 10:19, Luke 13:11–12

God will speak to this people, to whom he said,
"This is the resting place, let the weary rest"....
—Isaiah 28:11–12 (NIV)

After the Boston Marathon bombings, my daughters,
who both live in that city, found unexpected comfort
in their universities' use of dogs to distract and soothe
traumatized students. Charlotte's school enlists a herd
of therapy dogs, not only in response to tragedies but
also during finals week. And at Lulu's college, students
can check out dogs, like books, from the library.
(The dogs are listed by name in the library catalog!)

The petting sessions awakened the girls'
homesickness for their own dogs, and they started
begging me to send photos. "It's stress relief," Lulu
said. The next time she was home, she installed
Instagram on my phone and trained me in its use. I've
been posting daily photos of our four dogs ever since.

Photographing our dogs and thinking about their
capacity to soothe has taught me some valuable
things about finding rest. First off, whenever they're
not actively doing some important task, such as
eating what we provide, guarding our farm from deer
and other intruders, communicating with other dogs
(or ambulances or trains) in the dead of night, or
chewing whatever needs to be chewed, they're asleep
in the sun. Rest is, I would say, their default state.

Also, whenever I go out to where one dog lies sleeping and I squat to take a picture, the dog invariably rolls over, exposing his or her belly to be petted. Somehow, sleep, for a dog, is the state of being loved.

That's how I want to be: at rest whenever possible and keenly aware, even when barely conscious, of God's abiding presence and love.

Good Father, Provider of everything I need, help me to find rest and comfort in You. —Patty Kirk

Digging Deeper: Isaiah 28:13–16

Saturday, November 19

A man's gift maketh room for him, and bringeth him before great men. —Proverbs 18:16 (KJV)

It was a frosty day in Gettysburg, Pennsylvania, but the excitement of winning the Shaara Prize for best Civil War fiction had me feeling warm inside. I was a long way from home and glad my two children were with me to celebrate. We sat at the Gettysburg Battlefield as part of the commemoration of the great battle and President Abraham Lincoln's address. The irony of the moment was not lost on me: at least two of my great-grandfathers were born into slavery. And when historian Doris Kearns Goodwin and film director Steven Spielberg rose to address the crowd, I tried to convince myself this was not a dream.

Evening fell, and I made my way to the historic Majestic Theater to accept the prize given by Gettysburg College's Civil War Institute. When my name was called, I told myself, "You will not faint," then walked onstage to receive the award for my book *The Resurrection of Nat Turner, Part 1*. Though my eyes were blinded by the lights, I could feel the smiles of my family, my friends, and my ancestors. The audience laughed and embraced me. I relaxed. I was home.

Later, as I walked up an aisle in the theater, a woman stopped me. "Are you Sharon Foster? The one who writes for *Daily Guideposts*?" Soon we were hugging, and I added being part of the devotional family to the wonder of the day.

Lord, thank You for honors and for family of all kinds, because a welcome is the greatest reward of all. —Sharon Foster

Digging Deeper: 2 Samuel 22:20, Isaiah 61:7, Jeremiah 29:11

Sunday, November 20

Hope does not disappoint.... —Romans 5:5 (NAS)

I now have a homeless son.

I recently had to accept that truth. My twin sons, Jon and Jeremy, have led troubled, often dangerous, lives for decades. They have chosen not to go by the rules. Drugs, alcohol, imprisonment, and mental illnesses have plagued them.

Jon sleeps at a homeless shelter and walks to First Presbyterian Church to receive a big breakfast, sermon, and mail each Sunday. He calls me when he can borrow a friend's cell phone. Jon remains optimistic. He gets that from his father, not from me. Most of my life I've battled fearful thoughts. I can send him a debit card in care of the church. He doesn't seem to want or need much. He assures me he loves us, but he doesn't want to see us. Not now.

He phoned one day. "It's Jon, Mom."

How could I not recognize my own son's voice? He was joyful, as usual.

"I have to have a chest X-ray. My TB test didn't come back right. I can walk to a clinic in two weeks. I'm sure it'll be fine."

I called all our family to pray and battled my negative thinking. Two weeks and four days passed. I answered the phone early one Monday, a week before Easter.

"Hey. How are you?"

"Jon?"

"Yeah, it's me, Mom. I'm good. How about you? My chest X-ray was fine. I now have to get a driver's license for twenty-five dollars."

"I'll put a gift debit card in the mail."

"Thanks, Mom. As soon as I get my license, I believe I have a job and a place to live with a buddy."

"You never give up hoping, do you, son?"

"Of course not! You have to hang on to hope. I love you. Happy Easter!"

Father, almost everything I've learned about hope has come from my sons. —Marion Bond West

Digging Deeper: Job 13:15, Psalm 39:7

Monday, November 21

Trust in the Lord with all thine heart; and lean not unto thine own understanding. —Proverbs 3:5 (KJV)

A friend of mine is a chaplain in a hospital, and as we got to talking the other day, he closed his eyes and walked in memory through hospital corridors, pausing at each door and telling me who was in the room and why and what was said.

First door: girl, seven years old. No hair. Already lost right leg. Wants to know if God issues new legs if you ask very politely. Next door: man, age sixty. Former professional athlete, worried about some things he never quite told his wife. Will it hurt her if he tells her now or is it merciful on his part to let it go as he goes? Next door: girl, age twenty. Used to believe in what we call God. Now she doesn't, not after seven years of cancer. "Can you blame me?" she says to the chaplain. "Do you still believe, after all the pain and agony and loss you have seen?"

My friend, the chaplain, opened his eyes and said, "That's the daily question, isn't it? How can you believe in good when there's so much bad? Crazy to believe, isn't it? But I do. You see the flash of holiness and greatness of spirit and unimaginable courage and grace and tenderness sometimes, but if you are looking for proof, you are an idiot. You'll never prove God, but you see God all the time if you watch and listen. God's everywhere in light and music and kindness and living things. People get hung up trying to understand. You can't understand. Pain and loss are part of the gift. I don't understand why. So what? Why should it be small enough for me to understand? But I believe it anyway. So did I see God today? All day long, my friend. All day long."

Lord, I am blessed to believe in all I do not understand, like marriage and physics and You.
—Brian Doyle

Digging Deeper: Hebrews 11:1

Join us for our Thanksgiving Day of Prayer. Find out more at guideposts.org/ourprayer.

You hem me in behind and before, and you lay your hand upon me. —Psalm 139:5 (NIV)

Lonny and I were driving home. We'd been to an early-morning appointment, and the weather was wild. Heavy flakes swirled. The roads were thick with white. The sky opened wide, and it was supposed to snow all day. I felt safe with my husband behind the wheel. But after arriving home, he'd go one direction for work and I'd gather our younger sons and venture out in the other.

"Are you sure you need to visit your friend today?" he asked.

"We've planned this day for weeks," I said.

"I wish you'd stay home."

"You're sweet, but it's not far."

It wasn't—just up the highway and a mile along the Mississippi River. But once in the van with my boys, I wished I'd listened. The road had disappeared, and the choppy, brown ribbon of water was threatening and close. I moved slowly, anxiety curling my hands tight.

That's when I saw lights in my rearview mirror. Lonny had been following me; I was safe.

When I pulled into our friend's driveway, my husband pulled in too and tapped my window. "When you leave, call," he said. "I'll escort you home."

Lonny's chivalry reminded me of the way God has moved with us. We've had some rough roads this year, growing our teenage son. Often it has been hard to discern the path, and we have been afraid. But I can see that God has always been there for us, paving the way with His Word, protecting us from behind by sending sweet souls to support, to help, and to pray for us. We were hemmed in.

Lonny left, and the boys bolted to our friend's door. But I sat in silence for a moment, grateful for hemming, for safety within the seams.

When I'm afraid, Lord, help me to remember You're there. Amen. —Shawnelle Eliasen

Digging Deeper: Psalm 138:7, 1 Thessalonians 3:3

Wednesday, November 23

Thus Samuel grew and the Lord was with him and let none of his words fail. —1 Samuel 3:19 (NAS)

Much of our family history dwells in my three decades of writing for *Daily Guideposts*. I have wanted to be a faithful "scribe" in relating the many stories of God's presence with us, feeling it an immense privilege that His touch in my life could be helpful for others.

But there was a period of years in the early 2000s when just about everything was on the line. I was fighting a long and arduous battle in my personal life. Throughout this time I understood God to be "not far" (Acts 17:27, NIV), a lifeline when I felt distanced from many of those close to me.

I was honest with the *Daily Guideposts* editor about my conflict. Some people might have requested I not submit devotions until I had the difficulty resolved. However, this editor encouraged me to continue to write what I truthfully could.

All these years later, his decision abounds in my life. He kept the door open, believing my contributions would matter. My journey in making God-honoring choices was strengthened through his support.

Someone commented recently, "Your writing has changed. What happened?"

What happened is that I battled in the "good fight" (2 Timothy 4:7, NIV) of faith, fought to regain my footing with God beside me to help me prevail. God did not for one minute stop believing I would find my way in Him, that I would emerge from the fight with new depth of heart, wiser compassion, and a love for Him that fills my soul.

"Take words with you, and return to the Lord. Say to Him, 'Take away all iniquity; and receive us graciously'" (Hosea 14:2, NKJV). Hear this, my truest prayer, oh, God. —Carol Knapp

Digging Deeper: Psalm 145; Lamentations 3:56–58; Galatians 6:9–10; 1 Thessalonians 4:12–13, 17

Thursday, November 24

Oh, give thanks to the Lord, for He is good! For His mercy endures forever. —Psalm 107:1 (NKJV)

The turkey is on the table, my favorite green bean supreme casserole is beside it and, best of all, my extended family rounds our dining room table. It's a little crowded, I have to admit. Sometimes elbows rub and we've had to use every chair in the house, but we all fit—and the amazing aroma of Thanksgiving fills the house.

In a few minutes we'll share what we're thankful for, but this year, as the host, I'm adding a new twist to our family tradition. I suppose it all started at the beginning of the year when I was trying to think of a word to focus on. The phrase "Expect a Blessing" kept coming to mind.

I tried to shorten it to *expect* or *blessing*. I even looked for something else altogether. But again and again it came back to me. Browsing a cute little gift store in town, the same three words greeted me on a hand-painted sign, and I said to myself, *Okay, okay, I get it.*

I wrote "Expect a Blessing" on the inside flap of my journal and vowed to mean it. I said it whenever a worry came into my thoughts. Instead of going over the worst of any given situation, I countered it with the best. Even if a blessing didn't follow, I felt at peace.

So, in line with my theme for the year, and in addition to sharing gratitude for what's already happened, I'm asking everyone to give thanks for a blessing that's on the way—a goal they want to accomplish, a vacation down the road, maybe a raise at work, their hopes for tomorrow.

Dear God, on this special day of Thanksgiving, thank You for the amazing gifts You give us, most especially the ones to come. —Sabra Ciancanelli

Digging Deeper: Ephesians 1:16, Colossians 3:15, James 1:17

Friday, November 25

She watches over the affairs of her household and does not eat the bread of idleness. Her children arise and call her blessed.... —Proverbs 31:27–28 (NIV)

After a week of active kids, working full-time, cooking, and every other responsibility that lay solely on my shoulders, my home always looks disheveled on Fridays—my day off and my day to catch up.

This particular day it felt overwhelming. The pile of laundry loomed, dirty dishes filled the sink, and the table was a cluttered mess, mostly with bills. I could feel the negativity clouding me as I saw each responsibility as a curse. I sat on the couch and looked at my home—mainly the mountain of dirty laundry. "Look at all those clothes!" I whined to God. "So many clothes!"

What a complaint! I sound ridiculous, I thought. And with that, my bad attitude turned into gratitude as I tackled each responsibility for the day.

Thank You, Lord, for my piles of laundry.
My kids and I have plenty of clothes to wear.
Thank You for my sink full of dirty dishes.
It means I was able to feed my family
to their hearts' content.
Thank You for a home that is mine to clean.
Thank You for my bills.
You've allowed me the provisions
to pay them, and each one represents a service
I was blessed to receive.
Thank You for my job. It provides for my family,
and the people I work with have become
part of my extended family.
Most of all, thank You for my two little boys.
The love and joy they give me
will forever outweigh
the challenges of being their mom.
Without them, I would be well rested,
but I wouldn't have such an important and
precious reason to work so hard. —Karen Valentin

Digging Deeper: Matthew 25:23

"The Lord is my strength and song...."
—Exodus 15:2 (NAS)

I met Chuck last winter on the ice of the lake in my neighborhood. It happened, as we say, "by accident." I was walking the dog and the lake was frozen over, so Max ran onto it, scampering around in circles, delighted to be off-leash for a few minutes. Then I saw a small figure crouching over a fishing hole in the distance.

I was feeling a little depressed that day. Everyone in the house was fighting the winter flu, including me, and my work was getting me down. *Lord, I could use some encouragement*, I prayed.

I slowly approached the man.

"Howdy!" he said as I drew near.

"Hi. How are you? My name is Jon."

"Good to meet you. I'm Chuck." Then, in his next breath, he quoted to me the verse at the top of this page. Scratch that; he *sang* out the verse—with joy!

How did you know? I thought to myself. I said, "Thanks, man. I believe that. But I also needed to hear it just now."

We stood and talked for about ten minutes while Max continued to sprint around the lake. Chuck was out of work but searching for a job. He was the single parent of a difficult teenager. Chuck was joyful, full of hope.

"God is good, brother," he said as I prepared to leave, putting Max back on his leash.

"He is," I said. "Thanks."

I walk to that lake three or four times a week, and I've never seen Chuck since.

You are my strength, God. And especially when I feel down, You are my song. —Jon Sweeney

Digging Deeper: Daniel 6:19–22

First Sunday in Advent, November 27

THE GIFT OF SMALL MOMENTS
The Promise Fulfilled

"But you, Bethlehem Ephrathah, though you are little among the thousands of Judah, yet out of you shall come forth to Me the One to be Ruler in Israel, whose goings forth are from of old, from everlasting." —Micah 5:2 (NKJV)

"Let's try there," Margi said, "over that hill." My wife pointed up a steep incline. Three families trekked through knee-deep snow somewhere in the rugged woods of northern California. Armed with a permit, we searched for that most elusive quarry: the perfect Christmas tree. It had become our post–Thanksgiving family tradition. Each year, hot chocolate and strong coffee fueled our two-hour drive into the snowcapped peaks of the national forests.

The kids scrambled up the snowy hillside. The adults struggled along. Nobody complained. Tall pines frosted with snow, a cobalt sky, and rugged terrain made for a postcard vista. Add the laughter of children and a few snowball fights, and nothing could have been better.

"How about this one?" someone shouted.

"No, the back is bare."

"Or that one? Or the next one?"

My aching legs wanted us to settle for something scrawny, but I bit back my whining.

"I think the perfect tree is *always* going to be over the next hill," my daughter, Josie, said.

"Well, that's just where we'll have to go," Margi responded.

That's how hope is, I thought. It's a promise fulfilled over the next hill. Generations abided in Christ before Christ came. They pressed forward in hope, finding that confidence in future grace is never disappointed.

The next hill paid off. Our tree was perfect. Just like the Savior.

Lord, You promised a Savior and He came. As I trudge through life, may I rest my heart in future grace, perfectly fulfilled in Him. —Bill Giovannetti

Digging Deeper: Luke 2:1–6

Monday, November 28

"And why worry about a speck in your friend's eye when you have a log in your own?" —Matthew 7:3 (NLT)

I hurriedly steered my car into a parking spot. I was headed to dinner at a friend's house and had offered to bring bread, but I was running late. I opened my door to get out and noticed how close I was parked to the car next me. *Gosh,* I thought as I edged my way out, *that car sure is parked wrong.* It had, in turn, forced me to park outside the yellow lines. I looked at the odd angle. *Why can't people take the time to park their cars right?*

A woman who'd parked a few spots away looked over as she walked past. "Amazing how people just can't park straight, isn't it?" I called out, shaking my head as I walked into the store.

I paid for the bread, headed back to the parking lot, looked over to where my car was parked, and stopped short. "Well, would you look at that?" I said out loud, shocked. It was *my* car that was parked crooked, not the other one! I felt my face flush.

Of course, the woman whom I'd complained to earlier walked by. She hesitated and then turned to me and stopped. "I learned a long time ago," she said with an understanding smile, "that when I find myself in a place of discomfort and not-knowing, it's always better to be a learner instead of a judger."

As embarrassed as I am, Lord, thank You for this reminder that there's really no place in my world for criticism. —Melody Bonnette Swang

Digging Deeper: Matthew 12:36–37

Tuesday, November 29

Thy words have upholden him that was falling, and thou hast strengthened the feeble knees. —Job 4:4 (KJV)

For decades, I took my health for granted. I always prayed, of course, for dear ones who suffered from chronic pain or serious illness, but for myself, I hardly gave it a thought. After all, I danced a lot, hiked rugged trails, and easily hefted a suitcase and laptop when I traveled. I took care of myself: vitamins, exercise, the works. What could go wrong?

Then last year, occasional hip twinges turned into incessant pain and my knee complained constantly too. Doc tapped the X-rays with his pencil. "Yup. Osteoarthritis. About five on a scale of one to ten." I squinted at the telltale shrinking space in my hip joint. "Take ibuprofen. And when the pain gets too bad, come see me for a new hip."

I grumbled at my annoying new companion that demanded I wear sensible shoes and take the escalator instead of the stairs. Supplements and swimming helped a little, and although the arthritis never went away, it became tolerable. Some days I just ignored it altogether; I kept teaching, writing, singing, decorating cakes—in short, living my life.

Now I am grateful for the minor pinches and pangs of crabby, creaky joints. I recognize and empathize with friends who gingerly ease into the car or limp ever so slightly. More important, I give thanks every blessed morning that I awaken pain-free and that the rest of my vintage body works just fine.

Creator God, only You would use pain to remind me how healthy I truly am. I am humbled.
—Gail Thorell Schilling

Digging Deeper: Psalm 139:14, Isaiah 35:3, 2 Corinthians 4:16

Wednesday, November 30

Children are a gift from the Lord; they are a reward from him. —Psalm 127:3 (NLT)

When my daughter, Micah, was young, we spent nearly every moment together. We both looked forward to *Barney* on PBS but for different reasons. Seated in front of the television, Micah was mesmerized for thirty minutes while I took a much-needed break. At the end of every episode she'd shout for me. We'd hold hands, sway, and sing with the big purple dinosaur, "I love you. You love me.

We're a happy family. With a great big hug and a kiss from me to you, won't you say you love me too?"

Fast-forward a decade: Micah's a tween, and we no longer spend every day together. She craves independence. I entice her with destinations she likes to lure her into running errands with me. Instead of holding my hand and skipping, she wants me to walk a few paces behind her when we're at the mall. Once I planned playdates with families I thought were suitable, but Micah now chooses her own friends based on two criteria: "She's cool, and I like her." It can be a bit trying at times. I have to remind myself that autonomy is a natural part of growing up.

Cleaning out a pile of stuffed animals last weekend, I found a plush Barney. Waves of nostalgia hit me. I squeezed his stomach, and he began to sing, "I love you. You love me. We're a happy family...." Tears pooled in my eyes. Those precious times were long gone.

Suddenly, Micah burst through the door. Almost knocking me over with a hug, she belted out, "Won't you say you love me too?"

My relationship with my daughter has changed, but our feelings for each other have not, even though I'm relegated to walking a few steps behind.

Lord, thank You for the gift of children at all ages and stages of life. —Stephanie Thompson

Digging Deeper: Isaiah 40:11, Matthew 18:10

GOD'S ABIDING LOVE

1 _____

2 _____

3 _____

4 _____

5 _____

6 _____

7 _____

8 _____

9 _____

10 _____

11 _____

12 _____

13 _____

14 _____

15 _____

16 _____

17 _____

18 _____

19 _____

20 _____

21 _____

22 _____

23 _____

24 _____

25 _____

26 _____

27 _____

28 _____

29 _____

30 _____

December

For to us a child is born, to us a son is given;
and the government shall be upon his shoulder,
and his name shall be called Wonderful Counselor,
Mighty God, Everlasting Father, Prince of Peace.

—Isaiah 9:6 (ESV)

Spend your time and energy in the exercise of keeping spiritually fit. —1 Timothy 4:7 (TLB)

Many times, December through March, the temperature here on the west coast of Florida is in the fifties. Since my main exercise twelve months a year, six days a week, is the water aerobics class in the heated outdoor pool across the street, I hate to miss it. I'll go if it's fifty-five degrees out. My husband, Jack, says sixty is his bottom line.

One morning I woke up to a cloudy, gray, drizzly day and fifty-four bone-chilling degrees.

"Just one degree below my bottom line," I said to Jack. I looked out the window to see my friend Dodie's car in the parking lot and knew she was already in the pool. I didn't want my favorite octogenarian to be alone, so I pulled on my swimsuit and a long-sleeve pool shirt, slipped into my terry bathrobe, grabbed my towel, and headed out the door.

Dodie and I were the only ones doing jumping jacks, cross-country skiing, knee bends, twists, and arm stretches to the water aerobics tape that morning. Even during the sprinkling rain, we giggled. "Uh-oh, it's raining! We might get wet!"

When the tape was over, I felt like a new woman: refreshed, energized, strong, ready to tackle the day, and very happy. My knees, which had been hurting, now felt normal, and I walked home with a spring in my step.

I learned that sometimes I just have to do it: step into a little discomfort in order to reap rewards. Being kind to a friend and good to my body aren't always easy, but they're certainly always worth it.

Lord, when I want to stay home and forget about daily exercise, give me a push, please.
—Patricia Lorenz

Digging Deeper: 1 Timothy 4:8–10, Hebrews 5:14

Friday, December 2

And the shepherds returned, glorifying and praising God for all the things that they had heard and seen.... —Luke 2:20 (KJV)

This morning I picked up a delightful picture book I intended to read to a young neighbor: *The Birds of Bethlehem* by Tomie dePaola. It tells the Christmas story in the simplest terms. Eating breakfast in a wintry field, each of six pairs of birds—green, yellow, blue, red, brown, white—reports to the others their most significant memory from the day before: congestion on the roads, visitors at the stable, angels in the sky.

It reminded me of my own memory of yesterday, a snowy morning that churned up a feeling of spiritual doubt. *Is the bright God of the heavens here in my world on a dark, stormy day?*

I took an early lunch break, made a sandwich, and ate it while standing at the dining room window, looking out across my narrow yard and road through a heavy squall. A male cardinal, as red as the bird from *The Birds of Bethlehem,* had flown into a tree. And then a lone pedestrian appeared on the scene, walking down the sidewalk. She was well protected by winter boots and a long coat. But mostly I remember the sight of her expansive umbrella. Its scarlet color—and the red bird looking down from above—assured me that the Christ of Christmas is here with us always.

God, thank You for the tangible message that You, the bright God of the heavens, are with me today and always. —Evelyn Bence

Digging Deeper: Isaiah 52:7–10, Nahum 1:15

Saturday, December 3

Before a word is on my tongue you, Lord, know it completely. —Psalm 139:4 (NIV)

"Millie, lie down! I can't see." The entire rearview mirror of our vehicle was taken up by a large golden retriever's head with its tongue hanging out.

"Don't yell at her," my wife, Julee, said, reaching back and easing Millie down. "Besides, you're driving too fast."

"I'm going exactly the speed limit."

"This stretch of road is a mess. Millie doesn't like the bumps. That's why she's up. It's because of your driving. It makes her nervous."

I sighed and slowed down. Julee is quick to say she is a much better driver than I, but she almost always leaves the honors to me.

I shot her a look. She glared back. All of a sudden I felt a jolt. The vehicle lurched slightly left, provoking the driver who was passing me to lay on his horn. I swerved back into my lane. Millie popped up again. I tried to look composed, but my heart was racing.

"Potholes!" I snorted. But, really, I wanted to scream. If only Julee would keep quiet.

There was a long, tense silence. *Here it comes,* I thought. *An argument. One we've been having for years. Lord, does it always have to be like this?*

Then Julee surprised me. "Sorry if I distracted you," she said, coaxing Millie back down.

I almost didn't know how to respond. I was all ready to stick up for myself. Finally, I said, "I should have been paying more attention."

Julee patted my knee. "Let's both pay more attention."

Just then we hit a smooth, newly resurfaced stretch of road. Almost as if on cue.

Lord, You know how stubborn I can be. Thank You for defusing a situation I was determined to make worse...and for reminding me Who's really in the driver's seat. —Edward Grinnan

Digging Deeper: Psalm 12:7, Proverbs 10:19

Second Sunday in Advent, December 4

THE GIFT OF SMALL MOMENTS
A Perfect Plan

"Behold, the days are coming, declares the Lord, when I will raise up for David a righteous Branch, and he shall reign as king and deal wisely, and shall execute justice and righteousness in the land."
—Jeremiah 23:5 (ESV)

An eager crew unloaded a trailer full of Christmas trees and decorations. The annual ritual of decorating our church had begun. The biggest boxes contained about ten trees of different sizes. Each box was labeled: Tree 1, box 1 of 3; Tree 1, box 2 of 3; and so on. But we hit a snag.

There were at least two trees labeled Tree 1, and neither was complete. Other labels were wrong too. Some made no sense. Whoever had put away the trees the previous year hadn't labeled them correctly.

What should have been a simple task collapsed into a complex riddle. One volunteer said it felt like "sorting jumbled pieces from multiple puzzles without a box top."

I was frustrated. I believed we'd let down our volunteers. In that same moment, I felt God's gentle nudge: *Think of what it took to set up Christ's birth*. The painstakingly detailed prophecies. The astonishingly clear promises. The growing profile of this coming Savior painted by Old Testament sages over a span of two thousand years. Every piece was in its place. Every detail arranged perfectly.

The providence of God never shone more brightly than on the day the Savior was born. Tiny Bethlehem. The humble manger. Caesar's census. The virgin shall conceive. The birth of Christ was no afterthought. It was the outworking of a grace-filled plan from the ages of eternity past.

We might have jumbled Christmas, I thought, *but God doesn't*. And He didn't jumble the details of my life either. Not even the frustrations. Or the sorrows. God's saving plan rises above it all.

Thank You, Lord, for the meticulously coordinated, ages-long countdown to that first Christmas Day. May I abide every day in the certainty of Your perfect plan. —Bill Giovannetti

Digging Deeper: Isaiah 9:6

Train up a child in the way he should go, and when he is old he will not depart from it. —Proverbs 22:6 (NKJV)

It was December Holidazzle in downtown Minneapolis. Arriving early, my husband, Terry, good-naturedly decided to jump-start the short informal parade by walking down the street and waving to spectators, calling, "Merry Christmas!" Our grandson Clayton, nine, was thoroughly amused.

But when our family challenged him to go with his grandpa, he refused. It wasn't his personality to be in the limelight like that. Unfortunately, we kept after him about it. His eyes filled with tears, and he pulled his stocking cap over his face to hide from us.

My heart sank. I had to make it right with him. When Clayton next visited, I said I was sorry for pressuring him to parade down the street. Then I dealt my ace. "Remember when you wanted Papa and me to call the store to ask about that new computer game? You didn't want to talk with someone you didn't know. But we encouraged you to call because it was your game and your questions. And you did an excellent job! The difference between that phone call and the parade is there will be times when you'll have to talk with people you don't know and you need to learn how to do it. Papa and I were right to insist that you make the phone call yourself. But there was no good reason to insist that you be in front of a bunch of people you didn't know at a parade you weren't even in. We were wrong."

Proverbs 22:6—referring to training a child in "the way he should go"—is literally translated "according to his way." Each personality faces its own soft spots, exhibits its own strengths. Knowing when to encourage others and when to back off are things God wisely insists I learn.

Holy Spirit, guide me through the many nuances in my relationships. Let Your peace flow.
—Carol Knapp

Digging Deeper: Job 23:10–17, Proverbs 1:8, 1 Corinthians 13:11–12, Ephesians 6:1–24, Colossians 3:21

Tuesday, December 6

They prayed for the new believers there that they might receive the Holy Spirit. —Acts 8:15 (NIV)

An acquaintance sought me out at a big event and pulled me outside. She'd helped plan the party. "I feel lousy!" she sobbed. "I've worked so hard, and everyone seems to be mad at me about something."

I hugged her tightly and said all the reassuring things I could think of, starting with how it was a truly beautiful event that showed lots of work and planning, and finishing by noting that people often say harsh things whenever they care deeply because they want everything to be perfect.

"I know." My friend sniffled. "But I grew up in a family of alcoholics, and when things get stressful I try to take control. And then everyone gets angry at me."

I absorbed that news. With my children and spouse, it's mood disorders and anxiety that cause things to spin out of control. I know all too well the temptation to impose order on chaos by becoming authoritative. I've learned the hard way that it's wiser to be flexible than controlling.

As gently as I could, I offered, "Breathe deeply and find your grounding. You only need to control what's under your control. Remember what you believe in and hold it close."

"But I don't know what I believe!" she wailed.

"Breathe deeply and you'll remember," I replied. She did and, in a few minutes, was more peaceful.

She thanked me and wiped her eyes. "I wish I had the kind of grounding you seem to have," she said.

It wasn't the time or place for a theological discussion, so I sent up a prayer on her behalf. "You'll get there. Just keep searching for the truth...and then build your life around it."

Holy Spirit, enter the hearts and minds of those who don't know You and kindle in them the fire of Your love. —Julia Attaway

Digging Deeper: John 6:35–40

Wednesday, December 7

"Isn't this the carpenter's son?..." —Matthew 13:55 (NIV)

The museum was full of small decorative-arts objects from the seventeenth and eighteenth centuries: silver boxes, ivory statues, jewel-encrusted images, delicately carved figures. It was more my wife Carol's sort of thing than mine. As much as I appreciated the craftsmanship, nothing transported me.

Then I stood before a tiny figure carved in coral: a man holding a baby, reminding me of when my boys were young and I held them in my arms. I had felt both small and large at once, in awe at what God had made and overwhelmed by the challenges ahead. I often wondered if I was up to the task. "Thank You, Lord, for this child," I must have prayed a thousand times. "Don't let me blow it as a dad."

But this baby in coral wasn't just any baby, and the father wasn't just any dad. The title read, "Joseph holding the Baby Jesus." Talk about holding the world in your hands! Here was the man who held the Son of God. I imagined how he felt.

At first he was struck dumb by the role he was asked to play in the holy drama, but then he took to it graciously, marrying his betrothed, taking her to a stable in Bethlehem, dashing off to Egypt for safety, moving back to Nazareth, raising other sons mentioned in the Bible: James, Joseph, Simon, and Judas. Mary usually gets pride of place—for good reason. But here was Joseph, the earthly father of the Son of God, carrying his baby. "Look at this." I pointed it out to Carol. "Jesus and His dad."

"That's so sweet," she said. Like any good dad, Joseph took on an immense challenge and performed it admirably by doing the right thing, not loudly, not looking for praise, just listening to the angels and following their guidance.

Lord, thank You for blessing me with my sons. Give me the wisdom and courage to follow in Joseph's footsteps, to be the father You've called me to be. —Rick Hamlin

Digging Deeper: Matthew 1:19–21

Thursday, December 8

Whoever walks with the wise becomes wise.... —Proverbs 13:20 (ESV)

Cleaning out our mudroom, I hold on to a single kelly-green mitten. I bought the pair almost two decades ago at a church Christmas bazaar. The knitter, Flossy, told me she was ninety-five-and-a-half years old. I remember her smile when I said, "The green ones are gorgeous!"

She held out her wrinkled hand to hold mine and told me that when you get old, you go back to counting the years in quarters, just like you did when you were a kid. And then she shook her head and said, "You grow young again. You'll see."

She told me she had lost most of her sight, but she could still knit. I held up the mittens, admiring the intricate stitches, and noticed the low price written in wobbly handwriting on the tag. "Three dollars!" I exclaimed. "Oh, these are beautiful. Only three dollars?"

"I don't care about the money," she said. "I just like to make them. They keep my hands busy. Everyone should have a good pair of mittens, and you know what they say about idle hands." When I paid for them, she held my hand again and said, "Wear them with love."

I put on the mittens right then and wore them for years. Sometime after Solomon was born, I lost one. I searched and searched and thought it would turn up when we moved. It didn't.

I believed that maybe the other would go missing and then I wouldn't have to discard it. But here it is, the sole mitten of a pair that has lost its intended purpose. I think of Flossy and everything she said in those few minutes and how I cherish having something she made with love right here in my hands—and perhaps that is its true purpose.

Dear Lord, thank You for the wise people whom I encounter and the sole mitten that helps comfort and warm my soul. —Sabra Ciancanelli

Digging Deeper: Deuteronomy 6:6–7, Proverbs 10:4

Friday, December 9

Fixing our eyes on Jesus, the pioneer and perfecter of faith.... —Hebrews 12:2 (NIV)

I grew up with *Daily Guideposts* on the coffee table, a fixture next to the blue basket of potpourri. I remember dismissively thinking of it as my mom's book, a bunch of stories about old people doing old-people things. How could anyone over twenty possibly know what I was going through?

Then I got my wisdom teeth removed. Three days on the couch, sipping lukewarm water through a straw, has a way of driving even the most sensible teenager batty. In a moment of boredom verging on desperation, I reached over and grabbed the book.

I can't remember what that day's devotion was about, but I remember thinking that the writer seemed to understand me, which was saying a lot, considering I was a spunky, independent teenager and she was not. I flipped forward and read the next day's devotion. Same thing: the words felt like they were written just for me. I came to rely on *Daily Guideposts* for insight, direction, and hope.

Fast-forward ten years, and I was a new mom. It was a hard time, fraught with sleepless nights and endless days. But I clung to a hope that came only from Christ and was reinforced by the stories and prayers of others who knew, who understood. And so when I was asked to "audition" for *Daily Guideposts,* I said yes because I knew that I was walking this faith journey with friends.

Lord, thank You for the hope that comes from those who truly know You. Amen. —Erin MacPherson

Digging Deeper: Jeremiah 6:16, 1 Corinthians 1:19

Saturday, December 10

"A Savior has been born to you; he is the Messiah, the Lord." —Luke 2:11 (NIV)

My daughter Kendall e-mailed a photo this morning that made me laugh out loud and then feel sad for her. The caption read: "When we came downstairs this morning, here's what we saw." Their beautifully decorated nine-foot fresh Christmas tree was flat on the floor surrounded by shattered ornaments. What an exclamation point on a season of expectations already marred by two of their three little ones getting sick and a constant change of their festive family plans. It was a season of expectations edited by realities.

The picture touched something familiar within me as I remembered being a mom of three young children, entering the holiday season with visions of sugarplums dancing in my head, only to be disappointed by cranky kids as we ran from church activities to preschool parties to the mall, increasing my own fatigue because I felt responsible to make the magic of Christmas happen for them.

Have I learned anything from those years of experiences? I pondered that question as I dug deeper into my years of memories.

Maybe God intends purpose in our unmet expectations at Christmastime. Maybe they are meant to open up a wider space in our souls that can be filled only with Jesus. Maybe the longings are meant to prepare us to freshly receive the meaning of His birth each year and celebrate with deeper understanding. Maybe...

Could I tell my daughter about these maybes or will she learn them for herself when trees fall down and kids get sick? Perhaps both. I picked up the phone to call her.

Jesus, the responsibilities and unmet expectations of a busy Christmas season increase my longing for You and the meaning of Your birth. For this, I am grateful and pray that my daughter will recognize the same blessing this year. —Carol Kuykendall

Digging Deeper: Luke 2:10, John 3:15–16, Romans 8:32

Third Sunday in Advent, December 11

THE GIFT OF SMALL MOMENTS
Shepherds

Now there were in the same country shepherds living out in the fields, keeping watch over their flock by night. —Luke 2:8 (NKJV)

It was just a poinsettia, but to my wife it was a miracle. Margi had taken on the mammoth task of decorating the church for Christmas. Two large sanctuaries, lobbies, children's spaces, and massive outdoor plazas fell under her designing eye.

After months of planning, shopping, and recruiting, her army of decorators went to work. Dozens of trees graced our worship centers. Thousands of lights sparkled, and countless ornaments lent their gleam. It took over two weeks, but the mission was complete. Almost.

One task remained: placing poinsettias on tables scattered throughout the coffee area. Just the right number of plants had been purchased. Unfortunately, I miscounted the tables and one was left bare.

It wasn't a big deal in the great scheme of things, but to an exhausted worker all alone at night, it meant a lot. Margi summoned the energy for a final return to the store.

But first, on a hunch, she sneaked a peak into a box—and there, to her surprise, sat a poinsettia.

"Just a little thing," Margi said, "but it meant everything to me."

I thought of how God does His finest work through little things, unimportant things: like lowly shepherds, like a husband who miscounts, like a baby in a manger.

**No matter my life's station, Lord, may
I faithfully abide in the grace of Christ's love.**
—Bill Giovannetti

Digging Deeper: 2 Corinthians 8:9

Monday, December 12

So then, brothers, stand firm and hold to the traditions that you were taught by us....
—2 Thessalonians 2:15 (ESV)

I loved Christmas presents as a child. Otherwise, I never got into the spirit of the holiday. I didn't want to trim the tree, and I would groan when my mom turned on Christmas songs.

As I've gotten older, I have altered my attitude, focusing on Christ's sacrifice for us and learning to appreciate giving. But I still have no interest in the season's trappings.

My wife, Emily, is the opposite. She loves reminiscing about family Christmas parties in Austin, Texas, plays Christmas music incessantly, and fills the house with Christmas baubles.

I resisted her attempts to "Christmasify" our apartment. I complained about the music and fought her on fully decorating the house. I thought this was all silliness and had nothing to do with what Christmas was really about. It never escalated to outright spousal warfare, but we had our disagreements.

One day, while I dragged my feet about buying a tree, Emily finally had had enough. "I don't understand why you're being so difficult!" she said angrily, with a hint of a tear in her eye. "I'm going to spend my first Christmas ever without my family back home, and I just want to do something that reminds me of being with them. Why won't you help?"

I finally got it. All the trappings may not be about Christ, but they represent what Christmas is about: tradition, family, and expressing love. And if that was true for Emily, then it was time it became true for me.

Thank You, God, for the traditions that help us grow closer to You. —Sam Adriance

Digging Deeper: 1 Corinthians 11:2

Tuesday, December 13

Isn't it obvious that all angels are sent to help out...?
—Hebrews 1:14 (MSG)

My son Jeremy keeps our yard looking pristine. My husband Gene is picky about our two acres, and Jeremy makes a determined effort to keep him happy. He almost always succeeds. He even fills our bird feeders and cares for anything we no longer want to risk at our age. Usually, Gene and Jeremy get along perfectly. As Jeremy once stated, "Gene's been my stepdad longer than my real father lived." (Jeremy was barely fifteen when my husband Jerry died.)

Somehow on this icy day, Jeremy and Gene weren't hitting it off. Gene had been uptight with Jeremy. I suppose because Gene was getting older and depended on Jeremy so much. Who knows why men get bent out of shape? I knew my husband was ready to explode by the tone of his voice and his body language.

Jeremy knew it too. The ice was unusual for Georgia. Jeremy backed his old white truck out of our driveway and slid into the yard. Sitting at my desk, typing, I watched him try over and over again to get out, but his truck remained stuck. Gene drove up in his clean, waxed truck to observe Jeremy making ruts in the yard. The streets had been cleared, but our driveway remained covered in ice.

My husband was beyond furious. Jeremy was helpless as Gene climbed out of his truck. I laid my head on my typewriter. *Oh, Lord, please send someone quickly, even an angel…*

When I looked up, our neighbor Wilder had stopped by and phoned a friend. In just a few moments, a huge truck arrived and pulled Jeremy's truck onto the pavement. The four men burst into smiles and mock cheers. I did too.

Father, how often have I neglected to call on an angel? —Marion Bond West

Digging Deeper: Psalm 91:11, Hebrews 13:2

Wednesday, December 14

But if we hope for what we do not yet have, we wait for it patiently. —Romans 8:25 (NIV)

"You mean I *never* get to watch that movie again?"

"Brogan, I didn't say *never*. I'm saying not today. What about one of these other movies?"

My words didn't matter. Out came the lip-and-chin quiver. My five-year-old son could not get over the fact that I didn't want him to watch a particular movie that day. Never mind that he had a plethora of other ones to choose from.

"Buddy, let's not focus on the one thing you can't have."

As soon as the words left my mouth, I knew they weren't just for my son. I had been fixating on the one area of my life that God had said no to: another child. And it wasn't even a *no, never*; it was a *no, not yet*.

Maybe it was time to step back and see the broader picture and not let the truth become blurry and distorted. How quickly God's *yes* could slip into obscurity when His *no* becomes our focus.

Those words to my son became God's words to me, from a God Who pours out blessings, a God Who poured out His very life.

Lord, Your blessings are everywhere.
Give me eyes to see them and forgive me
when I don't. —Katie Ganshert

Digging Deeper: Genesis 3:2–13, 1 John 3:1

Thursday, December 15

Do nothing out of selfish ambition or vain conceit. Rather, in humility value others above yourselves, not looking to your own interests but each of you to the interests of the others. —Philippians 2:3–4 (NIV)

My son opened the little wrapped shoe box that was handed to him by a white-bearded man. He wasn't playing Santa Claus; he was part of a team from North Carolina who'd visited our New York City ministry to give early Christmas surprises to the children. Brandon was delighted with each simple gift. "Crayons!" he screamed. "Toothpaste!" His favorite gift was a yo-yo, and the two of them spent time playing with it. Brandon watched each demonstration carefully, and both cheered when he finally got the hang of it. I was especially grateful for the attention he was receiving since his own father had recently chosen to no longer be in his life.

A while later, I heard Brandon crying. His yo-yo had broken, and the bearded man was working hard to put it back together. Brandon cried even more when it was obvious it couldn't be fixed, but he calmed down when we handed out cupcakes. I wanted to thank his new friend for trying to fix his toy, but I couldn't find him. "Oh, he went to the store to buy another yo-yo for Brandon," one of the other team members said.

The store was more than ten blocks away, and it was snowy outside. When the bearded man came back holding a small bag, he gave Brandon so much more than a yo-yo. He showed my little boy that he was worth a long winter walk and deserving of such extraordinary loving-kindness.

Lord, thank You for the hearts of Your servants who go above and beyond. Continue to stir the hearts of Your people to demonstrate Your amazing and personal love for us all. —Karen Valentin

Digging Deeper: Acts 20:35

Friday, December 16

And seek the peace of the city whither I have caused you to be carried away captives...for in the peace thereof shall ye have peace. —Jeremiah 29:7 (KJV)

Some call it progress. After ten years of teaching and positive evaluations at my community college, new accreditation rules trump fifteen years of experience. I'm suddenly demoted to teaching remedial courses, which carry no credit. Forget teaching critical thinking, fallacies, and research. Oh no, I'll now teach parts of speech and punctuation. Yet because I have so much experience, I'm asked to mentor newbie PhDs with none.

I consider quitting, yet I'm drawn to these hard-luck students who need basic skills to enter college classes. Until then, their dreams are on hold. In some ways, we are in exile together, on the margins of where we wish to be. Along with grammar, these self-effacing students need confidence, positive reinforcement, a dose of humor, my rubber chicken. Yes, I can do this.

Slowly, my students gain traction and reveal their lives in their writing: the unplanned pregnancy, the car wreck, the lessons learned from a prison sentence. At home, I find myself praying for them, especially the young man who smells sour because he lives on the street. At the end of the semester, he gives me a thank-you note—a rarity. I read it in the empty classroom. "Sure you taught me the semicolon, but more important, you kept me in school."

It's taken a few years, but I now recognize that God has me exactly where He needs me. I teach remedial English not as a career but as a ministry of hope.

Lord, You bless me everywhere, even in places I think I don't want to be. —Gail Thorell Schilling

Digging Deeper: Psalm 31:1–3, Acts 8:30–31

Saturday, December 17

WHAT THE SAINTS HAVE TAUGHT ME
Hildegard, Companion When People Put You Down

Now to him who...is able to do far more abundantly than all that we ask or think, to him be glory.... —Ephesians 3:20–21 (RSV)

I first met Hildegard of Bingen on the radio. On a music station I'd catch a high, haunting melody by unaccompanied female voices. Eventually, I bought a

CD collection of this ethereal music and learned from the liner notes that the composer was the medieval abbess of a monastery in Germany. I bought a book about her life, discovering a woman astonishing in any age, unimaginable in hers.

Born in 1098 into a male-dominated world, she became an author, artist, botanist, healer, visionary, composer, and poet. She believed music represented the original harmony between God and man, and wrote of Christ as "God's song." At a time when women were considered incapable of understanding either theology or politics, Hildegard preached all over Germany, counseled kings, popes, and emperors, and insisted that the nuns at her abbey develop the intellect as well as the spirit.

So I was delighted when my husband and I came upon Hildegard's monastery on a hillside high above the Rhine, twin towers rising among the vineyards. We left the car in the parking lot and followed a narrow lane toward a massive ancient-looking brownstone building. In fact, a black-garbed nun explained, the present abbey was built in the twentieth century, replacing earlier structures destroyed in repeated wars. Fifty-five nuns, ages twenty-five to ninety-four, were now living there. It wasn't just the scenes from Hildegard's life on the walls of the church that brought her to life. The whole serene setting with its craft shops and study center radiated the spirit of the woman who, in answer to men's, "You can't," replied with God's, "Yes, you can!"

As I ponder my own potential, Father, let me hear no voice but Yours. —Elizabeth Sherrill

Digging Deeper: Philippians 4:13

Fourth Sunday in Advent, December 18

THE GIFT OF SMALL MOMENTS
Extravagant Grace

And suddenly there was with the angel a multitude of the heavenly host praising God and saying: "Glory to God in the highest, and on earth peace, goodwill toward men!" —Luke 2:13–14 (NKJV)

Though our kids are now teenagers, they haven't lost the magic of Christmas morning. My wife and I love it. When they come down the stairs, their eyes still bug out at the massive pile of gifts they see.

We make that pile as big as we can. We shove the coffee table beside the tree and stack gifts on it just to add height. We spread gifts out across the floor, beneath the tree, around the recliner. The pile is enormous, and we're not commercializing Christmas!

The vast majority of those gifts are basic needs: socks, toothbrushes, notebooks, shoes. We stock up all year on whatever the kids need, wrap it up, and add it to the pile. We use extralarge boxes for the smallest gifts just to make the pile bigger.

We still read Luke's Christmas story to recall the Savior's birth. We still snuggle with hot chocolate and classic Christmas movies. Our teenagers still embrace our traditions.

But best of all remains that wide-eyed wonder on Christmas morning when the kids see their gifts, because their sense of wonder helps me remember God's extravagant grace.

Father, You delight in giving, and this season is the proof. Open my eyes to the wonder of Your grace. —Bill Giovannetti

Digging Deeper: Luke 1:26–38

Monday, December 19

What can I take as a witness...?
—Lamentations 2:13 (JPS)

I've never thought of myself as particularly pretty, and when my husband, Keith, died, I realized that the only person in the world who thought I was beautiful wasn't there any longer. I began to actively turn away from mirrors entirely.

It had been more than three years since I'd had my eyes examined, and part of my resolve to carry on without my husband was to make an effort to take care of myself, because that's what he'd have wanted me to do. So I made an appointment with the optometrist.

It occurred to me that I still had Keith's glasses: a pair of trifocals and a pair of sunglasses. His frames were different from mine. I favored dark plastic, while he liked thin metal. Though our tastes differed, when the doctor gave me my new prescription, I decided to have the lenses put into Keith's frames so that I could begin wearing them myself.

When the new glasses arrived, I put them on and looked in the mirror I'd been avoiding. My face looked different and, to my surprise, I liked it. I was looking at myself through Keith's eyes.

Please keep finding ways of telling me that You think I'm beautiful, Lord. I need reminding.
—Rhoda Blecker

Digging Deeper: Song of Songs 1:15

Tuesday, December 20

Your Father knows what you need before you ask him. —Matthew 6:8 (NIV)

From the time they were little, I always tried to teach my daughters the value of a dollar and not indulge their every whim. When my older girl was four, she crawled into my lap one day after a trip to the drugstore and asked, "Mommy, next time we go there, can we look at that Peter Pan snow globe? I don't want to buy it. I just want to look at it again because it's so beautiful."

What Peter Pan snow globe? I hadn't seen it. "Sure," I replied. "Next time we're there, you show me so I can see it too."

A few weeks later, she led me to a display at the same store. I picked up one of the globes and shook it before letting her hold it. Her eyes sparkled as glittering snow fell on the Darling house while the children flew to Neverland behind Peter and Tink.

"Thank you for letting me look at it, Mommy," she said. "You can put it back now."

I saw the sign: *$9.99.* It was a lot to spend on a trinket she'd probably forget about within a week, but something urged me to get it anyway. I knelt down beside my sweet girl and said, "Mommy is going to buy this for you."

Every night for the next few years, my little girl fell asleep as the snow globe played "You Can Fly." Now, years later, whenever I hear that song, I am reminded of what a precious gift my daughter is to me and am so thankful that I listen to those urges that often bring such treasures.

Giver of all good and perfect gifts, thank You for knowing exactly what we need. —Ginger Rue

Digging Deeper: Matthew 7:11, James 1:17

Wednesday, December 21

God is our...source of all comfort.
—2 Corinthians 1:3 (NLT)

Everything had gone wrong. I didn't even smile when I glanced at the bright yellow rubber ducky I'd taped to the top of my computer monitor, a silly toy like a lot of the other employees had on display to lighten their moods. I typed in my password and sighed. Today my home computer had gotten a virus, so I drove to work to download a patch to fix it. I'd planned on not coming in because it was a holiday, but even that had gone wrong. *What next, God?* I thought.

The sounds of Sunrise's thundering feet echoed through the empty office. Since nobody else would be at work, I'd brought my golden retriever. Within moments, I'd become so engrossed that I didn't pay any attention to Sunrise as she raced through the building. Every once in a while she'd sweep under my desk and ask for a pet before she ran off again. Finally, she brushed past my legs and plopped to the floor.

When the computer screen blipped "Download Complete," I pushed back my chair, but the wheels caught on something. Frowning, I looked down and gasped. Sunrise was lounging on a pile of silly toys, including my yellow ducky! She'd raced around the office, collecting toys from everyone's desks. I chuckled and shook my head. "You'll do anything to get rid of stress!"

When I scooped up the toys, a strange thought drifted through my mind. *What about me? When problems pile up, I dwell on them and expect more. Why haven't I surrounded myself with things that relieve the stress?*

I pulled out my prayer journal when I got home, nestled in my personal messages from God, and found all the encouragement I needed.

Lord, thank You for giving us words of comfort. Amen. —Rebecca Ondov

Digging Deeper: Psalm 23

Thursday, December 22

In Your light we see light. —Psalm 36:9 (NAS)

It was minus-twelve degrees in Minnesota on December 24. You couldn't tell it was Christmas Eve at our house. My husband and I hadn't wanted to make more work for ourselves in the midst of packing for our move to north Idaho. We had no tree, no decorations, no lights, no gifts. I was trying my best to not feel glum during my favorite time of the year.

I slipped out early and saw the morning star outshining all the others, reminding me of Jesus, "the bright morning star" (Revelation 22:16). Coming inside, I looked up a Bible passage connecting Jesus's birth with light. I read out loud, "Because of the tender mercy of our God, with which the Sunrise from on high will visit us" (Luke 1:78, NAS).

A while later I decided to go walking. Layering up, I headed into the chilly dawn. In the ice and snow I hadn't been going all the way to the cul-de-sac, but this morning I did. Just as I got there, I was startled by a brilliant red-gold glow across the snowy field. On the open horizon, just appearing, was the "sunrise on high visiting me." What a moment of praise!

The glorious burst of morning light synchronizing with my earlier Scripture reading was like a gift from God tied up with a bow. He seemed boldly present with me. I floated in joy through the day into the night—the Christmas Eve that looked bare but was far from barren.

Jesus, You came to "shine upon those who sit in darkness" (Luke 1:79, NAS). Your light lifts me every time. —Carol Knapp

Digging Deeper: Psalms 87:7, 97:11; Proverbs 4:18; John 1:4; 2 Corinthians 4:6

Friday, December 23

They came...and found.... —Luke 2:16 (KJV)

Christmas was near, and I was longing for a place to smell the hay. That's my gateway to the real meaning of it all, when everything falls away and I'm standing at the manger.

My daughter, Keri, and I had just arrived at Spruce Street Baptist, a church on the edge of downtown Nashville, where serving those in need was priority. We were there to distribute toys. Nearby, the women of Spruce Street were preparing the free noon meal.

The church's annex looked like a toy store. First to arrive was a mother with a little girl. The child was beautiful and well cared for, and from the minute she walked in her eyes were fixed on a particular doll.

"Santa told me this was meant for a special girl... one with big brown eyes," I said. "I think that's you!"

She held it close. Then her eyes fell on a sleeping bag that was pushed under the table. Keri had brought it as an afterthought. The little girl carefully returned the doll to its place. "Look, Momma," she said, picking up the sleeping bag. "I should take this instead."

"Oh, honey," her mother answered, "won't that be wonderful to have in the shelter...like sleeping in your own bed!"

Keri and I froze. Our eyes met. This little girl and her mother were homeless? How could it be? Seeing them leave, clutching the doll and the sleeping bag (we'd insisted they take both) was little comfort. We looked at those still waiting: homeless mothers and children.

The next free meal was Christmas Eve. Keri and I arrived at the church with two carloads of sleeping bags. The women were cooking; the people were gathering. There was good food, Christmas carols, camaraderie, and plenty of sleeping bags to go around. And God was there with us. The smell of hay had never been so sweet.

Father, there is nowhere on earth I would rather be than in the manger with You. —Pam Kidd

Digging Deeper: Proverbs 19:1, 17; Jeremiah 22:16; Luke 2:16

Christmas Eve, Saturday, December 24

THE GIFT OF SMALL MOMENTS
Worth the Wait

[Jesus Christ] was chosen before the creation of the world, but was revealed in these last times for your sake. —1 Peter 1:20 (NIV)

When my family and friends sat down to dinner last Christmas, we tucked into a meal that had taken days to prepare. Cookies had been baked. Christmas platters had been cleaned. Snacks. Dips. Drinks. And the star of the show: standing rib roast, my personal love language.

The mad dash gave way to a beautifully set table. I said to my wife, "Honey, this should be in a magazine." Grandma agreed. We gathered round, gave thanks, and dug in.

Not thirty minutes later, I pushed away, completely stuffed. All that work was finished off in minutes. "Days to prepare, minutes to eat," Josie, my daughter, quipped. We smiled.

My thoughts traveled back to that first Christmas. The birth of Jesus took one day, but the prelaunch required all the countless eons of earth's dateless past. Because that's how God, Who loves me, sets the table of His grace.

I looked at my son. "You know, Mom went into labor for you on Christmas Eve," I said, "but you wanted to wait for Christmas Day."

Jonathan smiled. "Worth the wait, right?"

My wife chimed in: "Ask again after you clear the table."

Father, it took an eternity to set the table for the gift of Your Son. May I abide in faith, trusting that all of Your gifts are worth the wait. —Bill Giovannetti

Digging Deeper: 1 John 4:9–10

Christmas, Sunday, December 25

THE GIFT OF SMALL MOMENTS
The Lord Gives

Therefore the Lord Himself will give you a sign: Behold, the virgin shall conceive and bear a Son, and shall call His name Immanuel. —Isaiah 7:14 (NKJV)

My son raced down the stairs, and I immediately got a lump in my throat. Inside the tall, strong boy, I still see the child. He's a teenager now, but fourteen years ago on Christmas Day, he lay in my wife's arms, a helpless newborn. We named him Jonathan, meaning "the Lord gives."

As Jonathan tore into packages beside his sister, Josie, I put an arm around Margi's shoulders. We watched and remembered: Christmas Eve labor pains, our rush to the hospital, a Christmas Day son.

We saw then what we see today: both gentleness and strength, stubborn tenacity and easygoing joy. His qualities from that first day still shine through.

I can't help but think of Mary and Joseph every Christmas morning. What they saw then defined them forever. Infant Jesus, meek and mild, swaddled in a manger, would grow to manhood, strong and self-assured, independent. I feel a bit of what they felt.

My Christmas Day son is growing up. But he's still the same child, only wrapped in a larger frame. And Jesus, I know, is still the same Savior: approachable, human, wondrous.

"O Holy Child of Bethlehem, descend on us, we pray. Cast out our sin, and enter in, be born in us today." —Bill Giovannetti

Digging Deeper: Philippians 2:5–11

You have let me experience the joys of life and the exquisite pleasures of your own eternal presence.
—Psalm 16:11 (TLB)

My husband, Don, and I were eating lunch at a restaurant when a toddler came in, each parent holding one of his hands. "Wow!" he said when he saw all the people. He kept up a steady stream of "wows" as they walked to their table. I lost sight of him, but when the waiter brought their drinks—two ice teas and a pink lemonade—I heard a soft but joyful "Wow!"

When was the last time I experienced such pure joy? I wondered. Somewhere along the way I'd become so blasé that I failed to notice, much less appreciate, everyday wonders and little miracles such as the lovely color and tart-sweet taste of pink lemonade. Could I capture a bit of that child's awe?

I decided to try by paying more attention to everyday events and surroundings. My first success came when we arrived home. My dog Tarby ran to meet me and licked my hand, her tail wagging and her whole body wiggling with pleasure. She greets me this way whether I've been away a few hours or a week. She always lifts my spirits, but I'd never acknowledged what a wonder it was to experience her enthusiastic, slobbery love.

I began to receive other small wonders with joy: a steaming bowl of chili during a miniblizzard; a hug and a heartfelt "I love you" from a grandchild; the beauty of my husband Don's golden daffodils, ragged from wind and nipped by frost but still blooming bravely; our church's bells ringing out "Joyful, Joyful We Adore Thee."

"Seek and you will find," the Bible says (Matthew 7:7, TLB). How true that is! How wonderfully joyful!

Thank You, Jesus, for the "wow" moments that take place every single day. —Penney Schwab

Digging Deeper: Psalm 148:1–14, Galatians 5:22

Tuesday, December 27

"He changes the seasons and guides history...." —Daniel 2:21 (MSG)

I was first asked to contribute to *Daily Guideposts* in the late seventies. I was certain I had nothing inspirational to share. But a couple of my devotions appeared in the 1979 volume. (We used only initials to identify writers then.) Changes in the book and in my life have transpired, but one thing remains the same: each year I know I can't possibly come up with something worthwhile to contribute. I delay, argue with myself, avoid my office. Finally, begging God's help, I take the plunge and sit down at my typewriter (I still don't have a computer).

My office is cluttered: papers everywhere, many versions of the Bible open on the floor, *Strong's Exhaustive Concordance* at my feet. My aged cat, Girl Friend, my companion for the last sixteen years, sleeps on top of whatever papers strike her fancy.

Through the years I've written about my fears, inadequacies, frustrations, and failures as a mother; bits about my two daughters and twin sons, including the addictions, bipolar disorder, jail, and prison time my sons have endured; the death of their father at forty-six with brain cancer; widowhood; loneliness; and—*tada!*—God's bringing my second husband, Gene Acuff, into my life through his reading of *Daily Guideposts*. We've been married nearly thirty years. I've written about my beloved pets and what wisdom and inspiration they've taught me, what sweet love they've freely given me.

I've made precious friends through *Guideposts*. I've met a few; most I haven't. They crisscross from Washington to New Mexico. They understand me, encourage me, and pray for my family and me. Their letters to me are stuffed into old trunks, cardboard boxes, and a chest of drawers. It's because of these unseen yet treasured friendships that I've continued to write.

Father, I ask You in Jesus's name to bless the socks off *Daily Guideposts* readers! —Marion Bond West

Digging Deeper: Psalm 35:14, Proverbs 17:17

Wednesday, December 28

Pray without ceasing. —1 Thessalonians 5:17 (NAS)

I'd been hearing about this new habit of my four-year-old great-nephew for several months. It seems he talks to God about everything. Braxton and his mom pass an ambulance in their car? "Bless those sick people," he prays in earnest. Rain falls on Halloween morning? Braxton asks God to keep the trick-or-treaters dry.

Still, on Christmas afternoon when we all gathered at his grandparents' home in celebration, I was somewhat taken aback. Towheaded Braxton stormed through the front door with his cousins to the smell of something burning on the stove. "Lord, help the food!" was his plea. And when he learned that the family down the street had suddenly lost a loved one, with details too complicated for most adults to comprehend, Braxton simply whispered, "Be with them, Jesus."

After dinner, I sat at the end of the table and applied pressure to my eyes. "The medicine hasn't touched my headache," I remarked to my brother. I noticed Braxton on the sofa, looking up from his computer game. He didn't say a word, just lowered his head and moved his lips to the One Who hears every request from every believer, young or old.

Somehow I wasn't surprised when the pain behind my eyes disappeared.

In the new year ahead, Lord, help me to depend on You for absolutely everything. —Roberta Messner

Digging Deeper: Ephesians 6:18, Philippians 4:6, Colossians 4:2

Thursday, December 29

My sheep hear my voice. I know them, and they follow me. —John 10:27 (NRSV)

The waiting room was packed. I'd driven my eighty-three-year-old grandmother, Marge, and her sister, Virginia, to their follow-up appointments for cataract surgery.

We found chairs together on the back wall. A complimentary coffee bar was at the end of our row. I went to the counter and poured three cups. When I turned around, Grandma Marge was by my side. I figured she wanted to stir in sugar or creamer. Instead, she grabbed the carafe and carried it around, refreshing the cups of others who waited. My heart was warmed by her hospitality.

Moments later, the sisters went into the exam room. Busying myself with a magazine, I heard a shuffling sound near me. Gazing up, I saw a man making his way to the now-vacant chairs in my row.

I need another cup of coffee, I thought. Immediately a second thought followed: *Ask him if he wants some.*

The man sat directly in front of the coffee area. I got up and walked over. "May I pour you a cup while I'm here?" I asked.

"Thank you," he mumbled. "Fill it halfway—don't want to spill."

I offered him the cup. He lifted both of his hands to take it, and I saw that his forefingers and thumbs were fused together and his remaining three fingers merged into a vee shape. Our eyes met. "Thank you," he whispered as I gingerly placed the cup between his hands. "Don't often get the opportunity to drink coffee. Pot's too wide for my grasp."

Back in my chair, I heard God's voice: *You won't always understand why I ask you to do things, but know there's always a reason.*

Thank You, God, for the much-needed lesson that obedience to You is more important than understanding why. —Stephanie Thompson

Digging Deeper: Exodus 4:12; 1 Samuel 15:22; Jeremiah 7:23, 26:13

Friday, December 30

Forgive others, and God will forgive you.
—Luke 6:37 (CEV)

My mind was consumed with accusations as I heaped a pile of hay on the sled to feed the horses. *Can't my friend see what he's doing isn't working? I told him the solution!*

Sunrise, my golden retriever, dribbled a tennis ball next to me. I ruffled her fur. "Okay...when I'm done feeding."

I pulled the sled into the pasture and tossed the hay into the feeders. I frowned when I noticed Sunrise hadn't traipsed behind me, so I peeked inside the barn. She lay next to a wooden pallet on which hay had been stacked. Whining, she pushed her nose between the slats, trying to grasp the ball that had rolled just beyond her reach. I pulled it out to play with her.

Throughout the afternoon I rehashed the offense as I vacuumed and dusted. Then I saw a spot of blood on the carpet. I walked over to Sunrise; her nose had a friction burn where she'd pushed it repeatedly against the wooden pallet.

By dinnertime, my heart was sour. Sunrise bounded over when I set her bowl on the floor. All the skin on the bridge of her nose was gone! She'd spent the afternoon clawing slivers from the wooden pallet out of her nose—and I hadn't noticed. I grimaced. "You need tweezers!"

You do too, I heard. Instead of giving my friend advice and then letting it go, I'd held on to his contrary decision and taken it personally. The offense, like a sliver, hadn't hurt him at all but had festered within me.

It took time for Sunrise's wound to heal, but when I forgave, my heart was instantly as good as new.

Lord, thank You for the gift of forgiveness. Amen. —Rebecca Ondov

Digging Deeper: Psalm 86:5

Saturday, December 31

It is God's privilege to conceal things....
—Proverbs 25:2 (TLB)

My first contribution to *Daily Guideposts* was in 1988, twenty-eight years ago. There were only thirty-one writers that year. Ronald Reagan was president, and America was singing Bobby McFerrin's hit song "Don't Worry, Be Happy."

The first letter I ever received from a reader was from a middle-aged woman whose husband had just died. She was going back to college to learn some new skills. She wrote, "I feel like I am getting ready for something, but what I am getting ready for is a mystery."

She was not disturbed by the mystery. In fact, she seemed excited about it, as if the future was a series of Christmas presents to be slowly unwrapped with joy. I had never thought of mystery as a pleasure, but after reading her letter I began to see how mystery could be a gift from God, something to add a bit of zing to life.

After all, would I even want to go to a ball game if I already knew who would win? Would I enjoy a movie very much if I had seen the ending before? If I knew I would someday inherit a million dollars, would I become unhappy in my job?

Not knowing the future frees me to pay attention to the present, and maybe that's the best way to be ready for the future. There may be trouble ahead, but if I manage my money well now, I should be ready for it. If I make the people I love happy now, there should be a harvest of joy someday.

Bobby McFerrin was right. "In every life we have some trouble, when you worry you make it double. Don't worry, be happy."

About my future, Lord, surprise me.
—Daniel Schantz

Digging Deeper: Deuteronomy 29:29,
Ecclesiastes 3:11

GOD'S ABIDING LOVE

1 _____

2 _____

3 _____

4 _____

5 _____

6 _____

7 _____

8 _____

9 _____

10 _____

11 _____

12 _____

13 _____

14 _____

15 _____

16 _____

17 _____

18 _____

19 _____

20 _____

21 _____

22 _____

23 _____

24 _____

25 _____

26 _____

27 _____

28 _____

29 _____

30 _____

31 _____

FELLOWSHIP CORNER

Much has changed in the last year for **Sam Adriance** of New Haven, Connecticut, but the most important things have remained the same. Sam and Emily have settled happily into married life and have made a home with their cat, Crookshanks. "I love being married," Sam says. "Going through this journey we call life is so much better when you have someone to share it with." He just finished his final year of law school and began a yearlong position working for a federal judge in Bridgeport. When that commitment ends, Sam and Emily will join Sam's brother, Ned, in Washington, DC. Sam's parents, Anne and Matt, are still a major part of their lives, and Sam's in-laws, Nancy and Mark, have become integral members of the family.

Marci Alborghetti and her husband, Charlie, of New London, Connecticut, are newly infatuated with Baltimore's Inner Harbor neighborhood, which they can easily reach by train, and they enjoy their road trips throughout New England and New York. When they aren't traveling, they continue their involvement with the local homeless shelter and the friends they have made there. Marci also corresponds with several individuals through the Church of the Brethren's Death Row Support Project. Her twenty-fifth book was published, and she is now working on a series of Scripture-based books. "I am blessed by the number of opportunities God offers to do the work Jesus taught us to do," she says.

"Could this really be the year I turn 68? I still can't believe it," writes **Andrew Attaway** of New York City. "Maybe one of the reasons I can't believe it is our family: one soon-to-be teen (Stephen), one early teen (Maggie), one midteen (Mary), and two young adults (Elizabeth and John). There's truth in the saying that children keep you young—just by watching and trying to keep up with them. And when there are bumps in the road, I can't sit under my vine and fig tree and read a book. I have to keep moving. Amid it all, there's the knowledge that God abides with me in His Word, in life's quiet spaces and in its difficult moments, in the love of family, and in the incredible generosity of friends."

"I used to think that if I could plow through whatever obstacle I faced, I would be able to resume my normal life," writes **Julia Attaway** of New York

City. "But this year I realized there was another way of looking at things." In the midst of an extremely difficult series of family crises, the phrase "Abide in Me" began to take on new meaning. Instead of pushing against the rough stuff, Julia focused on simply moving toward God. This attitude had a huge impact on her faith. "My prayers shifted from 'Make this problem go away!' to 'Show me what I need to see and how to draw closer to You!' In that sense, it was a fruitful and wonderful year."

 A number of years ago, **Karen Barber** of Alpharetta, Georgia, met a remarkable physical education teacher with multiple sclerosis who accepted her limitations by trusting that God was there with her. "She told me that even though her physical disability sidelined her, she could still support her students by cheering them on," Karen relates. "Since then I've often had to remember to abide and make myself at home with God when I face a not-so-welcome 'new normal' in my life, such as high blood pressure, the divorce of our son Chris, or our son John's career move away from home." Karen learned that with a retired husband, three sons, and two grandchildren, there's always a "new normal" just around the bend, where God is inviting her to abide with Him once again.

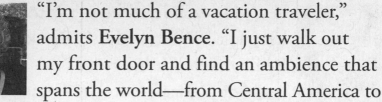

"I'm not much of a vacation traveler," admits **Evelyn Bence**. "I just walk out my front door and find an ambience that spans the world—from Central America to northern Africa and southern Asia. Where do I reside? In a diverse neighborhood in Arlington, Virginia. Where do I abide? Rooted in the life of Christ, hoping to bear the fruit of blessing." Two focal points of Evelyn's year have been table hospitality and spreading the word about her new book, *Room at My Table*, which is filled with meditations intended to inspire hosts as well as guests.

"I'm experiencing a profusion of blessings and healing, both spiritual and physical," says **Erika Bentsen** of Sprague River, Oregon. After a career-ending back injury two years ago brought an abrupt halt to ranching life as she knew it, Erika struggled to find the path God intended for her. "When I finally changed my prayers from 'But I want' to 'Yes, I will,' overwhelming peace followed—and blessings began to flow. I can still live in the country I love, surrounded by animals, but I'm taking a step back from the constant workload to savor life. Today is not only different from before—it's better. I want to thank all of the dear *Daily Guideposts* readers who sent prayers and letters of comfort. I am overwhelmed and humbled by their outpouring of support."

"I always wondered how Job could keep faith," writes **Rhoda Blecker** of Bellingham, Washington. "But now I really do understand. After Keith died, I found out that Los Angeles County had no record of our wedding thirty-five years ago. Then the bank couldn't find the power of attorney that Keith had signed to give me access to his account. When I tried to sell his truck, I discovered the state of Washington had never sent the ownership documents to us. On top of all of this, the cemetery buried Keith in the wrong grave and the headstone was installed facing the wrong way. I was starting to fray at the edges. Then, two months after Keith's death, our dog, Anjin, was diagnosed with cancer. It could have felt like the last straw, but somehow God gave me the strength and grace to cope. Anjin had surgery and was pronounced healthy. And I began to heal too."

"I'm hoping to unpack the last box!" writes **Lisa Bogart**. She and her husband, Rod, moved from San Rafael, California, to Scarsdale, New York, so Rod could take a job at HBO. They are excited to be in the same time zone as their son, Zach, as he finishes his last year at Boston University. During their relocation, they stayed in an apartment in Manhattan for three months. "It was quite the adventure," Lisa adds. "The city really doesn't sleep, but we learned to—despite all the noise in the street, thirty floors below. We enjoyed the museums, parks, and restaurants so much. I even figured out the subway system!"

Jeff Chu of Brooklyn, New York, is feeling pretty exhausted after a year of traveling more than he ever has before. He logged over 130,000 flight miles, with reporting trips and speaking engagements taking him across the United States, as well as to Australia, Canada, China, India, Indonesia, and Thailand. He remains grateful for the gift of other people's narratives, without which he couldn't do his work. Jeff says, "I am continually reminded of the power of stories—whether they are testimonies, dramas, or parables—to change hearts and lives."

Sabra Ciancanelli of Tivoli, New York, says, "Who knew that agreeing to my sons' pleas for a dog would bring such love into our home? Our new furry family member, Soda, came all the way from a shelter in Georgia, and he's teaching me that sometimes we don't realize what's missing in our lives until we find it. Soda is my constant companion, always willing to follow me wherever I go or happy to snuggle beside me on the couch. He's a breathing reminder of the unexpected blessings that come when I let go of misgivings and simply say, 'Yes!'" Sabra's new book, *Thin Places: Touching the Edge of Heaven*, is available at ShopGuideposts.org.

"Perhaps now isn't the time to bring this up," warns **Mark Collins** of Pittsburgh, Pennsylvania, "but the only reason I'm still standing is because of divine intervention, a loving wife and family, and modern medicine that helps to right everything that's miswired in my noggin. Love, the Almighty, and neurochemistry are lifesavers." Included on the lifesaving list are Mark's wife, Sandee, who is a seminary professor, and his now mostly grown children: Faith, Hope, and Grace. "I love the names we gave to our kids. I didn't know they would double as abiding prescriptions for a healthy life."

"This year, Elba and I celebrate our thirty-fifth wedding anniversary," writes **Pablo Diaz** of Carmel, New York. "I married my high school sweetheart as I began my final year of college, and we spent a great deal of time learning about each other and raising our two kids. Life wasn't always smooth, but through prayer, counsel, hard work, and love, we overcame tough times." Pablo and Elba enjoy each other's company whether they are on vacation or sharing a simple meal at their kitchen table. They love to sit and chat, which helps them sustain a friendship that keeps them deeply connected. "Elba and I look to the future with hope, knowing that God is with us. Because of Him, we are partners for life!"

Brian Doyle lives in Portland, Oregon, with his family and their dog, and Brian is the editor of *Portland Magazine* at the University of Portland. He writes, "These things abide in me: every moment in which my children ever laughed and giggled and snickered and wept and burbled and brawled; every moment in the savory company of my lovely bride since the moment she glanced at me in the street in Boston and then unaccountably smiled rather than sprinting away, shrieking; every slight gesture of kindness and grace I have witnessed, and these are beyond counting and measure. For I am a student of grace and kindness and laughter and endurance and defiant courage against the dark." Those are the subjects of his many books, most recently the essay collection *Children and Other Wild Animals* and the novel *The Plover*.

Logan Eliasen of Port Byron, Illinois, had a year full of transitions. "As I've reached the final stretch of my undergraduate studies, I've learned that the only way I can anchor myself in the midst of life's whirlwind is to abide in God. Whether I'm facing a stack of papers due tomorrow or the shifting uncertainties of the future, I know that only He can provide the strength I need to move forward step-by-step. God is so good! I'm continually amazed at how He not only gets me where I need to go but also slows me down to see life's beauty along the way."

"Raising a household of sons keeps you busy," says **Shawnelle Eliasen** of Port Byron, Illinois. "There are countless graces and joys. But there have been some tough times too. We're waiting on the Lord for healing." That's why this year's theme, "Abide in Me," is especially precious to Shawnelle. "We reach daily for sustaining grace. Staying connected to—and abiding in—Jesus is the only way." Shawnelle is learning how to delight in the gift of God's grace in everyday moments: a hand still small enough to fold into hers; a kiss on the cheek from a fast-growing boy; her husband's arms, safe, steady, and strong; and the goodness of a yellow Labrador puppy named Rugby. "God's kind compassion is all around us, all the time. Lord, give me eyes to see!"

Though this year has been full of challenges, **Sharon Foster** of Durham, North Carolina, has much to be thankful for. "As the old folks used to say when I was a child, we are each 'still clothed and in our right minds, with a reasonable portion of health and strength!' God is good. Anything we do bears fruit because we abide in Him!" Sharon's daughter, Lanea, is still fighting poverty at Southeast Community Resources; her son, Chase, is currently singing with the Chicago Lyric Opera; and Sharon is writing a movie script and working with girls at Bible Witness Camp in the summer. "Please pray for us, especially that our eyes, hearts, and spirits will be open to God's divine encounters and His will for our lives."

Katie Ganshert of Bettendorf, Iowa, is a slightly frazzled, ever-inquisitive midwestern woman who's passionate about Jesus, her family, adoption, writing, and all things romance—which is exactly what she writes: stories about flawed, broken characters who wrestle with faith and fall in love. When she's not plotting ways to get her hero and heroine to cross paths, she enjoys being silly and laughing with her husband, playing make-believe with her "wild child" of a son, dreaming and planning for the day her daughter from the Congo will come home, and chatting with women friends over coffee.

"With much fear and trembling, I began blogging from my Web site," says **Julie Garmon** of Monroe, Georgia. "Nothing has grown my faith like this form of writing. Each Wednesday morning, I post a short message from my heart. The scary part is pressing Publish and reading my words on the Internet. I always have flickers of doubt. *Lord, what if no one understands? What if I have nothing to say?* And each week, I'm reminded of 2 Corinthians 12:10 (KJV): 'When I am weak, then am I strong.' When we realize we can't do something on our own and ask God for help, He is faithful. He provides exactly what we need at the right moment, like manna from heaven."

"Though it's been a year of ups and downs, there's one thing I know for sure: God has blessed me more than I deserve," writes **Bill Giovannetti** of Redding, California. "One huge blessing is that Neighborhood Church, which I'm privileged to pastor, has just finished its first full year in a new worship center—God's answer to a very long-running prayer. And my two kids have officially become teenagers, thankfully, with minimal drama. Both amaze my wife and me every day with their humor and kindness." Their daughter, Josie, 14, continues to write her novel, and their son, J.D., 13, has become interested in computing. Bill's wife, Margi, homeschools their children and continues teaching business law and ethics classes at a local Christian university. Bill's newest book is *Grace Intervention*.

"Not to let the cat out of the bag," says **Edward Grinnan** of New York City, "but because of the long lead times in book publishing, most of us *Daily Guideposts* contributors prepare our little bios long before the year we're writing for actually arrives. So what I hope has happened by the time you read this is that the people (and dogs) I love are healthy, safe, and happy; that I have grown in my faith—even just a little bit; and that I have held on to my optimism, which is so sorely tested by the world today. I wish only the best for all of you too, and that we continue to abide in God as He abides in us." Edward is married to Julee Cruise. They have a golden retriever named Millie. Both appear regularly in Edward's blogs at Guideposts.org.

Rick Hamlin of New York City lives with his wife, Carol, and their very large cat, Fred. "Rumor has it that I will have entered another decade of life by the time this book is in print," writes Rick, "but I tell myself I'm a long way off from the age of Abraham, when God first called him, or Moses, when he had to bring the

Israelites out of Egypt. What I marvel at is that I still have so much to learn and so much growing to do. Every devotion feels like a chance to mark a step in my spiritual journey. I am glad I get to do it with all of the *Daily Guideposts* readers and writers. If I piled up every copy of *Daily Guideposts* I've contributed to since 1985, the stack would be higher than I am—a sure sign that as a community we are strong and standing tall!"

 **Carla Hendricks** lives in Conway, Arkansas, with her husband, Anthony, and their four children, Kalin, Christian, Joelle, and Jada. They adopted Christian at the age of 2 from Russia and adopted Joelle in this country as an infant. Carla directs the African American Church Initiative, which encourages African Americans to abide in the Christian's call to care for orphans, and serves the CALL, which trains and supports foster and adoptive parents. Favorite pastimes include curling up with a mug of sweet, bold coffee while watching a cathartic tear-jerking film, reading a novel, and abiding in God through Bible study and prayer.

 **Kim Henry** of Elizabeth, Colorado, had a year full of new beginnings and joy. She and her husband, David, rejoiced in the birth of their third grandchild, Madison Hope Henry, born to their son Kirk and his wife,

Courtney. Then, hip replacement surgery gave Kim a new lease on life. Within months of those events, she and her husband spent seven weeks traveling through ten European countries. Most of the towns they visited had been rebuilt beautifully after the devastation of war. "God blessed me with an even greater appreciation for His gift of new life," says Kim. "I'm thankful that God is a God of new beginnings!"

"You never know where God will lead you—maybe right back to where you started," says **Jim Hinch**. "Our family, after four years in California, moved back to New York when Kate accepted a job as rector of St. Michael's Episcopal Church in Manhattan. Not only did we return to our old neighborhood, we even moved back into our old house. We plan to stay here long term this time. Though we're westerners at heart, New York City is where our kids were born and where we spent the early years of our marriage. Most important, it's where we feel God calling us to work. For me, that means a return to *Guideposts* magazine as a staff editor."

The country of Oman, a TV production studio, and a classroom have been places of unexpected meaning and influence for **Jeff Japinga** of Holland, Michigan. A trip to Oman to experience how Christians can create a dialogue with Muslim people deepened his own faith in very tangible ways. Watching Lynn's and his son, Mark, on *Jeopardy! Tournament of Champions* was a reminder of the unique ways God has gifted each of us and an encouragement to explore his own gifts more fully. While their daughter, Annie, moved on to graduate school, Jeff's life continues to orbit around teaching and learning as a professor and pastor. "It's remarkable to see the faithful, and sometimes unanticipated, ways in which God continues to abide with us."

The word of the year for **Ashley Kappel** of Birmingham, Alabama, has been *peace*. There are days when Brian's and her newborn and toddler don't get the memo, but most of the time she can find peace in every aspect of her life, from her full-time job as a food writer to folding laundry at the end of a long day. "Choosing to see to-do lists as blessings instead of burdens has been a revolutionary shift," says Ashley, "and one I pray I can continue as I move forward, seeking God day by day."

"I feel like every year God enriches my life with a stronger cheering section," says **Brock Kidd** of Nashville, Tennessee. "Just the other day as I walked in the door, Mary Katherine, 3, was pointing excitedly out the window: 'Daddy, look at the *bootiful* sunset God gave us today!'

Her sister, Ella Grace, 1, also melts any stress I bring home as soon as she wraps her arms around my neck. My wife, Corinne, continues her rock-star mothering and volunteering for the community, and I couldn't be prouder of my son, Harrison, 14, who is now in high school. It's hard to imagine greater blessings!"

"Our daughter, Keri, was holding my mother's hand when Mom slipped away to heaven," writes **Pam Kidd** of Nashville, Tennessee. "I was standing with my husband, David, near her bed, and perfect peace surrounded us. To say I miss my mother is a vast understatement. No one calls me 'Pamela' now, or tells me I'm working too hard, or joins me for our traditional Sunday night popcorn dinners. But my mother's here in less obvious ways. I see that the refugee child Keri brings to preschool every day, the check my son, Brock, writes for the homeless, and my mother's husband Herb's continued care for shut-ins are direct reflections of her influence. Though I will never again hear her say 'Pamela' when I answer my phone, she will permeate my world in ways not yet imagined."

Patty Kirk of Westville, Oklahoma, finished a draft of her novel and transformed her previous struggle to find time to write into deep, restful pleasure. Kris's and her daughter, Charlotte, a recent college graduate, finally redeemed her high school graduation present: a trip to England. After a hectic week in London, Patty and Charlotte took the train to York, where they lounged in parks and cafés for a luxurious week of crocheting and reading. Their other daughter, Lulu, studying in Denmark all summer, traveled to Hamburg, Germany, and in reply to a frantic text about her whereabouts, concluded two decades of motherly worries with the curt command: "Calm yourself!" And Patty did.

 "Abide in me, and I in you." These words of Jesus in John 15:4 (KJV) have defined life for **Carol Knapp**. After her husband, Terry, retired and they moved from Minnesota to Priest River in northern Idaho (where they met and married over forty years ago), her mother, Ruth, declined in health. "I was hoping I would be her neighbor, but it was not to be," says Carol. "I cared for her at home and then spent five weeks with her in the hospital. On August 3, at almost 92, she entered into eternal life as I read to her from the Psalms." Meanwhile, their daughter Brenda worked through a concussion from a car accident and Terry began cortisone shots for back problems. "A gift smack in the middle of this eventful year was the birth of our eighteenth grandchild, Alice."

"As I walked my dog along the hilltop near my home, I thanked God for the blessing of consistency in my life," writes **Carol Kuykendall** of Boulder, Colorado. "For forty years, my husband, Lynn, and I have lived in the home where we raised our family on this same land where I grew up, and our marriage is still growing after almost fifty years. I am approaching another milestone birthday with a zero in it. We've experienced the joy of living close to our children, ten grandchildren, and a faithful circle of friends and still attend the church where we said our marriage vows. In a world full of change, I'm most thankful for the consistency of Jesus and a fresh awareness that all good things grow out of my relationship with Him, abiding with Him."

"It's exciting to know that *Daily Guideposts* has been inspiring millions of readers for forty years," says **Patricia Lorenz** of Largo, Florida, "and that this is the twenty-fifth time I've had the privilege of contributing to its pages. Sharing bits of my faith, family, friends, travels, passions, ups, downs, and adventures has undoubtedly been a highlight of my life." Her four children, their spouses, and nine grandchildren all live out of state, which means fun trips to California, Ohio, and Wisconsin. "My speaking career takes me to other states where I meet *Daily Guideposts* readers who strengthen my faith and remind me that we are all part of one big family abiding in God's love. It's an amazing, lovely life that I'm enjoying to the max with my husband, Jack."

"My husband, Wayne, and I are enjoying the fruits of our labors," says **Debbie Macomber** of Port Orchard, Washington. "In the last couple of years we've caught the travel bug and journeyed to Iceland, Scotland (where he bought himself a kilt!), Italy, and the Greek islands. We also traveled with members of World Vision to view their projects in Kenya, which was so humbling and eye-opening. When I'm not traveling for pleasure, I'm on the road, promoting my books and movies. At home, my most precious moments are those I share with family and friends. The Lord has blessed me above and beyond anything I could ever have expected or anticipated."

Finding time for just about anything has become a daily challenge for **Erin MacPherson** of Manchaca, Texas. With three kids in school (part-time homeschool) and a part-time job, Erin has made it her mission to find time to read, write, pray, and simply be. And through those glimpses of solace, she has been able to capture moments that otherwise would have gone unnoticed: those sunsets that brighten the kitchen table; those bright eyes glowing with hope; that moment when God speaks joy almost audibly into her heart.

 When **Roberta Messner**'s facial and brain tumors returned with a vengeance, her relationship with Jesus became dearer and more life-sustaining than ever before. Every breath became a prayer. One of the most surprising answers to these prayers was a visit from two faithful *Daily Guideposts* readers—a mother and daughter from New Martinsville, West Virginia, who traveled nearly five hours to visit her in Huntington. "We had the most amazing time together," Roberta recounts. "We shared what the Lord has been doing in our lives and then we sought Him for our futures."

 Over the last year, God has impressed on **Rebecca Ondov** of Hamilton, Montana, that the easiest way to find the answers to life is by doing one thing: abiding in Him. Rebecca says, "When I consciously began to focus on doing that, it was as if His hand moved in my behalf. This last year, I weathered some tough and stormy days with ease. Better yet, it was as if He poured out blessings on me." One of those blessings

included the release of her book *Great Horse Stories for Girls*. Spring, summer, and fall, Rebecca saddles up and rides the narrow trails of the Rocky Mountains with her golden retriever, Sunrise, by her side. She loves connecting with *Daily Guideposts* readers and invites you to find her at RebeccaOndov.com.

Natalie Perkins of New York City is wrapping up her final year at Union Theological Seminary and exploring innovative ways to combine her love of art and her new path in ministry. Recently, she led a happy-dance video through the halls of the seminary and explored what it means for folks to experience a God of happiness in the midst of sorrow. In her spare time, she still sings and dances in various shows and troupes, all while struggling to keep her plant, Otis, alive.

With a blended family of three children, **Ginger Rue** of Tuscaloosa, Alabama, struggled to find quiet time to pray, but this year she used a strategy a friend taught her. "After my husband leaves for work and the kids are off to school, I go into the children's rooms and pray for them," she says. "Being in their space helps me focus on each child and talk to God about my specific concerns and hopes for them." Ginger signed a two-book deal for a story about a middle-school girl who plays drums and forms her own rock band. "This was a challenge for me because I lack the coordination to be a good drummer. Luckily, my character is much more talented than I am."

Daniel Schantz and his wife, Sharon, of Moberly, Missouri, still reflect on their fiftieth-anniversary trip to England. Sharon has made several cross-stitches of London highlights, and Dan planted a couple of London plane trees in the front yard. They stay connected to Christ, the Vine, in several ways. They travel to Missouri churches, where Dan fills in for vacationing ministers. Sharon attends two women's Bible studies every week. And Dan often goes out to Central Christian College, where he taught for forty-three years, taking in the chapel speakers on Tuesdays and Fridays and encouraging the teachers as much as he can.

Gail Thorell Schilling of Concord, New Hampshire, said good-bye to her mother, 95, after years of failing health but determined spirit. "Mom was as frail as a kitten, but she sat upright and reached toward invisible arms just hours before she passed. I know she is safe and with Dad. The daughter of

Mom's flower girl, a great-niece and now a pastor, comforted us and conducted the service." On a more joyous note, Gail's son Greg married Nikki in California. "Not only do I gain a beautiful and talented daughter-in-law, but I can now claim her son, William, as my grandson!" That makes two weddings in one year, as Gail also joined Turkish family and friends to celebrate her son Tom's union with Canay for a moonlit dinner cruise on the Bosporus Strait. "I am blessed to have family on two continents!"

"Surgery for a ruptured appendix provided a valuable lesson on abiding fully in Christ," writes **Penney Schwab** of Copeland, Kansas. "As I trusted the hospital staff to care for my hurting body, I realized God longed for me to faithfully and totally trust Him to care for every aspect of my life. So through all of life's changes I'm striving to rely on God's Word to me: 'Take up your position, stand firm, and see what salvation God has in store for you' (2 Chronicles 20:17, NJB)." Penney and Don's youngest grandchild, Caden, is a teenager and plays hockey. Olivia graduated from high school, and David was commissioned second lieutenant in the Marine Corps. Ryan works as a pharmacy technician and is finishing a master's degree in business administration, while Mark and Caleb are college students with part-time jobs.

The highlight of the year for **Elizabeth Sherrill** and her husband, John, of Hingham, Massachusetts, was the marriage of their grandson Daniel to Suzanne in Geneva, Florida. "We like the coincidence of the town's name, since we were married in Geneva, Switzerland, sixty-eight years ago." Elizabeth considered the importance of place as their seven other grandchildren gathered, coming from New York, Illinois, Georgia, Oregon, Texas, and Tennessee for the wedding. "I was thinking that in this huge and restless country, our lives are not centered on a single place, as was true for most of our history. It reminded me gratefully of Jesus's invitation 'Abide in Me'—our sure center wherever our current dwelling happens to be."

It's a year of gratitude for **Melody Bonnette Swang** of Mandeville, Louisiana. "After a couple of difficult years dealing with the unexpected loss of my husband, John, God has given me the grace to heal and to begin again," writes Melody. "When something or someone we love has been taken away, it sure makes what we still have that much more meaningful." Among the things Melody is grateful for are the evening sunsets over her backyard pond. "I've always appreciated the sunsets, but now I make sure to thank God every evening for such beauty."

Jon Sweeney lives in Ann Arbor, Michigan, where he's a husband to Michal Woll, who is a rabbi; a dad to three children, two in college and one a preschooler; a book publisher at Paraclete Press; and a writer. He's grateful for all of those things, but not so much for the squirrels in his attic—although over the last year they've taught him patience. Jon's the author of several books, most recently *When Saint Francis Saved the Church*.

"I've taken intensive Bible Study Fellowship classes for three years and finally felt called into leadership," writes **Stephanie Thompson** of Edmond, Oklahoma. "But I worried about the time commitment. I'd have to devote two mornings a week, prepare at home for weekly training, and create lesson plans—not to mention still completing the in-depth Bible study pages. When I brought my concerns to the teaching leader, she encouraged me to pray about it and assured me that God would multiply my time when I served Him. It's been seven months, and she was right. I'm holding on to the words in John 15:5 (NRSV): 'I am the vine, you are the branches. Those who abide in me and I in them bear much fruit, because apart from me you can do nothing.' When I feel rushed or overwhelmed, I simply remind myself that I can't do it alone. It's up to Christ. He's the vine."

"I lounged lazily on the beach, watching my kids, Brandon, 6, and Tyler, 4, playing in the sand," writes **Karen Valentin** of New York City. "This idleness took some adjustment. I breathed in the sea air and thought about the last few years. The words that came to mind were *survival*, *change*, *lessons*, *stress*, *hard work*, and *exhaustion*. Yet with each year, the intensity of those words has decreased. The strong waves crashing down seem gentler these days—either that or I'm just stronger now. I looked out into the ocean, relaxed, hopeful, and waiting with anticipation for the next chapter of my life."

"I received precious advice from a recovering addict in my Sunday school class," says **Marion Bond West** of Watkinsville, Georgia. "Don had been a resident at a homeless shelter where one of my sons has slept all this year. 'I've been praying thirty years,' I told Don, who is now a vital member of the church. He locked his kind eyes on mine and smiled with the amazing love of God. 'Don't help your son,' he told me. 'Don't let him take you in. Don't stop loving him. When he reaches *real* bottom, he will bring healing to your entire family. I was in my midfifties before I allowed God to bring me to the end of myself. My mom didn't live to see my turnaround, but her prayers lived long after she died. Your son's going to make it.' My impatient heart settled down, thumping in joyful expectation."

SCRIPTURE REFERENCE INDEX

AUTHORS, TITLES, AND SUBJECTS INDEX

A NOTE FROM THE EDITORS

We hope you enjoy *Daily Guideposts 2016*, created by the Books and Inspirational Media Division of Guideposts, a nonprofit organization that touches millions of lives every day through products and services that inspire, encourage, help you grow in your faith, and celebrate God's love in every aspect of your daily life.

Thank you for making a difference with your purchase of this book, which helps fund our many outreach programs to military personnel, prisons, hospitals, nursing homes, and educational institutions. To learn more, visit GuidepostsFoundation.org.

We also maintain many useful and uplifting online resources. Visit Guideposts.org to read true stories of hope and inspiration, access OurPrayer network, sign up for free newsletters, download free e-books, join our Facebook community, and follow our stimulating blogs. To delve more deeply into *Daily Guideposts*, visit DailyGuideposts.org/DGP2016.

You may purchase the 2017 edition of *Daily Guideposts* anytime after July 2016. To order, visit ShopGuideposts.org, call (800) 932-2145, or write to Guideposts, PO Box 5815, Harlan, Iowa 51593.

Discover resources that help connect faith-filled values to your daily life

Digging Deeper

Enrich your devotional time with additional Scripture readings referenced at the close of each day's devotion.

 DailyGuideposts.org

Free Newsletters

Sign up for newsletters on positive living, faith in daily life, helping others, the power of prayer, and more!

 Guideposts.org/Newsletters

Free eBooks

Visit us to download more inspirational reading on subjects like prayer, personal growth, and positive thinking.

 Guideposts.org/SpiritLifters

Follow Us on Social Media

See what's happening with your favorite authors and more!

 DailyGuideposts

 DailyGuideposts

DAILY GUIDEPOSTS

Celebrating 40 years of spirit-lifting devotions